After work after play after all

A POLITICAL MEMOIR

John Cornwall

John Cornwall is a retired Labor politician. Following his early years as a veterinary surgeon he pursued a career in politics from the late 1960s. He was a Labor member of the South Australian Legislative Council for 14 years (1975-1989) and a senior member of the front bench for most of his political career. He served as Minister of Environment and Lands in 1979 and then as Minister of Health and Community Welfare in two John Bannon Governments from 1982 to 1988.

When his ministerial career came to an end in 1988 he wrote a book about the Bannon years (*Just for the Record*, Wakefield Press, 1989) and took up a career outside politics, moving to Sydney where he worked in senior executive roles for non-government organisations. These included Chief Executive Officer of the Australian Veterinary Association and Director of the Australian Youth Foundation. From 1997 he was General Manager of Delta Society Australia.

He formally retired in 2007 and joined the Horn of Africa Relief and Development Agency where he served in a voluntary capacity as President and Executive Director until 2013.

He lives in Sydney with his wife Patrice. They have one son, six daughters, six grandsons and two foster grandsons.

Few will have the greatness to bend history itself, but each of us can work to change a small portion of events, and in the total of all those acts will be written the history of this generation.

Robert F. Kennedy's Day of Affirmation speech, 6 June 1966

© 2017 John Cornwall

Printed by BookPOD

All rights reserved. Apart from any fair dealing for the purpose of private study, research, criticism or review, as permitted under the Copyright Act 1968, no part may be reproduced by any process without written permission.

Enquiries about this publication can be made to the author.
Email: cornwall@hotkey.net.au

National Library of Australia
Cataloguing-in-Publication data

Cornwall, John, 1935
After work, after play, after all : a political memoir

ISBN: 9780646944586 (paperback)

Cornwall, John, 1935-
Australian Labor Party--Biography.
Politicians--South Australia--Biography.
Health--Government policy--South Australia--Biography.
Veterinary medicine--Australia--Biography.

Dewey Number: 324.2942307092

The photographs in this publication are reproduced from the private collection of the Cornwall family.

Front cover: Media conference announcing resignation as Minister of Health and Community Welfare, 4 August 1988.

Contents

Chapter 1: A pocket full of dreams — 9
Chapter 2: Emerging ambition — 23
Chapter 3: Tall tales and true — 37
Chapter 4: High on the hill — 49
Chapter 5: The hard way — 63
Chapter 6: The practice, the principal and the pope — 75
Chapter 7: Swing to Labor — 91
Chapter 8: It's time — 105
Chapter 9: A waiting game — 123
Chapter 10: Follow the leader — 137
Chapter 11: Minister of Health — 149
Chapter 12: Social health, social justice — 165
Chapter 13: Tobacco, alcohol and other drugs — 177
Chapter 14: Medicare — 189
Chapter 15: Dismissal — 201
Chapter 16: An enigmatic Premier — 215
Chapter 17: Life after politics — 225
Appendix: Ancestry — 233
Endnotes — 239

As Captain John with brother, Pilot Officer Terry, on drill parade, Bendigo, 1942.

CHAPTER ONE

A pocket full of dreams

I was born in Melbourne's Queen Victoria Hospital on New Year's Day 1935, the third child and first son of Joseph and Edna Cornwall. My parents had come to Melbourne from the country two years earlier in the hope of finding work. Dad had been an enduring victim of the Great Depression, unable to find any stable employment for more than four years after he lost his job in 1930. However, less than four months before I arrived his luck had changed. He was about to start a new career as an insurance salesman and they had high hopes for their new born son. As a seventh generation Australian I was a robust mix of Anglo-Saxon and Celt, protestant and catholic, convict and free settler.

My mother Edna Bilston was born in 1907 at Gymbowen, a township in the Victorian Wimmera, the eighth of nine children. Her mother Ellen Ryan was a first generation Australian of Irish catholic immigrant parents. Her father George Stone Bilston was a direct descendant of convicts on the First and Third fleets. Edna grew up in the Wimmera, mostly at Gymbowen and Natimuk, where George worked as a self employed carpenter. After the First World War the family moved to Mildura where George bought the Arcadia cafe.

My father, Joe Cornwall, the second youngest of 12 children, was born in 1904, the grandson of Wilson Cornwall who was transported to Australia in 1839 following a conviction for robbery. Dad left school four months short of his 14th birthday to join his father working as a roustabout but anxious to escape life as a labourer he joined the Victorian Police Force as a 20 year old in 1924. He was probably attracted by the active recruiting campaign which followed the notorious Victorian police strike and the sacking of almost a third of the force.[1]

He was sent to Mildura, still a frontier irrigation settlement, where he met my mother, an attractive 18 year old who worked in her father's cafe after her day job as a junior clerk. They were married on 12 January 1927, six weeks before Dad's 23rd birthday and just before Mum's 20th. Shortly after their marriage Dad applied for a transfer to the Mounted Division and was posted to Ultima, a small township 20 miles from Swan Hill. The one man station was a mounted outpost, complete with horse, stable and all the tack and regalia necessary for a mounted constable. The young Edna Cornwall was a keen equestrian and for more than a year after arriving in Ultima took responsibility for exercising the big grey police horse virtually every day until her first pregnancy. My sister Margaret was born at the Ultima Bush Nursing Hospital in April 1929.

Dad's love for horses had a more unfortunate side: he was developing a gambling problem. One of his duties as the local constable was to collect money (presumably fines or state land tax) from local householders and landowners. In July 1930 he appeared before the Ultima Magistrates Court on three charges of 'larceny of money as a public servant', the alleged offences having occurred between July and November 1929. He pleaded not guilty, was committed for trial at the Bendigo Supreme Court in August 1930 and suspended without pay.[2]

Whether he mismanaged or misappropriated these funds is unclear but he was unable to account for a £27 deficit following an unscheduled audit. As many problem gamblers do, it is likely that he 'borrowed' the money with the genuine intention of replacing it when he backed the next winner. The trial of a policeman for larceny of public funds would surely have attracted public attention but I can find no later newspaper reports of a trial in the Bendigo Supreme Court. I assume the charges were dropped but the price was his resignation. His career in the Victorian Police Force was over and he became a long term victim of the Depression. Despite a desperate search for work he never found any form of stable employment for the next four years.

The Cornwalls moved to the relative sanctuary of Pakenham Upper where Aunty Vera Holdensen, Dad's widowed sister, had an apple orchard and tea rooms. For a short time after their arrival Dad found casual employment as a timber worker in the Gembrook Forest but he was soon forced onto the Victorian government's work for the dole schemes, the family surviving on the sparse, begrudging payments and the accommodation provided by Aunty Vera. By November 1931 when my second sister Denise was born in the Pakenham Hospital the adult male unemployment rate was approaching 32 per cent.

In 1933 the family decided to join Mum's parents in the Melbourne suburb of Pascoe Vale, believing that there must be more opportunities in the city, but things were even more difficult. It was not until the early spring of 1934 that Dad found a job as a commissionaire at Menzies Hotel. A good looking 30 year old and over six feet tall he cut a fine figure in his uniform and cap. It was the first luck the family had known since 1930 and quickly turned out to be the stepping stone to more good fortune. Within weeks of starting the job he met Alf Duffy, a guest at the hotel, who was the manager of the Temperance & General Life Insurance Company (T&G) in Albury. Duffy set him on a career path as a life insurance salesman and they became lifelong friends. Except for five years in the army, life insurance was to be his business for the next forty years.

Dad carried the scars of the Depression for the rest of his life. Although he never joined or participated in the Australian Labor Party (ALP) or its various forums, he was an avid and vocal supporter.

WE MOVED TO BENDIGO IN FEBRUARY 1935 six weeks after I was born, rented a house in suburban White Hills and Dad started work with the T&G. As a new agent, he rode a bike around Bendigo and well beyond its boundaries, looking for sales. Much of his early work involved selling so-called industrial insurance to the battling working families to cover the breadwinner; the insured person made a small weekly payment which the agent collected on his regular round. However, the real money for an insurance agent came from selling life policies with premiums paid quarterly or yearly. The agent got up to 50 per cent of the first year's premium and could negotiate his weekly drawing rate from his commission pool. Dad's early performance impressed the company and in a little more than a year he was selling term and probate life policies, displaying a real salesman's talent.

Joe Cornwall, always tall, articulate and intelligent, now had the added skill of artful persuasion. He was rapidly promoted to a superintendent's position and at a time when less than one family in five had a car or access to a work vehicle he was provided with a black four door sedan as part of his package.

Soon after arriving in White Hills the family met Ted and Rita Northway and the children Tom and Thelma. Ted was a First World War veteran, a carpenter by trade, an optimist by nature and an archetypal Australian male of his time - medium height, brown wavy hair, face a little weather beaten, easy going: a 'bonzer bloke'. He had served in France and while being demobbed in London in 1919 he met and married his first wife. Soon after they returned to Australia their son Tom was born but sadly his mother died from peritonitis when Tom was very young. Some years later he married Rita Schleiger whose German ancestors had come to the area that became White Hills at the time of the Bendigo gold rush.

Ted had built their family home, a neat weatherboard cottage in Cambridge Crescent. He still owned the vacant block next door and in 1937 he built a second cottage which he offered to rent to the Cornwalls for 10 shillings a week. The cottage had two bedrooms, a sleep-out, bathroom, kitchen, front hall and lounge room. Some years later when the Cornwalls purchased the house we weather proofed the sleep-out with louver windows all round to make a third bedroom and the back verandah was enclosed to make a vestibule and informal eating area. Most importantly, the lavatory was moved indoors, adjacent to the laundry, and Mum could dispense with the family chamber pot.

The person I remember with great affection is Rita Northway. She was a small woman with a large bust who wore her fine brown and later grey hair in a plain bob for all the years that I knew her. When I was a small boy she seemed to me to spend most of her time in a flour smudged apron baking cakes, biscuits and sausage rolls. Her specialty was what she called a 'kiss', two delicious shortbread biscuits joined to each other by strawberry jam.

I first faced the horror of war as a five year old in ways I found hard to comprehend. In 1940 Tom Northway joined the Royal Australian Air Force (RAAF). Less than three months later his shattered body was returned to White Hills for a simple funeral service after he crashed during pilot training at the RAAF base in Deniliquin. His father Ted was already over forty when the war broke out in September 1939. Both his age and his service in the First World War qualified him for exemption from any active service but he was among the first to re-enlist. He joined the 2/22nd Batallion and was sent to garrison Rabaul early in 1941. This was just a few months after Tom was killed and nine months before the Japanese attack on Pearl Harbour. When the Japanese overran the garrison at Rabaul early in February 1942 at least 130 of the 1,050 Australians taken prisoner were marched into the jungle near Tol Plantation in small groups, tied to palm trees and bayoneted by Japanese soldiers. Ted Northway was one of them.

Rita remained a dear friend of the Cornwall family for the rest of her life. She was in her apron again at my 40th birthday party at our home in Adelaide, looking a little frail but toiling in the kitchen to prepare the supper. Later she reminisced and sang in her soprano voice around the family's Wertheim piano. Almost exactly 12 months later I visited her in Melbourne where she was in St Vincent's Hospital with terminal cancer.

I STARTED SCHOOL IN WHITE HILLS just two weeks after the outbreak of the Second World War and three months short of my 5th birthday. The Holy Rosary School, which doubled as the church on Sundays, was a small weatherboard building, a simple wooden cross on top of the front porch the only external sign that it had pretensions to holiness. After Mass the men of the parish shifted the pews into an annex, rolled down a baize blind to cover the recessed altar and replaced the pews with school desks and portable blackboards. They then closed and bolted the two concertina folding partitions to make two classrooms.

The school was conducted by two Mercy nuns from the Bendigo Convent who travelled to White Hills each morning on Harry McMeekin's bus, an 18 seat Bedford. Each of the two classrooms accommodated four grades, one to four and five to eight. The children of the pious practicing families, the 'good Catholics', were captive pupils but our parish priest added to the numbers by rounding up the children of almost every defaulting catholic family in the district. He also collected the young rebels who had been expelled or suspended from the state schools to bring them 'to the one true faith'. There were 35 pupils in each classroom accommodated in double desks.

The walk to school took us past the local state school in the days when sectarian bigotry was still rampant. Catholic children knew they were God's chosen ones because the nuns and priests told us so but unfortunately no one had told the protestant kids at the state school. On information conveyed by their parents they believed just as fervently that we were an integral part of a papist plot to subvert all the things held sacred by a God fearing protestant society, loyal to King and Empire. Sometimes the more zealous state school kids would wallop a lone Mick on his way home. More often it was just taunting through the school fence. We were well versed in the art of survival and just occasionally if we had the numbers we gave a little better than we got.

The parish priest, Father Patrick Deegan, was a short tempered, florid faced red head in his mid-30s, direct from Dublin. He dedicated himself to the parish with great enthusiasm, pushing all the worst excesses of authoritarian, bigoted Irish catholicism. On one occasion when addressing a mixed audience at the school concert, he extolled the virtues of our faith and explained how it distinguished us from protestants who were no more than 'thinking animals'.

The school was supported financially by the parish and to ensure that the children were educated in the one true faith every working parishioner, regardless of age, financial or marital status, was obliged to make a weekly contribution over a six month period each year. Failure to meet this obligation when a collector from the congregation called to the door would result in a personal visit from the parish priest with a please explain.

On First Communion Day we were close to beatification as the children sang 'Softly and tenderly Jesus is calling' and the first communicants approached the altar rails. Not surprisingly we had difficulty understanding the Church's extraordinary doctrine of transubstantiation. The thin wafer ('the host') and the altar wine were not just blessed but became the Body and Blood of Christ ('unless you eat my flesh and drink my blood you shall not have life in you'). More prosaically, the saintly celebration was completed at the first communion breakfast, held in the local hall after Mass. Small children made themselves bilious on a cornucopia of pies, sausage rolls, cocktail sausages (with sauce), sponge cakes, lamingtons, cream puffs and fruit salad.

Seven was the 'age of reason'. From that time on it was not only possible but inevitable that a child would commit sins. Disobedience, questioning directions from parents or teachers were venial or lesser sins, although they did stain the soul a little and needed to be shriven in the confessional. Eating meat on Friday 'knowingly and willingly' was in the big league, a mortal sin for which a seven or eight year old could be condemned to the eternal fires of hell.

> Bless me Father for I have sinned. It is a week since my last confession and I accuse myself of…

In the likely event that children couldn't find any new sins to confess after carefully examining their consciences, they could and should confess 'sins of your past life'. It was preparation for a lifetime journey 'mourning and weeping in the valley of tears'. The first stirrings of pre-pubertal sex opened Pandora's Box. 'Immodesty in thoughts, words or deeds' were all mortal sins. Growing up was a minefield, the devil and his agents were everywhere.

Lest we should waver, our commitment to that one true faith was reinforced from time to time by the 'missions' conducted by visiting Redemptorist priests. The program ran for a week, with lengthy sermons and benediction each night and Mass at seven o'clock in the morning. Parishioners were reminded how good God had been to them yet how they, in return, had constantly offended Him with their sins. There was special, if euphemistic, reference to the very serious sin of contraception. This was not yet comprehended by us, the pious altar boys who were increasingly exhausted by the late nights and early mornings, but apparently offending against 'the natural law' attracted an eternity in the fires of hell.

If the positive attractions of the good Catholic life ('an increase in sanctifying grace') had not overwhelmed the parish by the final night, there was the ultimate weapon – the sermon on hell. The God of Love we had heard so much about in the earlier sermons suddenly turned nasty. Failure to obey His commandments and, by inference, the dictates of His church, would result in the God of Infinite Mercy casting us into the fierce flames forever.

WHEN TED NORTHWAY RE-ENLISTED as soon as war broke out in 1939 he persuaded my father to join him. After a brief stay in the army camp at Bendigo, Dad was transferred to Melbourne where the army had taken over the Caulfield racecourse. He was given a job as a driving instructor but army vehicles were scarce and improvisation was the name of the game. He delivered the introductory lessons to his trainee drivers by sitting beside them and going through the driving motions without a vehicle: 'Left foot depress clutch, engage first gear, right foot on the accelerator while slowly releasing clutch, double de-clutch and move through neutral into second gear …remember you haven't got a synchromesh gear box.' This was from a park bench near the Caulfield racecourse.

Soon afterwards Dad's battalion prepared to embark for the Middle East. This was more than 12 months before the Japanese bombed Pearl Harbour and the war was still in Europe and North Africa. Dad felt strongly about the way Australian troops had been used as cannon fodder in the First World War. His brother Robert was only 19 when he became one of the 46,000 Australians who died in the carnage on the Western front. As Hitler and the Nazi juggernaut moved to take over Europe, England and beyond, Dad's early comparison with the Kaiser's war was no longer valid but he was already 36 with a wife and four young children (brother Terry was born three months after the outbreak of the war in 1939). He transferred out of the AIF to the Australian Military Force (Home Defence) and spent the remaining five years of his military service in Australia.

When the Japanese began their thrust south early in 1942 there was a genuine and well based fear that they would over-run Australia. Even in Bendigo we waited with trepidation for strafing and bombing raids and prepared for them by digging slit trenches under the peppercorn trees in Creely's paddock adjacent to the school. I was aware of food rationing, blackouts, air raid wardens, the acts of extraordinary bravery and heroism on the Kokoda Trail and the invaluable support from the native bearers in Papua New Guinea – the Fuzzy Wuzzy Angels. That year Prime Minister John Curtin brought the Australian troops home from the Middle East and sought the support of the United States in the defence of Australia.

On 27 February 1942 the convoy carrying American troops of Task Force 6184 arrived in Melbourne and Bendigo was one of five major centres where the troops were billeted in private homes before being sent north to garrison New Caledonia. My 13 year old sister Margaret was very excited at the prospect of having a suave, handsome young American in the house, her expectations formed from Hollywood movies. In your dreams, Marg. We were allocated a very simple young man from Arkansas who had never previously been away from home. Desperately homesick he spent a lot of his time with our family sitting sadly by the kitchen window, looking at the lilac bush in the side garden. 'Reminds me of home, Ma'am'.

The propaganda for the war effort made it very easy for a seven or eight year old to feel intensely patriotic and stories of Japanese atrocities generated fear and loathing of the enemy. This reached a high point in May 1943 when a Japanese submarine sank the Australian hospital ship *Centaur* off the Queensland coast with the loss of 268 lives, including 11 Australian army nurses. The ship was clearly marked with large red crosses on a white hull and was brightly lit.

AS MORE MEN JOINED THE ARMED SERVICES manpower shortages on the home front brought most home deliveries to an end. Only the grocer's boy survived, calling to the house each week to take the grocery order. But as ever more resources were diverted to the war effort there were many shortages of the things that normally provided sustenance and comfort in peace time. Ration books with coupons were distributed, based on family size. In addition to food, rationing encompassed clothing, shoes, tea and petrol. There were also many serious shortages outside the scope of rationing, including toilet paper. A resourceful population soon discovered a substitute – daily newspapers cut into handy sized squares and hung on the lavatory wall with a piece of string through a hole pierced in the corner of the bundle. The paper squares were made more flexible and less harsh by crunching them into a ball by hand, then smoothing them out prior to use.

If the grocery order was substantial it was sometimes used as a lever to explore the availability of other goods that were in short supply. My mother was quite Victorian in her attitude to sex and bodily functions generally and in normal circumstances would never have discussed the availability of toilet paper with a grocer's boy. But these were desperate times. With the substantial weekly order completed she inquired in a soft voice whether there was any possibility of some toilet paper. The grocer's boy, a confident 14 year old school leaver, shot back without a trace of embarrassment, 'I'm sorry missus but you'll have to use *The Sun* like the rest of us!'.[3]

In pre-war Australia most women left work at the time of their marriage or less commonly during their first pregnancy but this was wartime and women were being called on to join the workforce as their patriotic duty. My mother's direct contribution to the war effort was at the Bendigo ordnance factory where she worked making and checking ammunition. It was the only time in her 57 year marriage that she experienced the luxury of having her own income. Rita Northway looked after my three year old brother Terry and my sister Margaret helped to run the house. Under the dual stress of shift work and family Mum eventually developed shingles and was forced to give up her paid work.

She now turned her talents and enthusiasm to organising and producing concert parties for the troops. She was no doubt influenced by 1930s Hollywood - musicals from Buster Berkeley at Warner Brothers, MGM spectaculars and Fred Astaire and Ginger Rogers at RKO. This was the golden age of the child stars, Shirley Temple, Judy Garland, Deanna Durbin, Jackie Cooper, Spanky McFarland and Mickey Rooney. She thought that her son John had special talents that could take him in the same direction and soon after my sixth birthday she enrolled me in the Ern Ross School of Dancing. Rossie, a dreamer and eternal optimist, taught tap dancing in a studio area behind his newsagency in Mitchell Street which was run by his wife and provided most of the sustenance for the family. I moved on to other more mundane interests after my eighth birthday but not before I had appeared in more than a dozen concerts in and around Bendigo.

Members of the Ern Ross School of Dancing entertained the troops in the Memorial Hall, appeared in benefit concerts at the Capitol Theatre (built with the 19th century riches from Bendigo's gold) and raised money for the Comfort Fund and the Food for Russia Campaign. The first solo act I performed was a song and dance routine, mixing Bing Crosby's *A Pocketful of Dreams* with a Fred Astaire dance routine. Just short of my seventh birthday I had a splendid wardrobe, top hat, white tie and tails. Other costumes and routines followed, an admiral's uniform for *The Fleet's In*, a cowboy's outfit and a ukulele for Tex Morton's *Rocky Ned*.

When Dad joined the Army we lost the Chevrolet, the new company car provided early in 1939. We were left with a local bus that provided a very limited night service, into Bendigo at 7.00pm, back to White Hills after the pictures at 11.00pm. Our alternative transport after dancing lessons, rehearsals and concerts was the electric tram to the Lake Weeroona followed by a half hour walk home in the blackout. We pressed on with costumes for every occasion. I was the family's solo act but both my sisters appeared in various routines. Mum worked with our dressmaker and next door neighbour, Eileen Jennings, to create something special for each occasion. She acquired enough khaki cloth for Mrs Jennings to tailor an army officer's uniform for me and a little later she commissioned a very swish air force uniform for my brother Terry who was still little more than a toddler.

At the height of the scare about Japanese bombing raids and possible invasion, my cousins the Jorys moved from Melbourne to White Hills where they rented a large house in Napier Street, adjacent to the Cornwalls. My mother's eldest sister Elsie Jory was a big, strong willed woman, handsome rather than beautiful. Her husband Holf was a slightly built, amiable but droll man who looked a lot like Percy Kilbride, the actor of Pa Kettle fame. Their youngest children, Harold and Jennifer, were in our age group, Jenny a simple eight year old, Harold a streetwise 13 year old who introduced a slick if limited Hollywood vocabulary to the neighbourhood, modelled on George Raft and James Cagney.

It was cousin Moira who brought real style to our community. She was a beautiful young woman, a Rita Hayworth look-a-like, the apple of her indulgent mother Elsie's eye. In 1942 she was already married but like many young married women whose husbands were away in the army she was a 'grass widow', although her role in raising the morale of the troops was more exciting than Barbara Paynter's contribution described in *The Grass Widow and Her Cow*.[4] Moira joined our concert parties where her body language, Dorothy Lamour sarongs and grass skirts brought a new meaning to the Bendigo theatre of the Pacific war.

DESPITE WARTIME RESTRICTIONS and rationing Dad made a special effort each year to organise a family holiday. If all else failed there was a trip to Melbourne in the steam train to stay with my mother's sister, Aunty Nell Widdicombe. Her large weatherboard house in Moreland was a permanent refuge for the Bilston clan. Towards the end of 1943 the war in the Pacific was turning in favour of the American and Australian forces and the threat of a Japanese invasion had receded. That summer we spent a holiday in

Melbourne's Dandenong Ranges. Dad was now seeing out the war in the safety, if not the comfort, of a small military police unit in Bendigo and he rented a well worn pre-war Chevrolet from an army colleague.

Wartime car travel was a unique experience; petrol was strictly rationed so kerosene was the standard fuel, boosted by power alcohol if you had the right connections. Our family connection was Dad's cousin, Harry Cornwall, who had started Ventura Bus Lines in Melbourne in 1924, running a service between Box Hill and the city with a 14-seat Reo bus purchased for £816. Ninety years later Ventura Bus Lines, still largely a family owned company, had grown to a business with over 1,600 employees and 950 buses and coaches carrying more than 30 million passengers across Melbourne each year.

Getting the Chev's motor started each morning was the big challenge. Dad would run the car down the four mile winding slope from our rented holiday house in Avonsleigh to Cockatoo, using the thrust from the transmission to push the cold motor into a reluctant start. After bouts of coughing on the strange petrol substitute, it would burst into a splutter, then into warmer life. On short trips it was essential to park the car on the nearest hill and never leave it long enough for the motor to get really cold. On longer trips, once the motor was warm we switched the fuel lines over to the gas producer, a large unit mounted at the back of the car. Gas producers were an ingenious but very cumbersome wartime invention, burning wood, coal or briquettes to produce a combustible gas to power the engine. With this great bulk fixed to the rear end of the car the boot was no longer accessible so the luggage was piled high in the pack rack on the roof. On the road, fully loaded, we looked like the itinerant gypsies who travelled in small convoys around Victoria in their old Hudsons and Packards, telling fortunes and forced to survive on petty theft.

During those two weeks we swam in the lake at Emerald, visited David Fleay's Native Animal Sanctuary in Healesville and travelled in Puffing Billy, the tiny narrow gauge steam train running between Fern Tree Gully and Gembrook. We walked among the tall trees and ferns in the rain forest, listening to the ring of the bell birds. And we fished for small trout in the tinkling, clear creek that bordered my Aunty Vera's' tea rooms and apple orchard at Upper Pakenham, once a refuge for Joe and Edna Cornwall during the dark days of the Depression.

Aunty Vera, who had been widowed at an early age, was a compassionate woman and the Cornwalls were not the only ones to have benefitted from her generosity. During the Depression an illiterate young man named Noel who had been a foundling was one of the many itinerants who knocked on her door looking for work. She took him in, provided him with a bed in a back room and set him to work for his keep in the apple orchard. He never married and stayed for the next 30 years, later managing the orchard and working on a profit sharing basis.

Noel was a humble man who became a first class orchardist. However, his early life had left him with a limited ability to comprehend the nuances of any conversation not directly related to his daily routine. During the season he loaded the fruit onto his tray truck and headed for Melbourne in the early hours of the morning to sell his produce to wholesalers at the Victoria Market. During one season the glut in the apple market was so serious that on one occasion he was unable to find a buyer at any price. One of the merchants with whom he normally dealt was sympathetic but unable to help. 'Noel, why don't you take the apples out to the orphanage at Abbotsford?' Noel drove out to Abbotsford, parked the truck and rang the bell at the front door of the orphanage. A Good Shepherd nun answered and Noel got straight to the point. 'I've got a truckload of apples over there. I took them to the market this morning but couldn't find a buyer and I wondered if you'd like to have them'. 'Oh, bless you' she exclaimed in her best convent manner. 'The Lord must have sent you'. Noel wasn't too sure what to make of this but he was quick to put her in the picture. 'No' he said 'it was Alex Comino at the Victoria Market'.

Riding 'Starlight' with brother Terry on 'Swanee' while home from Xavier for the school holidays, September 1950.

CHAPTER TWO

Emerging ambition

In 1945 I moved to Bendigo's Marist Brothers College, a Catholic boys' school. The principal in my first year was Brother Leopold, whose favourite way of delivering discipline was to walk up unannounced behind the offender and give him a very hard whack on the side of the head with an open hand. His other tactic was to publicly belittle or humiliate individual students, especially during school assemblies. Harsh corporal punishment was handed out by the brothers for a range of minor 'offences'. If I arrived five minutes late for school, even in winter, I was likely to be given four hard strokes with a cane on fingers frozen as I rode my small bike through a thawing Bendigo frost.

Yet others were talented professionals, dedicated to broadening our academic horizons while 'saving our souls'. In 1946 Leopold was replaced as principal by Brother Remigius who was also our maths teacher. Poles apart from Leopold, he was an outstanding teacher and a kind man who had little use for corporal punishment.

We were now moving into the world of Algebra, Geometry and Latin. We also learnt French, taught and repeated by us in strong Australian accents despite attempts to refine it through *dictee* delivered on the ABC radio schools programs. Brother Marcellin, our class teacher in year seven, was directly responsible for making us gentlemen, or at least giving us the chance. His lessons on manners, delivered to the tough, knockabout boys in our class were an integral part of our education. Many years later I met him in Adelaide where he had retired after more than 50 years as a teacher and school principal around Australia. It's impossible to estimate how many boys he had inspired to higher ambition and achievement in that time, this proud record now besmirched by the predatory paedophiles tolerated and protected for so long by the religious orders, senior clergy and covered up at the highest levels.

In those days the brighter students under 14 were selected by both state and catholic schools to compete for junior scholarships. Funded by the Victorian Government the scholarships entitled the winners to £5 a year and a small book allowance for the time that the student stayed in secondary education. The £5 was less than an average week's wage but for the Brothers it wasn't just the cash, more the kudos that came to their schools from producing scholarship winners. In 1947 five of us were promoted directly from grade seven to year nine to ensure that we got a major advantage over our competitors. We each won a scholarship at the end of that year and later we all became the first members of our families to complete university educations.

I HAD BEGUN PIANO LESSONS with Florence Hargreaves soon after my ninth birthday. She was a kind, middle aged woman dedicated to her music and her pupils. She was also a grand mal epileptic who was cursed by the prejudice of her time. On arrival I would always try to assess whether it was one of her good or bad days. During the lesson she sat close enough to me to be able to read my music on the piano stand and I would sneak quick glances to my right for any warning signs of a fit.

Florrie lived with her aging companion, Annie, a small, thin woman with white hair whose determined look was reinforced by plain steel framed spectacles. Annie followed a unique routine when Florrie had a seizure – she quickly removed her dentures, ensured her airway was clear, then slapped her about the face and berated her in a very loud voice until it passed. If this occurred during a lesson, I'd grab my music and bolt. Medication became available in later years which helped to control Florrie's epilepsy but by that time she was already an old woman.

It was more constant practice than musical genius that led to my early successes but for the rest of her life my mother held faithfully to her view that I once had the potential to become an Arthur Rubenstein or perhaps Jose Iturbi of the MGM musicals. Florrie had qualified through the London School of Music which was considered less rigorous than the exams conducted by Melbourne University's Conservatorium of Music so as I approached my 11th birthday I was transferred to Ruth Hillman. She was young, bright and beautiful with a degree from the Conservatorium. Ruth taught at Saint Catherine's, an exclusive Melbourne Girls School in Toorak, during the week and at her parent's home in Bendigo on Saturdays. I flourished under her tutelage, passing three consecutive exams with honours and winning the under 14 and under 16 Piano Sections of the relatively prestigious Bendigo Competitions at the age of 13. These were my golden piano days. I ultimately struggled to a pass level in practical music in my final year school exams, having lost both opportunity and motivation during my years at boarding school. Notwithstanding the realities of life, however, my mother's belief in my gift remained and many years later she frequently told my small children, to their increasing amusement, that I 'used to make the piano sing'.

Saturday morning was the time for piano lessons with Ruth Hillman but by midday between April and October I was sitting in the caddies' pen at the Bendigo Golf Club waiting to be selected to caddy for the members of the elite club. Saturday was competition day, members playing seriously against other members and their own handicaps. Women weren't allowed on the course, this was serious men's business. Sundays were the social occasions, men golfing with their wives in mixed foursomes.

There were four golf courses around the city boundaries but the Bendigo Golf Club (BGC) was the pick of them, beyond the financial and social reach of the battlers. By the age of 11 or 12 we were considered strong enough to carry a heavy golf bag and 12 clubs around an 18 hole course. At BGC caddies believed that being hired by our elders and betters showed real class and on dog-leg fairways we took up vantage points to ensure that our benefactors didn't lose their golf balls in the rough. The going rate for caddies was between two and three shillings for a round of 18 holes, the top of this range paid to older boys who had a permanent arrangement ('a perm') with one of the club members. The rest of us sat in the caddies' pen waiting optimistically for inspection and selection.

In this early post war period golf balls were in short supply and a ball in good condition brought more than a shilling, equivalent to nine holes doing it hard as a caddy. By keeping a sharp eye out during forays into the rough we would occasionally have a windfall, finding a ball lost by a previous player. However, there was a more reliable way. The long 14th fairway crossed a small creek on approach to the green and recrossed it on the par 3, 15th. Following a downpour, the creek became a minor torrent for an hour or two but for most of the winter it was a shallow water channel, an ideal trap for golf balls. As the last of the players were finishing their rounds on cold, wet Saturday afternoons, my mate Reg Jenkins and I would go back to the creek, take off our boots and socks and paddle in our short pants in the muddy, cold watercourse. We moved slowly, feeling with our toes for the balls that had been lost in the muddy water. Sometimes we found nothing but on good days we might each find two or three balls. As the winter darkness came I felt well satisfied as I headed for home to thaw out my feet in front of the kitchen stove.

SPON, STACKER AND SNOWY are colourful characters in my childhood memories of Australia in the 1940s. Spon got his nickname from an abbreviation of spondulicks. The second edition of the *Australian Oxford Dictionary* describes this is a 19th century colloquialism for money but we didn't need a dictionary to recognise that money was his business. Many years before off course betting became legal he distributed place cards each Friday inviting punters to invest anything from a shilling to 10 bob to pick three horses in the order in which they might finish in the main race of the day in Melbourne on Saturday. The odds were always tight enough, of course, to ensure that he had many more winning than losing days. Spon had droopy red eyelids, whiskery jowls beyond the reach of his cut throat razor and a deep, gruff voice. He always wore a grandfather shirt, open at the neck and without its detachable collar, and his appearance was complemented by a large, smooth and presumably benign growth on the back of his neck. Yet he was a caring family man, providing in the way he knew best for his wife and 'the Dean girls'.

During the War Stacker Lowe and Harry McMeekin were both busy running additional bus services to carry soldiers on short leave passes from the racecourse camp into Bendigo. Stacker had been known to carry up to three dozen soldiers in and on his 18 seat bus. 'Stack 'er up fellers' he'd say in his Aussie drawl. On Saturday afternoons he left the bus to provide an essential service as the starting price bookmaker at the Botanic Gardens Hotel in White Hills. He operated from the gent's lavatory in the backyard of the pub, sitting on the lid of a toilet seat while the punters came and went discreetly to transact their business. If one of his 'cockatoos', posted to warn of approaching cops, gave the alarm Stacker quickly flushed the betting slips down the toilet and emerged adjusting his braces.

Snowy Yates was our local barber. His bald pate, covered by a cloth cap whenever he ventured out during daylight hours, was untouched by the sun. Short back and sides was his standard haircut, followed by a two handed application of Californian Poppy hair oil or Vaseline Hair Tonic. His small barber shop was decorated with the mandatory photos of legends of the turf, Phar Lap, Peter Pan and The Trump. Snowy was a great story teller, many of his yarns no doubt enhanced over time, but his third in the Stawell Gift - 'Australia's Richest Foot Race' - 40 years earlier was a matter of record. At another stage of his varied career he took up horse training and in the desperate early years of the Depression, once walked 'a good horse' 100 miles from Bendigo to Melbourne to try his luck at Flemington.

My father was consistently devious with my thrifty mother about the true state of his finances as his gambling had him sailing close to the wind with creditors. He wrote prodigious amounts of life insurance during his lifetime, earning large commissions, but at the time of his death at the age of 79 his only assets were the little house in Cambridge Crescent, a five year old car and a small savings account to cover funeral expenses. Yet he was always a good provider. Whenever extra money was needed he would get an advance against commissions and take to the road, heading for the Victorian Mallee or Mildura on an intensive sales campaigns to rebuild his credit. He was the patriarch and benefactor for three generations of Cornwalls, his generosity to the large extended family legendary. He paid for my education at boarding school and supported me through six years at university. Later, when I needed a substantial loan to get established in veterinary practice in Mount Gambier, he didn't hesitate to mortgage the White Hills house as security.

My mother remained a keen horsewoman and continued her interest during the early days in Bendigo, occasionally riding track work at the Bendigo racecourse for Harry Mack before he decided there was a very limited future for country horse trainers in the 1930s. The track work ended when he purchased the Bedford bus and she became pregnant with my brother Terry in 1939.

BENDIGO'S HISTORY AS A GOLD RUSH town was still almost in living memory during my childhood. When I started primary school in 1940 it was less than 90 years after the great gold rushes that had been such an important part of Australian history. Many old Bendigonians at that time were first generation descendants of the gold diggers. Others had worked underground in mines like the Great Northern Deborah. Reminders were everywhere. Mine shafts that had been worked by two man teams of prospectors with hand winch and bucket still created hazards along the banks of the Bendigo creek, less than 500 yards from where I lived in Cambridge Crescent. Poppet heads and mullock heaps from larger scale mining operations still ringed the city.

A small community of direct descendants of the Chinese prospectors attempted to preserve symbols of their culture, the Joss House in North Bendigo and the Chinese dragon kept in Bridge Street the most obvious. The great dragon 'Loong' was always a feature of the Bendigo Easter Fair, taunted by fire crackers and clanging cymbals while more than 20 men sweated to carry him twisting and angry in the procession.

Our enthusiasm for the future after the war diminished our interest in the past. We were witnesses to 20th century political history in the making. Early in 1948 Dr McCarthy, the small, gentle Catholic Bishop of Sandhurst died. Catholics throughout the Diocese donated enthusiastically to a special appeal to buy a Packard Clipper for the new Bishop, Bernard Stewart, who came from Rome to Bendigo with the Pope's blessing. He became known as Bernard the Builder, the driving force in ensuring that Bendigo's Sacred Heart Cathedral was completed, a testimonial to his tenure in office in the European tradition. He also became influential in his support for the right wing group that split from the ALP in 1955 to form the Australian Labor Party (Anti-Communist), later renamed the Democratic Labor Party (DLP). The split caused great bitterness, not least among Catholic families in the Bishop's Diocese. The DLP's vehemence in opposing Labor and giving its preferences to the Liberal Party at successive federal elections succeeded in keeping the Labor Party out of government for 23 years.

THE IMMEDIATE POSTWAR PERIOD was a time of emerging ambition. In Bendigo the lawyers, doctors and local businessmen lived with their families in the brick and stone homes on the hills adjacent to the city. The rest of us lived in weatherboard houses in Eaglehawk, Quarry Hill, Kangaroo Flat and White Hills. Many of the children of the elite went away to boarding school where the girls developed social graces and the brighter boys made valuable contacts on their way to Melbourne University. I decided that boarding school was a must for me. Dad was initially puzzled by my determination but my mother, always impressed if a little daunted by the 'better people', supported my ambition enthusiastically.

In January 1949 we drove to Xavier College in the eastern suburbs of Melbourne for an interview with the Rector, Dad sweating in his navy blue suit, Mum elegant in her new summer frock with matching shoes and hat. Dad was back in his best form in the life insurance industry and driving a new Ford V8 to prove it. The Ford wound up the long driveway from Barker's Road, through the school playing fields with their well grassed surfaces and turf cricket pitches. It passed the main oval and the pavilion, then on past the beautiful chapel with its large cupola to the grey stone Rector's building. I was accepted to start my first term as a Xavier boarder the following month. This must have been a period in my parents' long marriage when they were very happy and well pleased - my brother Timothy was born nine months after this visit to Xavier, 10 years after brother Terry.

I had always been an avid cricket fan. When the 1946-47 England test team visited Bendigo I saw the great Walter Hammond bat against a Northern Victorian XI on Bendigo's Upper Reserve (later the Queen Elizabeth Oval). On New Year's Day 1948 Dad took me to the Melbourne Cricket Ground where I watched Don Bradman make 132 against India. Xavier had provided a comprehensive list of clothing and accessories for new boarders and families without previous boarding school experience followed it religiously, shopping at Myers or Buckley and Nunn. However, there was no mention of a dress code for aspiring cricketers. In Bendigo I had played with other 12 and 13 year olds, using composite cork cricket balls on concrete pitches and when I was selected to play for the under 15B cricket team against Wesley College I turned out in my best Bendigo rig - white shorts, tennis shirt and sandshoes. However, most of the 14 year olds in the team appeared in cricket boots, long white trousers and white shirts with rolled up sleeves, replicas of Bradman's Invincibles. I bowled two overs during which the Wesley batsmen punished me mercilessly. I was taken off and never played cricket again until the friendly inter-college matches at university.

Things were better but difficult in the classroom. From my earliest school days in Bendigo I had often been dux of my class but I found difficulty in adapting to the pre-university teaching style of the Jesuits, so different from much of the rote learning at the Marist Brothers. Coping with boarding school food was another challenge. The food, served from the top end of each long table in the refectory, was plentiful but less than a culinary delight. Cornflakes provided a reliable start for breakfast except when the bulk milk, delivered to the kitchen in ten gallon cans, was turning sour. The toast was cold and damp, the fried eggs cold and greasy. The other meals were culinary calamities, soggy cabbage with hot corned beef and boiled potatoes, boiled dried peas and tepid roast potatoes with thick outer hides. On Fridays it was tinned fish served with sliced boiled eggs in a claggy white sauce. Informal weekend meals included thick slices of white bread with apricot jam and on Saturday night meat pies with tomato sauce.

Then there were the Melbourne winters. The study hall housed 140 boarders with a small wood or briquette fire at each end. The younger boys were seated towards the back of the hall near the study supervisor and gained some benefit from the fire. The senior students were located at the front, close to the other fireplace. The rest of us had the benefit of the cheery glow of the fires but none of their heat. It soon became obvious why travelling rugs had been on the boarders' list. Doubled and wrapped around the waist they provided ankle length woolen warmth. There was no heating in the classrooms, indoor recreation areas, dining room, chapel or dormitories. We survived those harsh winters the hard way.

There was one bright spot in my first year. Xavier had an outstanding choir which sang in four parts, sopranos and altos whose voices had not yet succumbed to the changes of puberty, with tenors and baritones after the transition. I auditioned successfully for the choir and came to the notice of Father Montague, a stern but kind old Jesuit who was both the choirmaster and the director of the annual production of the Gilbert & Sullivan opera. *The Mikado* was the opera selected in 1949 and I got the role of the ugly Katisha which suited my voice if not my vanity. Then shortly before the scheduled performances the contralto began to break towards baritone. I just managed to hang on long enough to enjoy the applause of the audience, despite the odd yodel during *Alone and yet alive*.

Father James Boylen, the Prefect of Studies, and Father Gerry Owens, the distinguished, elderly Latin teacher, were kind and scholarly men whom I admired. but some of the others lacked the style, form and intellect traditionally associated with the Jesuits. Paul Keenan SJ, with his rolling athletic gait and aquiline features, was the antithesis of the traditional image, clearly more dedicated to sporting than academic excellence. He was the senior football coach and sought to bring the same tough regimentation to his role as the First Division Prefect, responsible for the maintenance of 'good order and discipline' among the senior boarders. This was a time when smoking was generally accepted as a sophisticated adult habit with scant reference to any health hazards, except that 'it might stunt your growth'. The Hollywood stars of the day boosted their images as suave, tough guys by chain smoking in their movies and as a rite of passage to adulthood it was singularly attractive to 15 year olds. But school rules classified it as strictly for adults. Students caught smoking were given six whacks on the backside with a thick black strap which the athletic Keenan wielded with considerable vigour.

One of the more interesting characters was the senior English teacher with the unlikely name of Ludwig Von Baer. His provenance was uncertain but he was said to support a large family on his modest stipend, a story given credibility by the well worn navy blue suit and ancient gabardine raincoat that he wore virtually throughout the four seasons. His teeth, in an obvious state of disrepair, added to the impression that he was totally indifferent about his personal appearance. Whatever his domestic tribulations or his personal idiosyncrasies, he was an outstanding teacher who gave me an appreciation of the beauty of language and literature.

My enthusiasm for team sports was dampened dramatically by my early experience in that cricket match against Wesley and having shown that I was no athlete I was often free on Saturday afternoons when everyone was involved in cricket or football. It was easy for a boarder to leave the school without permission and I became a regular Saturday afternoon patron at the movies, visiting the grand picture theatres of the day. At the State Theatre in Flinders Street Stan Bourne's 17 piece swing band rose on the hydraulic stage to play during the interval and at the ornate Regent Theatre in Collins Street the mighty Wurlitzer organ was the centrepiece.

Horse racing was a growing interest for me and during Melbourne's spring racing carnival in 1950 I had spectacular success as a 15 year old punter. John Sutton, a day boy and close friend who lived in suburban Brighton, asked his father to act as my 'agent' to invest five shillings on the great Comic Court which won the Underwood Stakes. The next week I had my winnings on Grey Boots which won the Toorak Handicap and bet the lot on him when he won the Caulfield Cup a week later. Within two weeks I had won £25, almost a year's pocket money. I bought a Leica camera, kept the £5 change and managed to convince my doubting parents that I had won the expensive camera in a Brighton Yacht Club raffle.

Because I was not yet quite 16 when I completed my matriculation I was considered too young and immature to attend university. A repeat year could bring personal honours and supplement the school's academic reputation. However, I already had six matriculation subjects at a level which in those less competitive days would admit me to virtually any vocational course that I chose and there was little practical incentive to improve on it. At 16 I was becoming more interested in girls than Latin and Physics. Selwyn (Sel) Murray's sister Judy was at Mandeville Hall, an upmarket Catholic Girls School. She was a useful social contact and on boarders' *exeat* weekends I sometimes managed invitations to stay with the parents of weekly boarders and get to Saturday night parties in fashionable homes in the eastern suburbs. Powerhousing, the preferred form of dancing for young Melbournians at the time, derived its name from the old powerhouse on the banks of the Albert Park Lake which had been converted into a dance club. The lights were turned down low, the band played *I'm in the Mood for Love* and young couples danced cheek to cheek, swaying rather than moving.

My three years with the Jesuits at Xavier might have been character forming but they were far from the happiest of my life. In my final year my nemesis was Buster Cook, the school captain who in my considered, if less than objective, opinion had few attributes for the position. His only achievements were a commission in the school cadets and active membership of the Sodality of Our Lady, both of which lay outside my ambition or inclination. He was appointed by the Jesuit masters and assumed the role of disciplinarian, always the cadet captain pursuing us for such dreadful breaches as talking in chapel or not wearing the school cap when leaving the college grounds.

Normally silence was enforced from the time we left the study hall at 9.30pm, through showers in the communal block to lights out in the dormitory. However, on the Friday night before the final exams we were in high spirits and skylarked on the way from the study hall to the senior dormitory. Buster, ever the authoritarian, was affronted by this breach of discipline and singled me out for a special reprimand. 'Our last school night, could you really be serious?' I laughed at him, raised my fists and ducked my head, sparring in a comic gesture of insubordination.

The Rector, Tom Costello SJ, tall, bald and corpulent, was rarely seen around the college after dark. Conventional wisdom among the students was that he was necessarily more concerned about the state of the college finances than giving the scholastic and spiritual leadership so prized by the Society of Jesus. On this unlucky night, all my stars were in alignment for the high farce that followed. I didn't see him but he was just behind me as I shaped up to Captain Cook and he interpreted it as the ultimate breach of discipline. Comedy turned tragic. 'Cornwall' he bawled in his tremulous, high pitched Irish voice, 'get to my study'. His ruddy face was on fire, blood pressure soaring. As he recounted my numerous sins I was distressed but flattered by the attention that my progress through the school had apparently attracted. I was a serial offender – smoking, preferring the pictures to sport on a Saturday afternoon, challenging school rules generally. The Rector recited the list of charges, although he was not aware of the essential service I had provided as the school's starting price bookmaker on Melbourne Cup Days, allowed no evidence in mitigation or rebuttal and asked me to leave that weekend.

All classes had finished for the year so there was none of the high drama of expulsion, just 'get out!'. Ian Stephenson was a weekly boarder whose parents ran a guest house on St Kilda Road, a slightly dilapidated mansion but still a fine example of Victorian architecture from more gracious days. I found asylum there and over the next three weeks sat for the matriculation exams for the second time in Melbourne's Exhibition Building along with thousands of students from the Catholic School system whom the authorities were presumably concerned might cheat without independent supervision.

By the end of 1951 I had completed two years of matriculation studies and was still just short of my 17th birthday. I left Xavier with good friends, some happy memories, mixed emotions and eight matriculation subjects, including first class honours in English Expression and English Literature. Latin, History, Physics, Chemistry, Mathematics and Music made up the remainder.

With Mum, Dad and brother Terry at the Essendon Airport before boarding the TAA Convair to fly to Brisbane and the University of Queensland, March 1952.

CHAPTER THREE

Tall tales and true

During my final year at school my boyhood aspirations for a big brick house on a hill had been replaced by fantasies of white posts and rails along the sweeping drive to the homestead of my thoroughbred horse stud. As a first step I decided to pursue a career as a veterinarian and had to choose between the only two veterinary faculties that existed in Australasia at that time. For a teenager who had never ventured far beyond the Victorian border, sub-tropical Brisbane seemed an exciting choice. More importantly the weekly accommodation at St Leo's University College was less than £4 a week, half the tariff at St Johns in Sydney.

In early March 1952, aged 17, I boarded a TAA Convair 240 at Essendon Airport bound for Brisbane. I was the first member of my family to fly and one of the first of the extended Cornwall and Bilston families to attend a university, seven generations after the arrival of the First Fleet. The Convair, powered by conventional propeller driven twin engines, was one of the first pressurised commercial aircraft to operate in Australia and the fastest of its day. The 'Rocket' service from Melbourne direct to Brisbane took just three hours and 10 minutes, one class, first class.

The City of Brisbane was initially a disappointment with little of the waving palm trees and tropical charm that had been painted for me from the uncertain recollections of Victorian servicemen who passed through it during the Second World War en route to Papua New Guinea. Apart from the City Hall and several fine public buildings from colonial days Brisbane's central business district in the early 1950s was uninspiring and I was puzzled by the weatherboard houses on stilts.

But with its population of just a little over 500,000 the city had a casual, unsophisticated character which quickly captivated me. I fell in love with Brisbane and the lifestyle of an undergraduate at the University of Queensland. This was the city of the home grown department stores TC Biernes and Finneys, predating Myers and David Jones; of silver trams with drivers and conductors in Foreign Legion style caps; of art unions (a Queensland euphemism for raffles) for every worthy cause from surf lifesaving to the Mater Hospital. And when most Australians who wanted a lottery ticket still had to send to Tasmania for a 'ticket in Tatts' Brisbane had a Golden Casket agency on almost every city block. The Cloudland Ballroom, with its uniquely sprung dance floor, was a Brisbane landmark; Sandro Merlini was singing at a supper club called The Havana (admission six shillings, bring your own hip flask); the Bellevue Hotel in George Street combined social grace with architectural charm and T-Bone steak and eggs at Nick's Cafe in the city cost three and sixpence. Temprite had not yet arrived from the south. In the hotel bars hooped wooden beer barrels were rolled out of the cool room, raised to a handy height on a stand, spiked and tapped, the beer then pulled directly into the glass. The barrels were colour coded, red for Fourex, green for Bulimba, commonly known among students as the green death. And in the early 1950s it was hard to find a two storey building on the Gold Coast where social life was centred on the Surfer's Hotel beer garden and the Cathay Cafe.

Prior to the winter racing carnival at Eagle Farm and Doomben each year Brisbane's two newspapers, the *Courier Mail* and the *Telegraph*, reported that senior detectives, led by Inspector (later Commissioner) Frank Bischof were meeting interstate flights and apprehending southern criminals who were swiftly returned whence they came. Despite compelling evidence to the contrary which would emerge later, it was still widely accepted that crime and corruption only happened 'down south'.

FRESHLY ARRIVED FROM VICTORIA I was prepared sartorially for university life as it was lived in Melbourne with a touch of Oxbridge, Fletcher Jones slacks, Harris Tweed jacket, woollen tie. I arrived in Brisbane with a new lightweight brown suit by 'Mr Whitmont' and soon after arrival somehow managed to find the money to buy a light grey tuxedo jacket from Rothwells Men's Store. Queensland male dress code was much more relaxed and students paid little attention to fashion. At St Leo's the students wore academic gowns to dinner but often over t-shirts, well worn rugby shorts and sandals. However, there were exceptions: Professor

Max Hickey insisted that his male medical students (there weren't many females) wear a white shirt and tie to his anatomy lectures and for black tie formals a dinner jacket or tuxedo, owned or hired, was *de rigeur*, a corsage for your partner mandatory.

The old St Leo's was on Wickham Terrace overlooking the city, one of the best and most sought after locations in Brisbane, but the accommodation was less than salubrious. Forty five students were housed in a series of partitioned and louvered balconies, rooms, cubbies and alcoves in two gracious but dilapidated mansions. Ten more lived in 'the hut', a fibro-cement structure of uncertain origin and poor repair, their rooms just able to accommodate a single bed, small wardrobe, study table and a chair. Nine more lived in rooms in the Sheehy Shed, an antediluvian structure which reflected a determination to relocate to the new Leo's proposed for the St Lucia campus as soon as possible. There was a large central area in the shed which contained a billiard table in a terminal state of disrepair and an ancient upright piano with only the slightest residual value as a musical instrument. Some years later it was broken up and burned by the students as a symbolic gesture of disaffection during a dispute with the recalcitrant Jesuit Rector. The large block behind the shed was overrun with weeds and labelled taipan country by the student body. A small, well worn path ran through it to Paolo Piccio's tiny corner store and it was a short walk to Ray and May's well patronised late night hamburger bar in Spring Hill.

The students came from diverse and contrasting family backgrounds, the sons of doctors, lawyers, publicans, bookmakers, salesmen, school teachers, graziers, cane farmers and storekeepers. The Rector in 1952 was an aging Vincentian priest, Father Gerry Power, a benign patrician who controlled his students with tolerance and good humour. He had an impressive ability to monitor a student's progress unobtrusively and give a quiet word of advice or a kindly gesture of support.

We were a generation rich in contradictions. There was little organised political activity on Australian university campuses in the 1950s. Yet this was the period of the Cold War, the rabid Senator Joseph McCarthy in the United States, and in Australia the Menzies Government's *Communist Party Dissolution Bill* and the Petrov Affair. Doc Evatt's destructive obsessions overshadowed his proud achievements at the United Nations just a few years earlier and were a catalyst for the bitter splits that would keep federal Labor out of office until 1972 and consign the Party to the opposition benches in the Queensland Parliament for more than 30 years.

The general student response to this climate of political reaction was a stoic acceptance: switch off, adapt to the leisurely academic pace of the 1950s and pursue the good life. For us this was considerably enhanced by Tony and Don Ridolfi, mine hosts at the City View Hotel on the corner of Wickham Terrace and Leichhardt Street, strategically placed between three university colleges, Emmanuel, St Leo's and Union.

In 1952 there were only 17 students in my first year and around 100 undergraduates over the entire five years of the veterinary course at the University of Queensland. Less than 10 per cent were women and the syllabus was markedly different from the way it is structured in Australian veterinary schools in the 21st century. First year was essentially pure science. Lectures and practical sessions in botany, zoology and physics were conducted at the end of George Street, adjacent to the Botanic Gardens, later the site of the Queensland University of Technology. Chemistry lectures and practical sessions were conducted at the main university campus at St Lucia. Physiology and biochemistry in second and third year were largely annexed to the medical faculty. Musculoskeletal, nervous, gastrointestinal, circulatory, reproductive and urinary systems; endocrine and exocrine glands; cells, membranes, nuclei, mitochondria, Mendelian genetics, chromosomes, enzymes and the Krebs cycle. There was an outline of the ongoing research but little detail about RNA (ribonucleic acid) and DNA (deoxyribonucleic acid) and vague references to but no insight into a new technology called computer science.[5]

The Professor of Physiology, W.V. McFarlane, had earlier worked with Nobel Laureate Sir John Eccles when Sir John spent a period as Professor of Physiology at the University of Otago, New Zealand. Eccles' book *The Neurophysiological Basis of Mind* was first published in 1953 and was compulsory reading for students in Vet II and III, although we were never too sure how this learned and challenging tome would relate to veterinary practice. Veterinary anatomy was taught over two years, Vet II and Vet III, at the old vet school at Yeerongpilly, Sisson's *Anatomy of the Domestic Animals* the standard text. Our only encounter with live animals prior to fourth year was in some practical animal husbandry sessions.

MY LOVE FOR GOOD HORSES in those days was matched by my passion for punting. Late in 1953 I had a run of luck betting with a senior veterinary student who was the inter-college starting price (SP) bookmaker. When he had difficulty settling I took over the book in lieu of payment and became the SP bookmaker for the residential colleges of the Queensland University. The wagers were small but plentiful, the punters were uninformed and on Saturday afternoons St Leo's student phone was available for incoming calls from students at the other colleges with approved credit. For a while I had a modest but virtually assured income in excess of my cadetship allowance but I mixed my bookmaking with punting and not only lost the lot but ran up a substantial debt. In less than 12 months I'd 'retired hurt'.

But I was ever alert for other ways in which my quarterly allowance of £50 could be supplemented or stretched. In 1954 I became aware that the University Students Union was relatively flush with funds and that a substantial amount of this money was allocated each year to pay the fares and expenses of students participating in intervarsity sporting contests. There was no chance of selection in any of the team sports but I thought I must be in with a chance of selection as a lightweight in the boxing team and that year the national university boxing championships were being held in Melbourne. This might be a way to get to Victoria and home for the second term vacation at the union's expense. I attended the gym three times a week, did a little road work, punching the air like a pro, and took some advice from an old timer who was training us – left lead, right cross, feint, counter punch, uppercut.

When my mate Tony Johnston queried the adequacy of my training regimen and more particularly my ability I assured him that I was 'good with my hands'. It was unfortunate for me that in 1954 the lightweight title was contested by a third year medical student, a skilled and lightning fast southpaw. All my instructions on defence and counter punching came to nothing and at the end of the first round I felt as though I had been run over by the proverbial Mack truck. I agreed enthusiastically with my seconds and the referee that it would be unwise and probably dangerous for me to emerge for the second round.

It was clear that I was not good with my hands so the time had come to use my head. The AGM of the Boxing Club was upon us and they needed an experienced secretary. My credentials for the job were impeccable - six weeks of light training and two minutes of boxing made me a clear choice! Within a month I was flying to Melbourne as secretary-manager of the very successful University of Queensland boxing team.

EVERY OTHER STATE CAPITAL in Australia conducts a Royal Agricultural Show but in Queensland it's called the 'Ekka', the Brisbane Exhibition, held for 10 days in August each year. In my first year I scored a job on the Mater Hospital Wheel in sideshow alley where we raised money for the Mater Mothers Hospital, 60 tickets for each spin, the winners picking prizes ranging from a large stuffed teddy bear to kitchenware. The wheel was alongside the Gyro Globe of Death where Daredevil Durkins and his partner risked life and limb on their motorbikes as they defied gravity on the hour every hour, roaring in circles, one vertically one horizontally, never colliding but always at fearful risk in the steel mesh globe.

In subsequent years I bought my compulsory Australian Workers Union (AWU) ticket and worked on the change windows. Our team exchanged notes for the coins that the crowds needed to work the admission turnstiles, and then made runs to the on-site bank to replenish the coin supply. Not as stimulating as working alongside Daredevil Durkins in sideshow alley but much more rewarding. In 10 straight days, working 13 hours a day with penalty rates courtesy of the AWU, I earned almost as much as the three month allowance from my cadetship.

During the long summer vacations in those pre-clinical years I worked on farms in Victoria. During the summer in which I had finished school and prior to starting university I served my apprenticeship working for Glen James, a tough old cocky on a mixed farm at Pyramid Hill. We worked seven days a week, milking 60 cows before breakfast, spending the day harvesting wheat and oats or cutting chaff, irrigating sown pasture for the dairy herd, then facing milking time again towards sunset.

All students who turned 18 during the previous calendar year were required to register for national service in the following January-March.[6] The university vacation was extended for students in that category but as my 18th birthday was on 1 January 1953 I missed the intake at the end of first year by one day. In subsequent years the authorities seemed to lose interest in me and by the time I graduated the scheme was being wound down. I never did get to be a 'nasho'.

In the summer vacations of 1953 and 1954 I worked on farms in the Victorian Wimmera and Mallee, pulling a Combine Harvester behind a John Deere or Fordson tractor, sewing oat bags, driving the bulk truck to the wheat silos, milking the house cow, a regular farmhand. At Natimuk I helped to build haystacks, now a long forgotten skill, using a pitchfork to turn the oaten sheaves to the stack builder who laid them at an angle to form a protective sloping sidewall, finished artfully with a thatched roof. When the wheat harvest finished in 1953 I picked up prunes for three weeks at Quantong, collecting the ripe plums shaken from the trees for drying. I fell in love briefly with the farmer's daughter, although sadly I never got to tell her. In February and March 1954 I also worked as a strapper in my brother-in-law Bert Honeychurch's racing stable in Berrigan while colleagues were doing their national service.

AT THE BEGINNING OF 1954 the spirit and charm of Leo's were shattered when the Vincentian Fathers relinquished their interest to the Jesuits who appointed Father Tom Johnston SJ as the Rector. He was a very strange choice; aged, ascetic and authoritarian he was determined to put his stamp on the College. The happy days under the benign guidance of Gerry Power had been replaced by the new autocracy. His deputy was Brian Buxton SJ, a vague, well meaning soul who was tormented by his imagination. He was a Victorian and a gentleman who failed to make the cultural transition necessary to understand Brisbane in the 1950s.

On the Thursday prior to Easter that year a group of us decided to celebrate the resurrection in advance. We set up a keg of Fourex in a vestibule in the Vice-Rector's building and partied until midnight when some of us moved to Kevin 'Frosty' Hale's room. It was Good Friday by now so when Denis Shanahan was dispatched on his Lambretta to Ray and May's Hamburger Bar his order was for egg burgers all round. Upstairs in his bedroom Brian Buxton was listening to the proceedings with trepidation. Towards 1.30am there was a loud knock on the door; the Vice Rector had arrived. Frosty retreated to his large, old fashioned wardrobe where he curled up among the shoes, baggage and dirty clothes and quickly closed the door.

When Buxton entered in his dressing gown he saw inebriated students munching on burger packs. He was convinced that we were committing the ultimate sin, eating meat on Good Friday. 'You are like the soldiers under the cross' he said in his most sombre manner. 'No Father', Edgar Ahern replied, attempting to look equally serious, 'this is more like the last supper'. Edgar, a tall, loose limbed medical student from a grazing property at Muttaburra in Western Queensland, was one of Leo's genuine characters, intelligent, amusing and a little eccentric. Buxton was aghast at his irreverence. 'I think there will have to be some expulsions' he said with anguish. Just at that moment Frosty lost his balance, fell out of the wardrobe, looked up from the floor and said profoundly 'I don't think that will be necessary Father'.

COMMEMORATION WEEK WAS an important occasion on the University of Queensland calendar, always held in the week leading up to May Day and the Labour Day weekend. There were a series of ceremonies and other celebrations important to university life and the week culminated on the Friday night with the Commem Ball at Cloudland. After a mid-week celebration at the City View Hotel to get into the spirit of the week several college men pressed on to the Havana supper club with their dates while I returned to Leo's quite unhappy at being left out because I didn't have a partner. However, my luck turned when I answered the student phone on the way to my room. It was Patrice Hourigan wanting to speak to her brother John, an earnest, amiable engineering student from Gympie whose room was adjacent to mine in the Sheehy Shed. I had never met Patrice but I convinced her that I was one of John's best friends and that I would really like her to join our party at the Havana. Within 10 minutes I was on my way to pick up my date in a Yellow Cab ('one shilling flag fall and a shilling a mile'). Within two years we would be married, a union that would last for more than 60 years.

Frosty Hale may have thought expulsions from Leo's were not necessary at that Good Friday party in April but Johnston SJ had other ideas. As his relations with the student body deteriorated he decided to get rid of the 'irresponsible element'. Just after midnight on Saturday 12 September John Moro and I made a rowdy return to College after attending a social in the nurses' quarters at the Brisbane General Hospital. We disturbed the Vice-Rector who called out from his upstairs bedroom window, ordering me to get to bed. I had an energetic and rather comical verbal exchange with him, helped along by a blood alcohol level that in these days of random breath testing would be described as mid-range; foolish but hardly a capital offence in university college life. I was summoned to the Rector's office at 9.30am on Saturday morning, ordered to pack and leave the college immediately.

Initially I refused, at least pending the opportunity for mediation or conciliation but Johnston then changed his tactics. 'I am just drafting a letter to your father' he said. His proposition was that if I complied with his direction and left quietly he would simply say that we had agreed I was not suited to college life. On the other hand, if I continued to resist he would have to paint a grim picture of an unruly student lurching out of control. I packed my belongings and left within three hours.

In fact Johnston had already posted his letter to my parents. It was delivered with due speed, arriving at Cambridge Crescent on Tuesday morning, just hours after my father had left on a business trip to Mildura. Rather than the low key 'unsuited to college life' proposition, it painted a picture of a rebel out of control. Meanwhile I had sought asylum at Beatrice Chappel's boarding house at Dutton Park. 'Beet' ran her establishment in the best tradition of the fifties - the tariff was reasonable, the food adequate and nutritious, the accommodation comfortable and the linen spotless. Beet was an attractive middle aged woman with a generous figure and assisted blonde hair who took an unobtrusive interest in the wellbeing of the bank clerks, students, teachers and apprentices who lodged at Dutton Park over the years. In the months following my expulsion it became a refuge for several victims of the Johnston purge.

I was unaware that the Rector's letter had been dispatched with such speed and treachery and spent the weekend wondering how to tell my parents why I had revised my living arrangements. On the Tuesday evening Dad contacted the President of the Leo's Student Council for details of my whereabouts and I was at Eagle Farm to meet him when his plane landed the next day. Father Cornwall met with Father Johnston within hours of arriving in Brisbane, conceded that my behaviour had been unruly and foolish but asked the Rector, in very blunt terms, why I had not been counselled rather than turned out into the street. He spent two days with us at the boarding house, made sure my bills were paid, then flew back to Melbourne. As he left he gave me the advice he always offered whenever I was in trouble: 'You'd better pull your socks up son'.

Despite the brave face that I displayed for the College Men on the day I left Leo's, I was wounded strategically and emotionally. I had already pushed my luck by leaving any serious study until third term and been thrown out just six weeks before the end-of-year exams. In what was to be a vain attempt to make up for lost time I was taking amphetamine tablets during the two weeks of 'swot vac', immediately prior to the exams, studying through the night until 3.00am, snatching three or four hours of disturbed sleep before breakfast, then returning to the books. Despite emerging concerns, dexedrine was being prescribed as an appetite suppressant in the fifties and some general practitioners were writing prescriptions for amphetamines without too many questions.

I struggled through the written exams in November but by the time I got to the *viva voce* question and answer sessions the amphetamine caused some bizarre distortions. During my anatomy *viva* I had a detailed mental picture of the illustrations in Sisson's anatomy text book but no names: 'I know the answer, Mr May. The illustration is on page 134 in Sisson, it's the nerve labelled 5b but I can't remember its name'. For the first time in my career I scored supplementary exams in anatomy and pathology, two of the big three subjects in third year. I spent three weeks at home in Bendigo, then flew back after Christmas to start six weeks of summer study.

Approaching the exams I was contrite but confident, having done almost as much intensive study in six weeks as I had done for the whole of the previous year. After the written and practical exams I felt that I had done well but the Dean, Professor Ewer, thought differently. T. K. Ewer was a Sydney graduate but he had done post-graduate work in animal husbandry at Cambridge and adopted the form and manners of a Cambridge Don; tall, slim, a full mane of abundant grey hair, silk handkerchief in the breast pocket of his well cut jackets. He had a rather pompous manner and an accent to match. I sought an appointment with him and pleaded my case. 'You're a young man, Cornwall' he said. 'A repeat year will do you the world of good'. I pointed out that losing my cadetship payments for a repeat year would cause me great financial hardship and when that failed to have any impact I compared my record in the previous two years with some of my colleagues who had advanced to fourth year. I asked for my performance in the posts to be reviewed independently but he was unmoved.

For the first time in my life I had failed academically. The wounds were self inflicted and very deep, with an equal mix of guilt, grief and resentment. My first impulse was to drop out and I even made preliminary inquiries about a job based in Toowoomba, on Queensland's Darling Downs, selling agricultural and veterinary chemicals. Following our first night at the Havana in May the previous year, Patrice and I had dated intermittently but by September she had become my 'new best friend'. Now it was February 1955 and for the first of many occasions in our long life together she gave me the stability and support that I needed. She urged me not to surrender, pointing out that if I did it would be an admission of failure that would impact on my life chances forever. She told me to repeat the year and to make some dramatic changes to my study habits. Then Dad came to the rescue. 'We can find the money. You just keep your head down and make sure it doesn't happen again'.

Cutting the cake at our wedding reception held at the bride's family home, Calton Terrace, Gympie, 19 May 1956.

CHAPTER FOUR

High on the hill

I was appalled at the prospect of a repeat year in 1955 but had to make the best of it. Patrice and I were now in a committed relationship but in the 1950s cohabitation was unthinkable, especially for a well reared Irish Catholic girl from Gympie, so finding suitable independent accommodation was my next priority. By this time Frosty Hale (of wardrobe fame) had graduated as a veterinarian and was working for the Queensland Department of Agriculture and Stock, based in Brisbane. He was a salary earner and creditworthy enough to sign a lease on a flat that we could share. The 'flat' was the upstairs portion of a dilapidated weatherboard cottage built on the downside of a hill at 20 Judge Street, Petrie Terrace, behind the Caxton Hotel and adjacent to the Police Barracks.

Frosty had not yet come under the influence of Agnes who later performed miracles in converting him into a devoted husband and father, a well-respected member of the veterinary profession and his local community. He was intelligent and clever, graduating from the five year course before his 22nd birthday, but in 1955 he was a very rough diamond who paid scant attention to personal appearance or freshness. In those days when white shirts were standard rig, Frosty often chose his shirt of the day from the soiled clothes bag, selecting one that could be worn just one more time – or longer. As a new graduate with the department one of his first projects was an investigation into infertility in dairy cattle in the Brisbane Valley. Among other things this involved a lot of pregnancy testing, done by rectal examination in the days before shoulder length disposable plastic gloves were available - Velvet soap and water were the only lubricants. After a hard day at the rear end of innumerable cows and heifers Frosty would repair to the Lands Office Hotel with his mentor Col Craven, his right arm still bearing the stains of the day's work, and sink a few beers. Then he would head for home to cook some simple fare – sausages, potatoes and beans a staple – and relax in a lounge chair cleaning his finger nails.

By and large I was keeping my head down in my repeat year as Dad had advised but I was not averse to an occasional party. Tony 'Storky' Johnston never needed any encouragement and we were well supported by Ben Benaradsky. Ben's father had been a young veterinary officer in the Czar's cavalry and fled to Peking with his wife after the Russian revolution. Ben was born there in 1932, survived the Japanese occupation but in 1948 the family fled again, this time to Hong Kong when it became clear that Mao Zedong and the communist party would gain control. The refugee family eventually came to Brisbane via Manila. Ben had spent the immediate post war years in an American High School conducted for the children of United States military and diplomatic personnel in Peking. He completed his secondary education on arrival in Brisbane and joined us in first year in 1952.

Ben's father arrived in Australia with very limited English and with no prospect of registration as a veterinary surgeon. He was employed as the kennel man at the vet school, medicating, feeding and providing general care for the cats and dogs in the small animal hospital. Ben's mother, who came from an aristocratic family in the Czar's Russia, worked as a cleaner at the Mater Hospital. Father Benna's life experience as a student and in the officers' mess in the old Russia had taught him all you need to know about a good party. The Benaradsky house in suburban Stones Corner was the venue for some great parties. Mrs Benna was always supportive and solicitous for our welfare and improvised bedding for anyone who needed to stay the night. Then half way through Ben's course his father, aged 62, had a fatal heart attack.

In 1955 the flat at 20 Judge Street had also become an occasional party venue. The necessities of life at the parties were alcohol, salted peanuts and a haze of cigarette smoke. Ben had good connections with the student nurses at the Mater and could be relied on to ensure a gender balance if recruits were required. Patrice added a touch of class and provided supper. One of our regular partygoers was Maurice Furtardo, an Indian medical student from Goa, at that time still a Portuguese colony. He had been an active and popular member of the 'Leo's push', had a great sense of humour, loved a beer and was always happy to be where the action was. In those days of the White Australia Policy Maurice was often a victim of racism. From time to time nurses at the Holy Spirit Hospital would accept his invitation to accompany him to social functions, then withdraw at the last minute; in the White Australia of the 1950s it took courage to be seen socially with a black man. On one occasion he was identified generically as a 'blackfella' by a barmaid and barred from Brisbane's British Empire Hotel.

A lot of beer was drunk and peanuts were crunched on the cheap linoleum at the Judge Street wingdings. If the party was on a Friday night we tried to run a mop over the floor and empty the ash trays on Saturday morning before the landlords, a husband and wife team, arrived to service the flat. But occasionally they came early – or we slept late. After one of our parties they let themselves in and came upon Maurice sleeping on the ancient couch, stripped to his boxer shorts for comfort. The large, semi-naked black man stirred from his sleep, glowered at them and demanded in a deep voice and Goan English accent 'Who the bloody hell are you?' There was a very happy ending to the Furtardo story. He graduated in medicine, married a Gympie girl, Peggy Riek, became an Australian citizen, gained his specialist qualification as a radiologist, reared a family and practiced in Queensland for the rest of his professional life.

At Easter I was invited home to Gympie to meet Patrice's parents, in November I passed all the third year subjects with credits in pathology and physiology and at year's end Frosty and I relinquished our lease on Judge Street. I returned to Bendigo for the long summer vacation and Patrice flew to Victoria on New Year's Eve to see in the New Year, help me celebrate my 21st birthday and join us for a family holiday.

BY 1956 I WAS IN FOURTH YEAR where we began our clinical training. The day started early with treatment of the animal hospital patients, then lectures from 9.00am to 11.00am followed by two hours in the small animal clinic or operating theatre. After lunch there were more practical sessions in surgery, parasitology, animal husbandry and bacteriology; eight hours of contact followed by evening study.

We were paired for some of the practical projects. In second term I joined Chong Sue Kheng, a popular mature age Malayan Chinese student who later became the Director of the Veterinary Research Institute at Ipoh, to conduct an artificial insemination project in poultry. With the introduction of laying cages in the 1950s, artificial insemination in hens was being explored commercially in Australia. It never found practical application in the long run but aspiring veterinarians were supposed to be familiar with many species and techniques. Chong and I proved to be less than proficient at collecting roosters' semen by manual stimulation, a technique requiring considerable sensitivity and dexterity, and we were even less successful at inseminating the hens. After four or five days, eggs which were being incubated could be identified as fertile, infertile or bad by 'candling', working in a darkened room with a candling torch which gave a bright light to illuminate the contents of the egg through the shell. Less than 25 per cent of our incubated eggs were fertile when we candled them, proving again that I was not good with my hands.

John Francis, the Professor of Preventive Medicine (and later Dean of the Faculty) had been recruited from the United Kingdom during 1952 and came with an international reputation for his work on bovine tuberculosis. He came to Brisbane with the fair complexion, manners and accent of an English gentleman but he was determined to adapt to the local environment. Shortly after his arrival he set out on a trip to acquaint himself with the very different culture of the graziers, jackaroos, stockmen, shearers and roustabouts of Western Queensland. On the second day of his trip he breasted the bar in Dirrinbandi, ordered a large, cold Fourex beer and struck up a conversation with the local drinkers. 'I'm told this is great sheep country but very different from what I'm used to. Tell me, what's the annual rainfall?' An old stockman along the bar gave a wise nod, winked at him and said 'It's 16 inches mate but we never bloody well get it!' Later he adapted to the local customs and culture so well that he spent the remaining 50 years of his long life in Brisbane.

RHG (Robby) Burns, Chief Lecturer in Veterinary Studies and Senior Surgeon, was described by Dr Peter English in the July 1986 volume of the *Australian Veterinary Journal* as 'the founding father of the post Second World War Veterinary School'. We called him 'Burnsy' but never to his face - Mr Burns was not a man to encourage familiarity. He had been a commissioned officer in the Australian Army Veterinary Corps during the Second World War and his face was well worn in a way that reflected a keen taste for Scotch whisky, drunk sometimes with officers and gentlemen at Brisbane's United Service Club but more commonly at the Morrison Hotel in South Brisbane. He wore thick horn rimmed glasses, affected a rather detached manner and gave some peremptory descriptions in his lectures which were very short on detail. All equine lameness below the knee, for example, whether involving a sesamoid, pedal bone, tendon or suspensory ligament, produced 'a typical lower limb lameness'.

Virtually all 'lotions, tinctures, ointments and rubefacients' had become available premixed and packaged by this time but as our lecturer in *Materia Medica* Burnsy also insisted we learn and practice the apothecary's dispensing art. It was no doubt an interesting historical diversion but during 20 years in practice after graduation I never once used a mortar and pestle or prescribed *tinc opii camph* (camphorated tincture of opium).

Despite his apparently detached manner we reckoned that RHG Burns missed nothing and forgot even less. It was widely accepted, if not well based, that if you wished to graduate you must make every effort to stay on side with him. Animal liberation was not on the horizon in those days and Friday afternoons in fourth year were devoted to a practical surgery period using live animals. Abandoned and stray dogs from the RSPCA which were destined for euthanasia were induced into deep anaesthesia with long acting intravenous Nembutal (pentobarbitone). Four students were allocated to each dog and over the course of a little more than two hours, working at each end or in the middle, we conducted amputations, exploratory laparotomies, gastrotomies, intestinal anasthomoses and cystotomies to name but a few. If the animals had not succumbed to surgical shock during this onslaught they were euthanased with a lethal dose of Nembutal at the end of the period.

Mr Burns would wander in and out during the session keeping what he affected to be a casual eye on the students. That I was not good with my hands was about to be reinforced yet again during my first practical surgery session. Burnsy was walking past just as I made a deep mid-line abdominal incision and slashed the engorged spleen which lay in my path. Apart from the liver, nothing bleeds quite like a spleen incised by a sharp scalpel. He grunted, asked me to explain just how I would salvage the patient in this life threatening emergency and moved on. I was ribbed unmercifully by my colleagues who got repeated laughs from recalling the episode and I remained just a little nervous that the senior surgeon would eventually bring me to book for it. More than 18 months later, as I completed my surgery *viva voce* at the end of final year, he looked at me through his heavy horn rimmed glasses, gave a half smile and said 'Now that you're about to graduate you'd better remember where to find that spleen'. Still missing nothing, forgetting even less!

Most of the veterinary graduates in the 1950s were destined for private rural practice or the state departments of agriculture. The New Zealanders returned home, the smart graduates established or joined the lucrative dairy practices in Victoria, particularly Gippsland, the Goulburn Valley or Western Victoria while others saw their financial futures in small animal practice. Among my contemporaries, Peter Spradbrow became a distinguished virologist with a well deserved international reputation and my best friend Tony Johnston joined the CSIRO and gained the award of Doctor of Veterinary Science (DVSc) for his distinguished work in protozoology and immunology, especially tick fever (babesiosis) in cattle.

THERE WAS LITTLE ORGANISED political activity among the students and staff on the main campus of the University of Queensland and even less at the vet school. It was not only populated largely by conservative or apolitical students but located at that time in isolation in suburban Yeerongpilly. However, there were exceptions. I was already a rusted on ALP supporter, despite the bitter splits, Professor Francis was a dyed in the wool Tory and John Auty, a returned serviceman, studying under the Commonwealth Reconstruction Training Scheme, was a civil libertarian and a political provocateur. In the mid-1950s the Cold War was at its peak and the Menzies Government was running hard on an anti-communist platform. Having failed to win the referendum on constitutional change to outlaw the Communist Party of Australia, Menzies stepped up the hunt for 'reds under the beds'. In this political climate staff and students were surprised when Auty, always the champion of free speech, organised a lunch time meeting at the vet school with barrister Max Julius as the guest speaker. In the 1950s Julius was one of the most controversial, skillful and high profile members of the Communist Party in Australia.

After graduation John Auty eschewed the promotion of party political ideologies but for 50 years played Jiminy Cricket to the Australian

Veterinary Association's (AVA) Pinocchio, ever pricking or puncturing the veterinary profession's conscience. He retired in the mid-1980s as Deputy Director of the Federal Bureau of Animal Health after a long career as a government veterinarian but continued to press his alternative views in the forums of the AVA, including advocating a ban on live sheep exports, for the next 20 years.

My political profile was much lower than Auty's but I did enjoy good natured jousting with John Francis, sometimes as an aside during lectures or whenever he expressed opinions that created the opportunity. My colleagues were convinced that this would be to my detriment, likely to be reflected in my exam results. However, my new found application to study was rewarded in fourth year when Professor Francis gave me a distinction in bacteriology and I was awarded the faculty prize in preventive medicine.

Jack Hourigan, Patrice's father, was old school country, self made, a man of substance and integrity. He supported her three brothers, John, Hugh and Kevin, through boarding school and university and all three had successful careers in their professions. On the other hand, though money and ability were not issues, he saw little value in tertiary education for girls whose destiny was to marry well and raise a family. Patrice spent three years as a boarder at Stuartholme Convent, conducted by the *Sacre Coeur* nuns in Brisbane, learning to be a lady. She also did well academically but when she finished her Senior (Year 12) she was repatriated to Gympie where she socialised unhappily, looking beyond her parent's expectations that she would make what they would consider a good local marriage. She was determined to escape.

Her parents could hardly argue against a career in nursing, living as a student in the nurses' quarters under the watchful eyes of the nuns at Brisbane's Mater Hospital. However, in less than three months she discovered that nursing was not her *metier*. She transferred to the Graham Burrows Institute in Sydney where good catholic girls lived in and were largely protected from the temptations of the big city while they completed a diploma in physical education. She returned to Queensland in 1953 and was employed in the catholic education system as a visiting teacher, travelling by train between Nambour, Gympie and Maryborough and, on one day a week, catching the early morning paper plane that flew the *Courier Mail* to Bundaberg. In 1954 she escaped again from Gympie, transferring to Brisbane where she taught in catholic schools in the suburbs.

When I first met her that year she was still working as a physical education teacher but losing her enthusiasm for it. A few months later she resigned and took a job as a receptionist at the Belfast Hotel in Brisbane's Queen Street. The shock of having to repeat third year had almost made me the conscientious student that I should have been from the beginning of the course but on weekends we were still able to indulge our shared enthusiasm for life and the living of it.

ON 19 MAY 1956 PATRICE and I were married in St Patrick's Church, Gympie. The reception was held at the home of the bride's parents high on the hill at Calton Terrace, well above the record 1956 flood that had submerged Gympie's Mary Street a few weeks earlier. On the same day there was a state election and the Gair Labor Government was returned with 60 per cent of the seats in the Queensland Parliament.

Tony Johnston and Don Glasgow represented the fourth year vet students at the wedding. Tony had sought my advice about a present in the weeks leading up to the wedding but I had no previous experience in these matters and gave no thought to the usual etiquette surrounding wedding presents: 'Tone, I've always wanted a Borsalino hat'. Tony took me at my word, no nonsense about cutlery, crockery and canisters for us, and he presented me with the hat a few days before the wedding.

Gerry Forde, a brash young Australian law student with a Canadian accent, had arrived at St Leos in 1954. He had developed his accent in Ottawa where his father, Frank Forde, spent seven years (1946-1953) as Australia's High Commissioner to Canada.[7] Gerry's tales of adventure, often exaggerated a little to give full effect, and his enthusiasm for life had soon established him as a player in our circle at Leos. We thought he was having us on when he told us that his fiancée was coming to Australia the following year to marry him but Leneen, a tall attractive blonde, did arrive and I was the groomsman at their wedding. She had a Canadian Diploma of Medical Technology and was employed as a medical laboratory technician at the Brisbane General Hospital until the arrival of their first son, Michael, in 1956.

Early in April that year, six weeks before Patrice and I were to be married, Brian Buxton had re-emerged to cast a fleeting shadow over my reputation. When he went to Gympie to act as a weekend locum for the parish priest he made it his business to call on my future mother-in-law, Eileen Hourigan. On the face of it that was unexceptional as John and Hugh Hourigan were both students at St Leos. But tortured soul, as always, he felt compelled to tell Eileen of what he described as my 'rough passage' through Xavier and Leos. Eileen assured him that the marriage had the family's blessing but was sufficiently concerned about Buxton's gaucherie to tell me about it. That's where the matter might have ended had I not met Gerry Forde for a drink at Vandeleurs Lands Office Hotel the following week. Gerry was now in the third year of his arts-law course and once we had been fortified by a few beers he was able to confidently inform me that I had been seriously defamed and must seek redress. Armed with this advice I made my way to the nearest public telephone, accompanied by my learned friend, and rang Buxton SJ. I told him my advice from senior counsel was that I had been seriously defamed and that I should seek redress at law for the grievous damage he had done to my reputation. However, if he were to write to Mrs Hourigan withdrawing his defamatory remarks and apologising unreservedly for the hurt and distress that he had caused I might be prepared to stay my action. Three days later Eileen received a lengthy, tortuous letter which served to extricate if not exonerate him.

Gerry and I remained good friends for the rest of my undergraduate years. Tragically, he died of acute leukaemia just 10 years later. In an extraordinary display of courage and fortitude following his death, Leneen not only coped with her young family but enrolled in the Faculty of Law at the University of Queensland and graduated in 1970. Her stellar career over the next 35 years included her appointment as Governor of Queensland (1992-1997) and Chancellor of Griffith University.

Our wedding was never going to be the number one item on the Queensland social calendar for 1956. Nevertheless, Patrice's sister Syra promoted it to the social editor of the Queensland edition of the *Women's Weekly*. I was described as coming from 'White Hills', presumably my family's grazing property in rural Victoria rather than a modest suburb in Bendigo. Due to the generosity of my father-in-law who paid for our accommodation we spent an idyllic week at Hayman Island, captivated by the beauty of the Whitsunday Passage and the coral wonders of the Great Barrier Reef. Our pleasure was diminished only by the thought of imminent poverty but we overcame this in the short term by cashing the cheques we had received from generous wedding guests. Acquiring the essentials of a well-equipped household kitchen for which the money was intended would have to wait.

Hayman Island was being developed under the personal supervision of Reg Ansett who was a regular visitor. In 1947 Ansett fell in love with Hayman and bought the lease for £10,000. The resort, grandly named the Royal Hayman, opened in 1950. A few wealthy guests flew by Sunderland Flying Boat from Rose Bay in Sydney and Redland Bay in Brisbane, a service operated by the Ansett subsidiary Barrier Reef Airways. Hayman was especially popular with honeymooners and most of us took the Sunlander train or flew from Brisbane to Mackay, then travelled by coach to Shute Harbour and made the 18 mile crossing from the mainland by launch.

It was already being promoted as an exotic tropical location but Hayman was a very different place from the luxury resort of the 21st century. Reg Ansett was an old fashioned capitalist entrepreneur and he met capital or operating budget deficits at Hayman from the profits of a busy but illegal poker machine recessed into a wall of the resort bar. Staff were given warning if any members of the friendly Queensland Gaming Squad were expected on a visit and avoided any potential embarrassment by concealing the 'pokie' with a sliding panel that converted the recess into an integral part of the wall.

Ansett later became a major player in the airline business following his takeover of Australian National Airlines (ANA) which was flying in tandem with Trans Australia Airlines (TAA) under the federal government's two airlines policy. However, in 1956 he was still flying DC3s along the East Coast from Brisbane to Melbourne. They flew through the weather rather than above it, to land at Coolangatta, Coffs Harbour, Sydney and Wagga, a journey (known as 'the milk run') that took more than eight hours. The upside from my perspective was that Ansett was the only airline offering 50 per cent student fare concessions.

Patrice and I returned to Brisbane from our honeymoon and settled into the little flat in New Farm that I shared with my friend John Moro from the good old days at St Leos. After our marriage Patrice worked for nine months until the mid-term of her pregnancy when, according to 1950s social norms, 'decency' dictated that she should retire from the workforce. By this time our social activities were based mainly on an occasional meal in a Chinese restaurant and a night at the movies. We were about to become young parents.

Our first child and only son, Mark, was born on 20 July 1957, the first Hourigan grandchild and the first grandchild in my family to bear the Cornwall name. This was just two weeks before the state Labor government was decimated in the election held on 3 August. The government had been hopelessly split after the Queensland Central Executive of the ALP expelled Vince Gair who took 24 of his colleagues with him. Labor was to remain in opposition in Queensland for the next 32 years.

THIS WAS MY FINAL UNDERGRADUATE YEAR and large animals dominated the curriculum. Apart from work in the vet school's large animal practice there were short term internships with practitioners (for me a dairy practice on the periphery of Brisbane and three weeks in a mixed practice in Kingaroy), three weeks with the meat inspection team on the beef chain at the Cannon Hill abattoirs and a trip to South West Queensland. George Osborne had pioneered a contract animal production practice in the Goondiwindi-Dirranbandi area as an outreach service from his veterinary practice in the New England area. When he joined the clinical staff at the vet school he retained his clients and used to take several final year students on each working trip to grazing properties in South West Queensland. There were virtually no other private veterinary services in that region at the time, except for those provided above and beyond their job description and duty statements by one or two enterprising government vets, keen to supplement their modest salaries.

George Osborne's services encompassed everything that could be done in two busy days on a grazing property, including examining rams for fertility, advice and strategies to improve lambing and marking percentages, some elective surgery, advice about nutrition, internal and external parasites, vaccination programs and gelding any colts bred from the station stock horses. To really establish credibility in those days the vet must be able to geld a colt quicker, more efficiently and more humanely (although this was a secondary consideration in the bush at the time) than the local 'colt cutter'.

Physically examining rams for testicular abnormalities was a crude indicator of reproductive health, its effectiveness later to be greatly enhanced by blood testing and programs to eradicate ovine brucellosis. Feeling for lumps and bumps on the end of rams' testicles in hot, dusty sheep yards was one way to pass the time but far more interesting for me were the customs and lifestyle of the graziers and their families, still rich from the wool boom. The young jackeroo had the status of an apprentice manager. He lived and ate with the family and, in the absence of the owner at any time, he sat at the head of the table to carve the mutton. 'Roast or boiled' was the question to each of the diners, the formalities observed despite the tough merino meat.

The head stockman was the central figure in the day to day livestock management but was in a different social class. He came to the homestead each morning, knocked on the back door, then sat with his vehicle under the shade of the nearest tree waiting for the boss to emerge. A far more attractive custom for visitors like us was to sit on the wide veranda with our host at sunset, drinking a cold beer or two before dinner, discussing the events of the day and discussing the schedule for tomorrow's work.

Mark in the back yard at Swan Hill with the unlined weatherboard garage that served as my clinic and surgery in the background, December 1960.

CHAPTER FIVE

The hard way

The graduation ceremony was conducted in the Brisbane City Hall early in December. As we were about to move to Victoria, Patrice and I had sold the few items of furniture we purchased when we returned from our honeymoon the previous year and used the money to pay for a week at the Gold Coast before the presentation of degrees and the dinner for the graduating class of '57. Now almost flat broke we were checking in with baby Mark and 30 pounds of excess luggage to fly to Melbourne where we would be met by my parents.

Many of my colleagues had arranged employment prior to their graduation. Tony Johnston, who later joined the CSIRO, began work immediately as a junior house surgeon at the vet school, Big Bob Meldrum, who later found his real place in the profession as the principal of a successful beef cattle practice based in Rockhampton, joined Ben Benaradsky to work with small animals at the Lort Smith Animal Hospital in Melbourne. Don Glasgow flew to Port Moresby with his new wife Jan to begin his career working for the Australian Government in the mandated territory of Papua New Guinea, still 18 years away from independence.

I was in Bendigo with Patrice and baby Mark, waiting to get started and to receive my first salary cheque from the Victorian Government. I rang the Chief Veterinary Officer to tell him I was available, wished to start immediately and anxious to get on the payroll. In the slow moving world of the agriculture bureaucracy this caused some amusement. Nothing could possibly be arranged before Christmas. My orientation would begin in the second week of January so my first fortnightly pay cheque was seven weeks away. My memory of the financial details during that period has become benignly vague over the years but I do remember that survival depended on regular £5 and £10 notes from Dad and several money orders that Eileen sent to Patrice.

In January department officers at Treasury Place in Melbourne took me through my role and responsibilities as a District Veterinary Officer (DVO) - the duty statement, weekly activity reports, mileage records, compensation reports and procedures, the realities of department life. The following week I travelled to Albury on the Spirit of Progress ('Australia's Wonder Train') to spend a three week induction period with John Bourke, the DVO at Wodonga. John had been a third year student at St Leo's when I first began the course and had acted as my mentor in first year. He later joined the Victorian Racing Club as Australia's first veterinary steward, a position he held with distinction for 40 years.

Patrice and Mark had joined me, living in a pleasant, friendly boarding house in Albury, across the Murray River from Wodonga. However, we were soon moving again. I was sent to Benalla to begin work as the DVO, boarding in a local hotel, and Patrice went to stay with Ben Benaradsky and his mother in Melbourne. In 1958 young graduates in the department received little support in their professional work and none with accommodation so my first challenge on arrival in Benalla was to find affordable rental housing for my wife, by then 10 weeks pregnant, and baby Mark.

I found a new but extremely modest fibro-cement Housing Commission cottage on the outskirts of the town with two small bedrooms, a lounge-dining area and a tiny kitchen with a wood stove. The house block was surrounded by a low cyclone mesh fence on all four sides. There were no roadside kerbs, no paved footpath and the yard surrounding the cottage was bare soil except for a few hardy weeds that had survived the dry summer. As the season turned to bring the first April rains the yard and the roadside turned into a quagmire.

The Housing Commission estate was unsewered, the woodshed doubling as a country lavatory from which the dunny man retrieved what was euphemistically called the night soil in a large black can. During a trip to Melbourne we bought some furniture on hire purchase - a bed and mattress, two teak Fler chairs, a kitchen setting and a charcoal grey Frigidaire, one of the first square look refrigerators. But there was a three-week wait for delivery and during that period we camped in the house, Mark in his bassinet, Patrice and I sleeping on two camp stretchers loaned to us by the Sheep and Wool Advisory Officer in the Benalla office. He also provided us with two canvas chairs and a folding card table which the newly acquired dachshund pup knocked over during his first week in the household, scattering the roast dinner on the floor.

For a couple trying to survive on £44 a fortnight, grey box or red gum blocks for the wood stove (or the open fire place when the bitter winter came) were too expensive. Instead, I carried an axe in the Agriculture Department's FJ Holden and filled the boot with stump wood, cut on the roadside as I travelled through my district. Patrice had never lit a fire in her life and took some time to develop a talent for it. Eventually she learned that the newspaper must be crumpled and lightly teased, the kerosene applied strategically and the kindling pine split finely. My Queensland bride eventually acquired an essential skill for surviving a Victorian winter in the 1950s.

Our first daughter Deborah was born in the Benalla hospital on 27 August 1958, following many hours of cruel, poorly managed labour. She was just 13 months younger than her brother Mark who was being cared for by his Cornwall grandparents. Patrice's mother made an epic journey by bus from Gympie to Benalla to care for her daughter and new born granddaughter, leaving the dry warmth of Queensland in early September to arrive in time for the last excesses of a wet, cold winter. She was particularly unimpressed by the thunder box in the wood shed: 'Whatever has my daughter come to?'

My first task as the Benalla DVO was to join colleagues from Shepparton in conducting a three week footrot eradication program at Dookie Agricultural College. Treatment in the Dookie project involved using secateurs to pare back the sheep's hooves to the edge of the quick, exposing any residual or sometimes active necrotic and smelly pockets of infection. The sheep were then run through a formalin footbath, a valuable treatment for them but hardly meeting my clinical or surgical aspirations. If any exotic diseases like foot and mouth eluded Australia's strict quarantine laws government vets would be deployed as the frontline troops for their detection, control and eradication. On a day to day basis, however, virtually all their field work involved the routine diagnosis and management of the common diseases in sheep and cattle. The clinical and surgical work throughout the area was done by private veterinarians who provided services across the species great and small. Some of the clients who used the Department's services were from the upper echelons of the grazing fraternity with political connections to the Country Party. Others were battling farmers who couldn't afford to contract veterinary services from private practitioners and struggled to implement good livestock management.

My territory ranged from the north-east of Victoria, down through the Ovens and Mitta Valleys to Mansfield and Yea in the south, almost 15 per cent of the state. I tried to organise my visiting schedules to minimise travelling but much of the working day was spent in the car, driving long distances at unsafe speeds. Friday afternoon was the time to process the paperwork and complain about the Department's restrictions on mechanical maintenance of the well worn FJ Holden, 'the one with the waggly tail'; smart drivers often carried a bag of sand in the boot of their FJs to stabilise them on corners.

I began to review our position soon after moving to Benalla. As a government vet I had no opportunity to develop my clinical skills, my salary allowed for little more than subsistence with no hope of saving, our accommodation and living conditions generally were intolerable and we seemed to have little prospect of developing any sort of social network. I was out of town on most working days and Patrice spent her time isolated from the world in our fibro cottage. I established a good working relationship and personal friendship with Benalla's private practitioner, veterinarian Joe Carruthers, who was both older and wiser than I was. However, in my day to day work I was missing out on the diversity and stimulation that a new graduate needed for professional development and job satisfaction.

A major consideration in any decision about leaving the department was the bond. Under the conditions of my cadetship I was required on graduation to 'work for the Department of Agriculture for a period of four years, if required, or practice continuously for three years in the State of Victoria.' The key phrase was 'if required'. With the only two veterinary faculties in Australasia producing less than 60 graduates a year in the 1950s, the bonded cadets in Victoria were all 'required'. The amount repayable was £1,350, equivalent to a year's salary, but the conditions of the contract meant that the bond money was probably interest free. The unknown factor was how hard the Victorian Government might press for a lump sum repayment. I decided to chance my arm, offered them £10 a month and began to look for an escape route. As it turned out financial fortune favoured the brave. Over the next eight years I made intermittent bond repayments totalling around £500 ($1,000). The Department must have then misplaced my file. It was not until 1973 that it was retrieved and the auditors pressed the department for recovery of the balance. I arrived at my small animal surgery in Adelaide one morning to be greeted by two bailiffs who delivered a summons demanding payment of the remaining $1,700. The bond had been treated as an interest free loan.

Arthur Vickers was an Edinburgh graduate who had been enticed into a rural practice in Myrtleford by the board of the local dairy cooperative with active support from local farmers. Myrtleford is situated on the Alpine highway, the gateway to the Ovens Valley and the snowfields of Mount Buffalo. In the 1950s the town population was a little more than 2,000 people. It was a rural centre for farming and grazing, sheep, dairy and beef cattle, timber, hops and tobacco. Arthur, a man of sober habits and frugal lifestyle, had flourished. Now approaching his 40th birthday he was about to enter 'the holy estate of matrimony' and wished to take his bride home to Scotland for an extended honeymoon. He offered me a six month locum at £30 a week, mileage paid at one shilling a mile (petrol cost two shillings a gallon) and a rent free house. In early November, nine months after arriving in Benalla, we packed our modest furniture and household belongings into a removalist's van, got into my second hand Volkswagen Beetle (my first car) and headed for Myrtleford with our two babies, Mark and Deborah.

Myrtleford was predominantly a cattle practice, very busy during the calving season in the autumn and winter but quiet in the summer as the cows approached the end of their lactation period and the heifers, already vaccinated against brucellosis (contagious abortion), began the third semester of their first pregnancy. There was ample time to enjoy the generous hospitality of friendly neighbours and clients. The Ovens River rises in the Victorian Alps and flows along the beautiful Ovens Valley past Bright and Myrtleford to Wangaratta where it joins the King River. The historic Mount Buffalo Chalet was still working at full capacity in the 1950s and when the snow melted on the ski runs horseback riding became one of the favourite summer activities for guests. Visits to treat the horses and ponies at the Chalet are among my happiest memories of the six months we spent in Myrtleford.

There were occasional calamities. Tobacco growing was still a major industry in the valley and, incredible as it may now seem, lead arsenate was still being widely used as a pesticide by tobacco farmers. The large farm sheds housed everything from machinery to fertilisers and often the residues of lead arsenate were left in cut down mixing drums. Many of the Italian farmers who grew tobacco in the Valley also milked small dairy herds, an incendiary combination if the farm sheds were not secure. Cattle seemed to find the lead arsenate as palatable as a salt lick, with terrible results: it could kill a cow within hours. I saw a dramatic and tragic demonstration of this soon after I arrived in Myrtleford when I responded to an urgent call to find six cows and heifers already dead with another four *in extremis*, half a small milking herd wiped out.

Dogs and cats were a small segment of most rural practices 50 years ago and the Vickers small animal practice was very small indeed. Surgery was done on a wooden kitchen table in the sleep-out at the end of the back veranda of the house. The dog was anaesthetised with a Nembutal injection, the dose predetermined by the animal's body weight and recovery was slow, sometimes uncertain. We made sure the animal was kept warm and watched anxiously for the shivering that indicated the return of muscle tone as the long acting anaesthetic wore off.

By mid-summer I was half way through my Myrtleford locum and anxiously examining my prospects. Would I seek a position as an assistant or associate in an established rural practice or attempt to establish my own practice in an area with identified needs? I applied for associate positions and travelled for interviews to Scone in the Hunter Valley and to Wagga but failed to negotiate satisfactory conditions, particularly housing. At that point I began to consider establishing my own practice, despite having only a few months of clinical experience since graduation.

The graduates who had opened practices in the lush, intensive dairying areas of the Goulburn Valley and South Gippsland, only four or five years ahead of me, had taken on prodigious workloads and quickly established themselves at the affluent end of the profession. Shepparton, Kyabram, Tatura, Rochester and Echuca were among the most spectacular success stories. Dairy practice in the Goulburn Valley was the place to be but where was the place for me? My father suggested Swan Hill on the Murray River ('I never knew a bad river town') where the directors of the butter factory were keen to recruit a private practitioner, although not so keen to provide financial incentives. Two young veterinarians who had preceded me in Swan Hill had struggled to make the practice viable and left town but conventional wisdom was that this was because they were single and therefore lacked the stability of a home base (and presumably the mandatory wife as an unpaid receptionist and practice manager).

The butter factory offered a modest house to rent and a prominent local pharmacist, who was also styled as the veterinary chemist, guaranteed a £500 overdraft at the ANZ Bank. With little more than a framed veterinary degree, a second hand Volkswagen Beetle and a £500 line of credit we headed for the unknown, pioneering a practice from which we would escape sadder but wiser two years later.

A carport was constructed in the driveway of the rented house and plans were drawn to replace the large, single garage door with an attractive frontage and entrance. The interior of the garage was to be lined, converted into examination and surgical areas and a kennel room for sick dogs and cats or recovering surgical patients was to be added at the rear of the small clinic. However, the butter factory manager's understanding of these undertakings was quite different from mine. He saw no reason to provide 'luxuries'. I was there for the benefit of his dairy farmers. My small animal 'clinic' when I arrived consisted of a cold water tap over a large stainless steel trough with an iron carpenter's work table on the cement floor that was to double as an examination and operating table in a bare, unlined garage. To further reduce the cost of a kennel room, the butter factory's handyman-carpenter built two cyclone mesh dog pens at the back of the garage. They were roofed but otherwise open to the extremes of the harsh Swan Hill climate – frosty winters and dust storms driven by hot north winds in summer's heat waves.

Distemper, a highly infectious viral disease, was endemic in the local dog population despite the relatively recent but widespread availability of safe attenuated vaccines. One distemper remedy in Swan Hill was still the 'bushman's pill' - a ground up copper penny mixed in lard – and Keith Dunoon (who styled himself as 'the veterinary chemist') provided over the counter medications which were just as useless. In the early stages dogs presented with a high temperature, nasal and eye discharge and pneumonia. Antibiotic treatment for the secondary bacterial pneumonia that accompanied the viral infection often produced temporary clinical improvement. Despite good nursing, however, affected dogs almost invariably developed viral encephalitis which caused uncontrollable epileptic convulsions or generalised muscle spasms up to six weeks after the onset of the infection. After a long and dreadful illness, the pup almost invariably had to be euthanased.

Dairy farmers on the irrigated river flats at Murraydale and Tyntynder were my primary target. However, Swan Hill's river flats were already among the first casualties of the salinity that was to become a serious problem in many of the irrigation areas. Reduced to marginal viability, many of the farmers could understand the cost but not identify the benefit of professional veterinary services, whether for individual animals or herd problems. When a heifer was in trouble delivering a large calf, the farmer or his friendly neighbour might even employ the brutal traction of a fencing wire strainer to force it through the heifer's small pelvis, often resulting in post calving (obturator nerve) paralysis or a ruptured uterus. Vibriosis, a venereal disease of cattle in which the bulls act as the vectors, was widespread but the resulting infertility problems were often 'treated' with over-the-counter medications like vaginal douches rather than implementing effective veterinary treatment and control.

Away from the irrigated river flats the country was semi-arid. The Victorian Mallee to the west grew wheat and produced some fat lambs while the pastoral country over the river in New South Wales produced merino wool. The annual rainfall in both areas was around 12 inches and in the 1960s veterinary practice in this low rainfall country was very limited. I would go anywhere I could find a case or a client – a house cow on a wheat farm 50 miles away at Sea Lake; a 250 mile round trip to treat a sick stud bull at Bunumburt Station, dodging kangaroos in the VW as I drove home at dusk; a flight in a single engine Cessna for a day's work on a distant sheep station in New South Wales; gelding colts for harness racing enthusiasts on Mallee farms at Chinkapook or Chillangollah.

There were several small thoroughbred racing stables in the district and I particularly enjoyed working for Kevin Wynne. He trained for Buster Livingston, one of the Livingston Brothers in the family butcher shop but better known as a clever and well informed punter on Victorian country and provincial racetracks. His horse Khorumi's win on the first day of the three-day Warrnambool Cup Carnival in 1954 was the stuff of legend. The horse was a real smokey - little previous form, trained by the bush trainer Wynne and ridden by a young apprentice jockey from Deniliquin called Roy Higgins. Roy would soon become Victoria's leading rider and one of the all-time greats but Buster had spotted him first. The horse was backed in to favouritism after opening at 12/1 and won by three lengths.

In the mid-1960s Kevin moved to Bendigo where he reached the peak of a successful career when he won the Caulfield Cup in 1968 with Bunratty Castle. Sadly, he died just a few years later.

Swan Hill had little of the social pretensions of Benalla, the recently introduced Fosters handy cans a boon for the thirsty Mallee drinkers in an egalitarian society with a certain frontier mentality. The hotels in Swan Hill were still closing at six o'clock under Victoria's licensing laws but the Federal Hotel, just over the river in New South Wales, closed late, sometimes very late. Drinkers who were still thirsty when the other pubs closed drove 300 yards across the river to the sanctuary of the hotel where the nearest towns, Moulamein and Balranald, were distant enough to ensure that there was very little concern about either liquor or gaming laws. On Saturday afternoons, long before legal TAB betting, Jack Wilkinson set up his stand on the small river flat across the road from the Federal Hotel, displayed the prices on the board and swung his bookies bag in the shade of a large gum tree.

Despite all my efforts the practice was struggling. In late summer the cash flow dried up as the cows dried off, prior to calving again for their next lactation and we had neither the diversity nor the volume of work from other species to carry us over. The situation was further complicated by my guarantor. Keith Dunoon was a wily old glad-hander who had conducted a thriving pharmacy in Swan Hill for longer than anyone could remember. As the veterinary chemist he offered all sorts of advice and sold all sorts of over-the-counter remedies, frequently even less useful than his advice. He referred his customers to me ('that young vet we have brought to Swan Hill') only when his medications failed and his patients were moribund. Nor was he above dispensing some antibiotics without veterinary prescriptions. Perhaps I should have reported this to the Victorian Pharmacy Board but I was seriously compromised by his guarantee of my overdraft at the ANZ Bank. Our financial affairs were so tight that had the guarantee been revoked and the loan called in I could have been bankrupted.

Our professional and financial concerns were accompanied by an increasingly desperate moral dilemma that would persist for almost another decade. Our second daughter Amanda was born in February 1960, nine months after our arrival in Swan Hill. In less than four years since our marriage Patrice had endured three pregnancies and was coping with three children less than three years of age. We were tormented by the Pope's injunction that as Catholics we must follow 'the natural law'. Artificial contraception was absolutely forbidden but there was the Billings rhythm method in which we were enjoined by the catholic church to predict the date of ovulation by taking vaginal temperatures, measuring the pH of vaginal mucous and planning intercourse accordingly. In couples with a high natural fertility and matching libido this was a spectacular failure, bedtime roulette in which the croupier was the consistent winner.

Towards the end of 1960 I began to look for opportunities in safer, higher rainfall areas and applied for a job as an associate in a dairy practice in the small town of Allansford in Western Victoria. The package included rent free accommodation, a generous mileage allowance and rostered days and weekends off duty. I made an appointment to meet the principal who seemed enthusiastic but a few days before the scheduled trip for the interview I ran my VW Beetle off the road, hit a white post, flipped and did a double corkscrew roll, rear end first. I escaped unharmed but my new car, with just 7,000 miles on the speedometer, was written off.

Soon afterwards I heard from one of the pharmaceutical reps who visited us on a regular basis that Alf Humble was anxious to lease his Mount Gambier practice in the South East of South Australia. Alf was an ex-RAAF pilot who was still very keen on flying and owned a small twin seat Auster plane. The little high wing plane was ideal for flour bombing the players during the annual Legacy golf tournament but he couldn't find much use for it professionally in a closely settled farming and grazing practice. Alf had been offered a job with the Department of Primary Industries in the Northern Territory that would involve a lot of flying hours and was keen to take up the appointment.

Patrice and I seized the opportunity, had our baby sitter live in for the weekend and travelled to 'the Mount' early in the New Year. This was a mixed one man practice conducted from home, formerly a doctor's residence and surgery, and the three year lease included an option to purchase the practice and the house as a package, the price to be negotiated prior to the expiry date. The contract between the Humbles (husband and wife) and me set 1 May 1961 as the date of commencement. We returned to Swan Hill to wind up our affairs.

With Patrice on the beach at Maroochydore in Queensland on our family holiday, December 1966. Jennifer and Geraldine are playing in the background.

CHAPTER SIX

The practice, the principal and the pope

The autumn rain came early in 1961 while the soil was still warm. When we arrived in Mount Gambier in May the pastures were succulent and the mood among farmers and graziers was optimistic. The plentiful rain brought abundant demand for veterinary services in a practice that had something for every season. Calving in dairy and beef herds began in the autumn and continued to mid-winter, in spring the brood mares and foals in my equine stud practice kept me busy. Strain 19 vaccination of heifer calves, TB testing of dairy herds and pregnancy testing in the beef herds filled the summer program. Stable work with racehorses and my small animal clinic completed a mixed general practice.

Hypocalcaemia (milk fever) in dairy cows is caused by a sudden drop in the level of calcium in the cow's bloodstream due to the very high demand on calcium for the new milk being produced around the time of calving. In the early stages the cow has difficulty standing, staggers and soon falls. At this stage the farmer can inject a calcium solution under the skin and the cow normally recovers uneventfully. In advanced cases, however, the animal becomes comatose, lying on her side with body temperatures as low as 32°C. If she has gone down overnight she might already be on her side, comatose and close to death when found in the pre-dawn light.

During the winter the phone would often ring before dawn with an urgent call to a case of milk fever. Careful injection of a calcium solution directly into the bloodstream through the jugular vein (while carefully monitoring the heart rhythm) could produce spectacular results in most cases. As the blood calcium levels returned to normal the cow would regain consciousness, sit up on her sternum and might even be up and walking before I left for home.

One of my regulars had a small farm just outside the town boundary.

Francesco Palmieri had an amazing work ethic and a temperament that reflected his Italian heritage. He rose at 4.30am each morning to milk 30 cows, then put in a hard day's work as a timber faller in the radiata pine plantations, arriving home in time for the evening milking. His beautiful Jersey cows were especially prone to milk fever and when he got out of bed for the morning milking and found one down he'd jump in his car, drive to our place less than five minutes away and ring the bell at the surgery entrance, anxious and excited. I tried to explain to him how adjusting the diet was one of several ways which could help to reduce the incidence of the problem, providing good quality hay and calcium supplements to balance the intake of lush green pasture. It didn't seem to make much difference to his management practices or his habits but at least he had a name for his problem. From then on whenever he rang the bell in the early hours he'd tell me in a voice loud enough to wake the household 'too much grass, too much grass'.

Caesarean section in cattle is performed through an incision in the left flank with the animal restrained but standing. The pain is controlled by local anaesthetic injections – an epidural and a series of nerve blocks along the spine to deaden the nerves that supply the flank. In the field there was no time or opportunity for the luxury of surgical drapes or autoclaved instruments. The surgical instruments were placed in a container of disinfectant and the area for the incision was clipped, shaved and disinfected. The incision through the skin and muscle wall was large enough to grasp and make a cut in the uterus to deliver the calf. The uterus and muscle wall were then sutured with catgut and the skin with synthetic suture material. The animal was released into the stockyard, hopefully to mother a live calf. Speed was one of the important elements in a successful outcome.

The Australian veterinarian in rural practice was a very different person from the avuncular British gentleman vet in the BBC television series who spent a lot of time working in a warm barn. Winters in Mount Gambier were cold and wet and in beef heifers the surgery in my practice was done in the cattle yards open to the elements. Edgar Pick was one of my favourite clients, aging, affable and wise. His property was near the Victorian border not far from the southern coastline, cold, windy and wild in the winter. On one of those days I had delivered a live calf by caesarean section and was suturing the uterus, exposed through the flank incision, when a wild rain squall blew in. Undeterred, Edgar took off his broad brimmed grazier's hat and used it to keep the freezing rain off the uterus and out of the abdominal cavity. We pressed on to complete the surgery and soon had the heifer mothering her calf which was struggling unsteadily to its feet.

Locals used to say that the red gum country around Mount Gambier loved 'to get its feet wet'. Strawberry clover thrived in the wet conditions and stayed green long after pasture in other areas had dried off in the late spring. It was excellent cattle country but during the wet winter months some of the low lying areas held patches of water that were almost waist deep. Good managers always had calving cows on higher ground close to the cattle yards but this client wasn't one of them. I was called to a calving heifer on his property at the aptly named Dismal Swamp one July afternoon to find her still at large in a back paddock. The little Aberdeen Angus was especially feisty, fear mixed with aggression, and all we could do was to loop a rope over her neck on the run, reconfigure it as a halter and tie her to the client's Land Rover. A manual examination established that the calf was alive but simply too large to be delivered through the pelvis of the heifer, estimated to be not yet two years old.

She was given a tranquiliser and the instruments were sterilised in surgical disinfectant diluted with fresh swamp water. With the epidural and nerve blocks completed we began the surgery but half way through the operation the patient suddenly lay down, frustrated that all her previous efforts to beat us had failed. Despite the difficulties the caesarean was completed and we produced a lively bull calf. Now was the time for mother to tend her baby boy but for the moment she had other ideas. When the restraining rope was released she headed straight for the swamp and waded for more than 60 yards to the other side with her wound partly immersed in swamp water. Remarkably the sixteen inch wound survived intact and after we left the scene she circled back, this time around the swamp, to take up her duties as a nursing mother.

With my keen interest in horse racing I worked hard to establish a reputation with trainers throughout the Lower South East. There were no large stables and some of the smaller trainers were very slow to pay their bills but I enjoyed the work and admired their ingenuity. Frank Murphy, one of my aging battlers, maintained a delicate balance between survival and penury through his job at the State Sawmill. He never had more than two or three horses in work at any time and his wins were infrequent. When his veterinary bill was in the very overdue category he would avoid me around town and on race days he'd keep well clear with some artful dodging during the afternoon. However, on one occasion when he inadvertently found himself next to me in the bar after the last race he hastened to reinforce his honesty and good intentions with some great Irish logic: 'About that bill old fella, don't worry about it. I'd owe it to you all my life rather than not pay it'.

Ray Smith, with his olive complexion, ample jowls and generous girth, was known universally as The Rajah. He lived in a small dilapidated cottage across the road from the Mount Gambier racecourse with his wife, a pleasant, uncomplicated woman considerably younger than he was. They had five or six children, simple kids who wore perpetual grins. Half a dozen horses were stabled in more adequate accommodation at the back of the large yard.

The Raj had served with the AIF in the Second World War and would often tell me 'the ticker's not too good'. In the 1950s he was classified as totally and permanently incapacitated and given a TPI pension. His health was not enhanced by constantly smoking 'roll-your-owns' but he had learned the art of survival. He trained his fair share of winners from his small team and supplemented his income by rearing and selling dressed ducks and poultry, cash and carry. The ducks were free range, waddling, quacking and defaecating in the back yard. Rajah dressed the poultry in the kitchen, sitting with a decapitated bird between his splayed legs, plucking the feathers with the aid of a large tub of hot water and removing the innards onto newspaper. He was very hospitable and invariably offered me 'a cuppa' and homemade cake whenever I visited the stables: 'Plain black tea thanks Ray. I've just had lunch'.

Some years after I arrived in the town the Raj had a good run with his small team and built a new Mount Gambier stone house at the front of the block with the aid of a war service loan. The cottage was demolished and the family moved into the house, nicely finished with drapes, floor coverings and new furniture. The poultry dressing was then resumed in the new eat-in kitchen.

Vince Teranto came from an Italian family who had fished in the Mediterranean Sea for generations. Now he was fishing for rock lobsters out of Port McDonnell. He was a *cavaliere*, horseman and gentleman, as well as a *pescatore*. As an owner-trainer he had the good fortune to get hold of a very versatile mare called Princess Pura who in her early career won over six furlongs at Morphettville, the headquarters of racing in South Australia. A little later she won several mile races on country tracks and in the twilight of her career she was winning 'over the jumps', two mile hurdle races. She was a beautiful mare who finished her racing days virtually unscathed. Vince had two very attractive habits: he always paid his vet bills in cash and gave me one or two crayfish as a bonus.

Walter Jenkins of 'Nayook' and his adult sons Allan, Bob, Wally and David were a very successful family of graziers and among my best clients. When one of their valuable young Hereford bulls appeared in the paddock one morning with a seriously stiff neck I made a very tentative diagnosis of sprained apophyseal joints high in the cervical spine, probably sustained when head butting with an older bull in the paddock. Apophyseal joints are the hinge-like joints on both sides of each vertebra that interlock them with adjoining vertebrae to make the spine more stable and allow flexion and extension of the neck. The bull was in considerable pain but mobile and steady on his feet. I could only recommend pain control, yard rest and observation. Local physiotherapist Ray Gallagher suggested I try the technique he used - gentle extension and short, sharp but careful manipulation of the cervical spine (in selected patients with healthy bone structure).

A volatile Irishman, Ray served with the Royal Irish Fusiliers during the Second World War before migrating to Australia in the 1950s as a chartered physiotherapist and came to his Mount Gambier practice via Whyalla. He was short in height with a temper to match, had a fair gaelic complexion, ginger hair turning grey and an expanding waistline. Ray always dressed more like a Harley Street specialist than a country physio - tailored tweed suits and vests, Crombie overcoats, Church's shoes and Borsalino hats. He was a man to be avoided late at night when, full of Jamison's Irish Whisky and patriotic fervour, he played and sang his Irish rebel songs, flushed and tearful.

My personal experience as an occasional patient was that his technique worked well in a relatively relaxed human being who weighed 70 kilograms but how could you successfully manipulate the cervical spine of a 700 kilogram bull? The Irishman convinced me that it was worth a try. The patient was prodded gently into the crush and the two sides of the neck yoke adjusted to hold it securely, the head and horns protruding forward. I sedated the young bull and Ray grasped the horns with his soft white hands, extending the neck with his right leg on the front of the crush to give him extra purchase, grunting and sweating under the unusual strain of dealing with his giant patient. Continuing to hold the right horn in his left hand, he moved his right hand to the bull's chin and very quickly and adroitly twisted the head to the bull's left, then repeated the procedure on the other side. Ray assured us that he heard the characteristic click this usually induced in his human patients as the apophyseals were realigned. Whether because of or (more likely) despite the manipulation, the bull was grazing happily in a small holding paddock within four or five days.

Frank and John Livingston were wealthy graziers and keen yachtsmen. They took line honours in the Sydney to Hobart Yacht Race in 1954, 1956, 1957 and 1960 in their yacht *Kurrewa IV* and in 1964 they were involved with *Sovereign*, the British yacht that challenged for the America's Cup. The brothers had a property near the coast and were clients of my practice but they spent much of their time abroad or at their other property in Queensland and I dealt with their manager. However, I always dealt on a personal basis with their sister Emily, a single woman *d'un certain age* who lived alone in the gracious homestead on her grazing property just five miles out of town.

Emily employed a man full time who was described as her manager but his lack of organisational skills reflected the fact that he was more a knockabout stockman. The only other regular was a casual employee whose principal job was to clip and shape a rather amazing eight foot hedge which ran for 300 yards across the property's frontage to the main road. Emily played an active role in the day to day affairs of the property and on the manager's day off took responsibility for the care of the livestock. She was a trifle eccentric and unworldly but her eccentricities were more amusing than annoying; over time I came to expect the unexpected. This reached a high point on a very busy day when she called me to a calving heifer but failed to tell my wife when she phoned that she was on her own and the heifer was still in the paddock. I arrived with the normal expectation that the patient would be yarded, ready for the obstetrician to get on with it. Instead, Emily offered to help me saddle a stock horse so that I could get the heifer in from the paddock. It took me almost half an hour of bumping, propping and turning in the saddle to get the heifer into the yard where I delivered the calf (which was presenting rear end first) with Emily assisting. I added the extra time at penalty rates when I made up the bill but what I couldn't charge for was pain and suffering.

Helen Lesley Gebhardt was a prominent Mount Gambier identity, another single middle aged woman who made her mark in the real estate business. She had done this through diligence and fair trade but especially by what I charitably called force of personality. She had been a keen horsewoman and, although her days in the saddle following the hounds in Mount Gambier's version of The Hunt were over, she was still a keen member of the Club. She was a tall, big boned woman and jodhpurs, jacket and well polished elastic sided riding boots were favourites in her wardrobe. She bred and raced thoroughbreds and took me on, as both client and critic, from my earliest days in Mount Gambier. I did quite a lot of work for her and she was a loyal client, never trading me off against the other veterinary practice in the town. However, she was very hard to satisfy, always challenging my opinions and confronting me about treatments.

Patience has never been one of my virtues, despite intermittent attempts to practice it, but I did appreciate her loyalty and the prompt way in which she paid her bills. Eventually, however, I'd had enough. We had been taught as undergraduates that veterinarians should never refuse to treat an animal for a client unless they had given prior notice that they would no longer be at their disposal. For the only time in 20 years in practice I followed this advice. I wrote telling her that after careful consideration I felt it would be in our mutual interest for us to terminate our client-practitioner relationship. 'I am therefore giving you notice that I am no longer available to treat any animals owned by you or in which you may have an interest'.

Helen Lesley rang within 24 hours, sought an appointment, made the best qualified apology she could manage without losing face and asked me to reconsider my decision. I reinstated her and although she continued to ask probing questions about all manner of things there was never another confrontation.

THE AGREEMENT I HAD SIGNED with Alf Humble and his wife Betty was to lease his practice and their house (from which the small animal practice was conducted) for three years. The contract included an option to purchase the house and the practice as a single package at a price to be negotiated at the end of that period. The practice was doing well but towards the end of 1962 we were flattened financially by our first large provisional income tax bill. It became clear that it was going to be very difficult for me to get sufficient finance to purchase both the practice and the house within the next 18 months. I wrote to Alf telling him this and canvassed the possibility of splitting the contract into two parts, purchase of the practice on the expiry date and an extension of the lease on the house (including an option to purchase it) for a further two years. His reaction was immediate. He flew down from Alice Springs and angrily confronted me, asking bluntly if I was 'trying to steal the practice?' Either I met the terms of the agreement in full or he would return when the lease expired, resume practice and enforce the binding out clause that would prohibit me from practicing within 20 miles of Mount Gambier for two years. Nothing was negotiable.

I was shocked and disappointed. I wanted to negotiate in good faith to be fair to both parties. I thought he would be unlikely to want to return to the grind of working a seven day week in a single man veterinary practice; on the other hand I was 15 years younger than Alf, keen to continue to build the practice and take on an associate or partner. I decided to seek legal advice and try to negotiate rationally through independent third parties.

The legal advice, however, changed the basis and balance of our dispute quite fundamentally. Under the terms of the agreement lease payments were calculated at 10 per cent of the gross income of the practice and were split equally between Alf and his wife Betty. But in the 1960s legally enforceable restrictions on commercial conduct in professional practices were fundamentally different from contemporary regulations.

They included the prohibition of partnerships or any other arrangements that shared income from a professional practice with any person who was not qualified and registered in that profession. The inclusion of Betty Humble in the lease as a co-lessor meant that profit sharing was at the heart of the agreement which made it unenforceable. The solicitors should have drawn two contracts, one with the Humbles, husband and wife, for the lease of the house and one in which Alf Humble, veterinarian, leased the practice to me as a separate entity.

Notwithstanding this advice, Alf continued to play hard ball, insisting that the spirit and intent of the agreement should stand despite what he described as legal technicalities. He considered that I had set out to do him down. As a negotiated resolution of the dispute seemed unlikely, I moved to protect our position. Patrice and I purchased a five bedroom house on the northern boundary of the city. It needed renovation but the price was right and it suited our needs. My father acted as our guarantor, providing the deeds to the family home in Bendigo when we were unable to find a deposit large enough to satisfy the bank. The garage, linked directly with the house, became a small clinic and office and later a new double garage was built as an extension to the house. Within 12 months I made an ex gratia payment to Alf, notionally for the goodwill of the practice, and he sold his house on the open market. But I think he remained convinced for the rest of his life that I had short changed him, despite the ex gratia payment.

OUR DAUGHTERS JENNIFER AND GERALDINE were born in 1962 and 1964. By the time our fifth daughter Louise was born in 1966 Patrice had been pregnant for half of the previous nine years – 54 months out of 108 – despite continuing but futile use of the Billings' so-called rhythm method. We had spent the first 10 years of our marriage constantly agonising over the Catholic church's authoritarian teaching on birth control, reinforced by the threat of the fires of hell. Most Catholic couples have long since discarded this nonsense and live with their own consciences. Our children's generation think it is extraordinary that in the 1950s and 60s the church had such cruel control over our bedrooms and our consciences but it was a very real source of despair for many of us. Following the Second Vatican Council, convened by John XXIII, Catholics were optimistic that his successor Paul VI would accept the Papal Commission's recommendation that it was morally licit to use chemical or mechanical means to prevent conception provided this was 'in the overall moral context of a couple's openness to children'. However, the Papal Encyclical *Humanae Vitae: on the regulation of birth* released in July 1968, reaffirmed the church's ban on all 'artificial' means of birth control.

Despite Paul VI Patrice had decided that she could not face yet another pregnancy and I supported her decision with enthusiasm. She consulted Dr Mary Patterson, a plump, happy Scotswoman who was the obstetrician in our group medical practice and she prescribed Serial C, a predominantly oestrogenic contraceptive pill. It seemed to suit Patrice very well, the only side effect initially caused by the parish priest who refused her absolution unless she promised that never again would a contraceptive pill pass her lips. That was the final cruel blow. She has stayed in distant communication with the rituals of the religion of her childhood but, good woman that she has always been, was ultimately guided by her own conscience. Personally, I have not subjected myself to the cruelty of the confessional for 50 years and have serious doubts about a deity of any kind but it took a long time to finally leave behind the hang ups of a Catholic school boy.

There was an interesting epilogue to the story. In 1968 there was still considerable controversy about side effects of the pill and Serial C was said to be the problem solver for many women. Pregnancies aside, Patrice always maintained a constant weight but early in 1969 she began to put on weight, well rounded breasts, expanding waistline, perhaps side effects of the hormones in the pill? The ABC was running an exercise program on television at the time featuring Sue Becker, an energetic gymnast with a commanding voice and personality to match. Around nine o'clock every Friday night for six weeks we bounced energetically on the lounge room carpet during her program but Patrice continued to gain weight. At that point, despite Mary Patterson's assurance that she could not be pregnant, Patrice insisted on a pregnancy test. Our sixth daughter, Anna, was born five months later. Patrice had been in the very early stages of her seventh pregnancy during that confrontation with the parish priest in the Mount Gambier confessional box.

IN A MIXED VETERINARY PRACTICE without an associate the only practical way for me to provide a 24 hour service was to conduct the practice from the house. The downside of this arrangement was that I was never off duty and Patrice was constantly on call as the receptionist, answering the phone and the door bell and doubling as a surgical assistant for small animal emergencies at all sorts of odd hours. With a 24/7 practice there wasn't much time for socialising but we had domestic help and reliable baby sitters and did get out sporadically on Saturday nights to dine and dance at Jens Hotel or Giffords. An Australian wine renaissance began in the mid-1960s and no South Australian man with any pretension to sophistication would be without a suede jacket and an appreciation of the red wines of South Australia's Barossa Valley or Southern Vales. But for now sophistication meant white burgundy and beer and we danced to a trio playing popular standards on clarinet, piano and drums. Cabarets were held from time to time in the large hall at the showgrounds where the dancers drank flat jug beer and took to the floor to jive, twist and stomp. The vocalist helped us get into the spirit of the occasion by singing the Big Bopper's *Running Bear* with other members of the band chanting 'uga, uga' and providing the Indian war cries.

The Mount Gambier Club's premises were very modest, four rooms on the first floor of a two storey office building, one of which was reserved for two snooker tables and another for the poker games that we played on Friday nights. The club had neither the resources nor the need for staff. It didn't serve meals and was unlicensed. Alcoholic beverages were provided on an honour system – chits gentlemen please, no cash. Nevertheless older members saw it as something akin to the gentlemen's clubs of the capital cities. For many years membership had been largely restricted to graziers, members of the professions and business men and the Christmas dinner was the one night of the year when women were welcomed. Wives accompanied members to dinner and we danced at Jens Hotel. It was held in early December and although Mount Gambier had cold winters and cool, erratic spring weather, it was not unusual for the dinner to occur during the first of the heat waves that characterise southern Australia's summers. Jens had no air conditioning but the Club's dress code had to be maintained. Men sweltered in dark lounge suits in the best tradition of the early colonials.

During the sixties the membership criteria of the Club were relaxed to the extent that Tom and Kevin Preece, successful dairy farmers and respected members of the general community, were nominated and accepted as members. However, the old guard was keeping an eye on them. Walter White, a retired architect approaching his 80th birthday, had the demeanour and social attitudes of a retired colonel. In the week after the dinner in 1966 I overheard him discussing it with George Freeman. George, already in his seventies, was still conducting his dental practice, playing golf regularly and was quite switched on generally. 'I thought it was a splendid night. What did you think Walter'? 'I think so George, but I do worry about Club standards. Do you know that during the night one of those young Preece chaps asked me if it would be alright if he removed his suit coat.'

The big social event on the calendar was the two day Mount Gambier Cup carnival. Regrettably it was held in June in the cold, wet winter, although this didn't seem to diminish the enthusiasm of the local gentry. There was a race club dinner on the eve of the carnival and a grand ball the following night before the Cup. I was the Mount Gambier Racing Club vet I so I had my overalls in the car in case there was an accident or emergency. However, this was always an occasion to dress up. My race going outfit was a green tweed suit and mustard vest from Georges (at that time Melbourne's most fashionable department store) topped with a snap brim felt Stetson, Sinatra fashion. In the 1960s no man of any standing would be seen at a race meeting without a hat.

BRUCE GYNGELL MADE HISTORY on 16 September 1956 when he presented the first television program in Australia from the TCN9 studio in Sydney. In Melbourne HSV7 went to air on 4 November the same year, in time for the Melbourne Olympics, and Michael Charlton introduced viewers to ABC television from its Sydney studios the following day. However, viewers in rural and regional Australia had to wait. Mount Gambier, almost 300 miles from Adelaide and Melbourne, was an impossible distance away for anything remotely resembling reliable line of sight television transmission.

Limited reception was possible when BTV6 Ballarat began transmission in April 1962, although to get any reception it was necessary to have large twin phased antennas with a masthead amplifier (the technicians' description) mounted on top of an 80 foot latticed iron mast. This was anchored in a cement base with supporting steel guide ropes. The brave and the foolish among us invested more than £300 to acquire our masts and antennas and just occasionally we got good reception but most of the time we had more 'snow' than picture, viewed through the mandatory transparent blue paper over the TV screen. This was supposed to reduce the visual impact of the snow but as far as I could tell had little discernible effect. The sound came in waves, between bursts of static.

The antennas could be rotated to face Ballarat, Adelaide or Melbourne and from time to time on a dry summer night when the atmospherics were favourable we got some pictures from the capitals. Just occasionally, regardless of where the antennas were facing, we received simultaneous reception of different programs from Ballarat, Melbourne and Adelaide. They waxed and waned in a very confusing contest for our attention.

SES8 began transmission in Mount Gambier in March 1966 and the ABC regional station began later that year. Apart from news and live to air variety shows most of the popular programs broadcast on commercial television in the 1960s were produced in the United States while the ABC bought its drama and comedy from the BBC. Despite limited resources in these early days SES8 produced several programs that went live to air as well as a local news service. The children's program was presented by Enid Chapman, a local woman who taught elocution and voice training privately and was a part-time teacher at the Mater Christi primary school. It was produced with a studio audience of little people. She had no television or professional acting experience but I thought she did a good job by the pioneering standards of rural and regional television. This was no doubt a biased opinion because she saw me as potential talent and invited me to do a weekly segment talking about pet care. Each week I went to the studio with Blacky, the Cornwall's family cat, or with Timmy, a good natured Welsh Corgi borrowed from a client. My props were flea powder, brush, disposable syringe, a lead, cat collar (with a bell) and some harmless tablets for Blacky and Timmy. We did 10 short weekly programs, keeping it simple for six to 10 year olds – behaviour and training (good dog, bad dog), feeding, grooming, exercise, vaccinations, controlling worms and fleas. However, I clearly lacked Dr Harry's magic and we never had a repeat series.

My twin antennas and amplifier became redundant when SES8 and the ABC began regional transmission from Mount Gambier but when I installed a two-way radio I already had an 80 foot transmission tower ready to go. The base was established on the kitchen bench adjacent to the telephone with an extension to the office. Patrice could now answer the phone, use the two-way radio, rock the baby in a bouncinette and cook dinner almost simultaneously. We were told that because of the limited channels available for individual transmission it was essential that we use the standard operating procedure proscribed in the licence: 'Base to mobile, are you receiving me, over' and the response 'Mobile to base, receiving you, over'. It was believed that the Postmaster General's Department monitored the channels regularly and failure to work this way could result in the licence being revoked but the younger children were undeterred and soon worked out how to press the button in the kitchen to send me messages in the car. Allegations of hitting, pinching and other acts of petty cruelty were frequently transmitted without any introduction.

In 1965 I decided that an annual holiday had to be worked into our schedule so around Christmas each year (when the large animal practice was quiet) we took the family away for three weeks, everyone crammed into the Holden or Valiant sedan. The bench seat in the front could accommodate a child in the middle, one on Mum's lap if necessary and the rest in the back seat, no seat belts or air conditioning. In December 1965 and 1966 we headed for the Sunshine Coast in Queensland, a three day trip each way. These were simpler times and the holidays with our small children at Maroochydore were quite special. We rented a small, rather dilapidated Queensland weatherboard house on stilts, less than 100 yards from the beach, and bought watermelon from the back of a local farmer's truck for threepence a pound. However, by 1967 we decided that spending six days on the road for two weeks in sunny Queensland was just too demanding. Besides, Louise had made the first trip *in utero* and the second as a baby but she was now 18 months old and there were too many of us for such a daunting trip in the family car. We took the simpler option and began to explore Adelaide's southern beaches.

BY MID-1968 I HAD BEEN CONDUCTING the Mount Gambier practice on my own for seven years, working seven days a week; farm animals and horses during the day, a small animal clinic between 7.00pm and 8.00pm on week nights and on Saturday and Sunday mornings. Not infrequently there was a call to a farm animal emergency after eight o'clock at night to round off the day. I decided that I must get an associate vet, advertised in the *Australian Veterinary Journal* and was surprised when I received an inquiry from California.

Connor Jameson was a graduate from the School of Veterinary Medicine at Davis (University of California) and had done an internship in large animal practice at Cornell University in New York State, the top rated veterinary schools in the United States. He was interested in travel and looking around the world generally before settling down in his native California. Good looking, friendly, easy going and single, he was an instant but evasive target for the young women on Mount Gambier's A list. He hadn't come to Australia to find a wife. Connor was an outstanding clinician, a skilled surgeon and a dedicated professional. He was raised on a small cattle ranch in California and quickly developed a special relationship with members of Mount Gambier's farming community. For the first time in more than seven years I had the luxury of rostered time off, although Connor wasn't keen on what he called 'mutts and pussy cats' and increasingly I took on most of the small animal work.

A promotional family photo taken in 1968 as Labor's candidate for Prime Minister John Gorton's 'early election', and Amanda holding baby Anna who arrived 15 months later.

CHAPTER SEVEN

Swing to Labor

Historically Mount Gambier was a service centre for the district's farmers and graziers, Scotch Presbyterians and Irish Catholics with a solid core of German Lutherans. However, plantation based forestry was to play an increasingly important role in the economy of the region. As early as 1876 it had begun in a small way and relatively large planting of radiata pine from California began around the turn of the century. Private sector interest grew during the 1920s, stimulated in 1928 when the CSIRO perfected techniques to make paper from pine. During the Depression in the 1930s the rate of development of the plantations doubled through the efforts of men who were working for the dole.

South Australian Perpetual Forests (SAPFOR) was established in 1935 and Softwood Holdings followed in 1937. In 1958 the state government built and operated the Mount Gambier State Sawmill, at that time the largest in the southern hemisphere and in 1960 the large Apcel pulp mill, later owned and operated by Kimberley Clark, opened near Millicent. Panelboard Pty Ltd, which manufactured particle board, opened in the same year. This growing industrialisation inevitably had an impact on the character and political complexion of Mount Gambier as it grew from large country town to small provincial city. John Fletcher had held the state seat as an independent MP from 1938 to 1958 but when he died in office that year the Australian Labor Party (ALP) ran a strong campaign and Ron Ralston, a local councillor, claimed the seat for Labor. Ralston was the archetypal MP from another age, ample waistline, thumbs stuck in the armholes of his waistcoat as he held court with his constituents on Mount Gambier's main corner. He died of a heart attack in 1962, just four years after his election, with no heir apparent.

The ALP needed a candidate at short notice to contest the by-election and drafted Allan Burdon, a supervisor at the State Mill and a former member of the Mount Gambier City Council who retained the seat for Labor. Balding and bespectacled, Allan was a big man who moved slowly and his critics claimed he thought at a comparable pace. He was quickly dubbed 'Lively' Burdon by Des Corcoran, the member for the adjoining state seat of Millicent who became Don Dunstan's Deputy from 1970 and briefly the South Australian Premier when Don retired in 1979.

Early in 1963 I had been introduced to Russ Murrell, the secretary of the local sub-branch of the ALP. Russ was a self-employed carpenter who, like so many rank and file members of the Party in those days, was a well informed and dedicated foot soldier for the cause. I paid my 10 shillings annual membership fee and became a nominal but not yet an active member.

At the state election in 1962 Labor had secured more than 54 per cent of the two party preferred vote but was defeated by the notorious South Australian gerrymander: two thirds of South Australian voters who lived in or around Adelaide elected only one third of the members of parliament. Saturday 6 March was the date of the 1965 state election and the polls were indicating that the ALP had a commanding lead which might be large enough to see them overcome the gerrymander and return at last to government after more than 30 years in opposition.

After the polling booths closed I joined more than 20 (all male) campaign workers and supporters at Allan Burdon's home for an election night party while waiting for the results. Allan's wife Mildred wasn't keen on having the rank and file spoil her carpet so the party was conducted in the garage on a chilly autumn night. Allan had forgotten to organise a radio for the 'outsiders' so we had to rely on a runner who went inside the house at regular intervals to listen to the results and return with an update from the tally room. Shortly before 10.00pm he emerged to announce with suitable formality, 'Gentlemen, we have the Treasury benches'. The incoming Premier, Frank Walsh, would govern with a two seat majority.

Walsh was a social conservative. He was uncomfortable with the media, particularly television, and was a master of malapropisms and tangled syntax. Among many other gems in the parliament he referred to the winding up of the affairs of 'a diseased estate' and an opposition member who displayed 'a complete lack of apathy' with his constituents. When Tom Playford retired in 1966 Steele Hall became Leader of the Opposition.

At 37 the telegenic Hall provided a stark contrast with the bumbling Premier and the ALP heavyweights became convinced that Labor couldn't win the next election with Walsh as leader. In May 1967 Clyde Cameron (of whom Jim Killen reputedly once said 'the softest part of Clyde Cameron is his teeth') made a pre-emptive strike when he publicly thanked Walsh for making 'the noble decision to retire to make way for a younger person.' No one was more surprised than Walsh when he read this in *The Advertiser* but he saw the heavy artillery coming and within two weeks had announced that he was relinquishing the premiership. It would be Don Dunstan vs Steele Hall in 1968.

That election resulted in a hung parliament with Labor and the Liberal and Country League (LCL), as it was known in South Australia at that time, winning 19 seats each, despite Labor winning 53.8 per cent of the two party preferred vote. Hall formed government with the support of the Independent Tom Stott but Dunstan led a high profile public protest demanding fair electoral boundaries. Although it was not based on one vote-one value, Hall introduced legislation that provided a move towards a more equitable distribution for the House of Assembly. At the 1970 state election Labor won 27 of the 47 seats with a two party preferred vote of 53.7 per cent.

HAROLD HOLT HAD BECOME Prime Minister when Robert Menzies retired on Australia Day, 26 January 1966. In June that year he visited the United States and made his 'All the way with LBJ' speech on the White House lawns. When President Johnson made a reciprocal three day visit to Australia in October he assured us that 'Every American and LBJ are with Australia all the way.' He was met with large demonstrations against the Vietnam War in Sydney and Melbourne but in 1966 the threat of 'the yellow peril and the downward thrust of communism' still resonated with many voters.

In November that year Australia went to an election in which Vietnam was the central issue. The Leader of the Opposition, Arthur Calwell, first elected to the seat of Melbourne in 1940, had been a member of the House of Representatives for 26 years. Now 70 years old, he looked and sounded even older. Clips of Calwell's political ads during the campaign show why cartoonists had dubbed him 'Cocky' Calwell, caricaturing him as an obstinate Australian cockatoo. Calwell argued strongly (and presciently) against Australia's involvement in the war but he was an old-fashioned stump orator from the days when election campaigns were conducted through rowdy public meetings in town halls. Apart from his image problem in the new television age there were still deep divisions in the ALP and many voters feared that withdrawal of Australia's support for the war would be an affront to the United States, 'our great and powerful friend'. With Democratic Labor Party (DLP) support Harold Holt's Coalition Government scored a landslide victory.

The size and manner of the defeat caused me real concern. By the time of the next federal election the conservatives would have been in government for 20 years and unless there were some radical changes in leadership and organisation of the Party federally it seemed possible that Labor could become more an institutionalised opposition than an alternative government. I thought perhaps I could have some impact locally and decided to do my bit as an active member. I started to attend the Mount Gambier sub-branch meetings regularly and, among other things, took on the far right branch of the League of Rights through correspondence in the pages of the *Border Watch*, Mount Gambier's local paper. By the middle of 1967 I had become the sub-branch president.

I was on a steep learning curve in 1967 when I attended my first annual South Australian ALP Conference as Mount Gambier's sub-branch delegate. Under the card vote system the affiliated trade unions were allocated block votes based on the number of members for whom they had paid affiliation fees. This guaranteed them the majority of the votes on the conference floor but most of the important deals were done in advance (particularly pre-selections for state and federal seats) or dealt with between sessions at the conference. The Party's elders, led by old school Labor stalwarts Clyde Cameron and Senator Jim Toohey, ran the state branch as a guided democracy. Delegates from the sub-branches usually got to move their agenda items and have them passed or defeated on the voices or on a show of hands, although the machine men were very much in charge and set the agenda in advance of the conference. However, they were conscious of the need to broaden the base of the Party and the political imperative of preselecting candidates from a range of backgrounds and life experience. The South Australian branch had avoided the disastrous splits of the 1950s, the DLP was a very small shadow of its counterpart in Victoria and the formal faction system had not yet been entrenched.

WHEN HAROLD HOLT DISAPPEARED while swimming in heavy surf near Portsea on 17 December 1967 political commentators and the public generally assumed that Billy McMahon, Treasurer and Deputy Leader of the Liberal Party, would be his automatic successor. But John (Black Jack) McEwen, the hard man of the Country Party, announced that he and his party wouldn't serve in a government led by McMahon. In the subsequent leadership struggle, the Liberal Party turned to John Gorton, the only Senator in Australia's history to become Prime Minister. He resigned from the Senate on 1 February 1968 and was elected as the Member for Higgins (Harold Holt's seat) in a by-election held three weeks later.

Gorton was an ex RAAF fighter pilot, a veteran from World War II, with a face that told the story of the injuries he received when his Hurricane crash landed on Bintan Island early in 1942. He liked to portray himself as a man of the people who enjoyed a beer or three. He continued to support Australia's involvement in Vietnam but in other areas he pursued independent foreign policy and set new directions for federal-state relations, to the dismay of some of his more conservative colleagues and Liberal state premiers. He was initially a very popular Prime Minister and there was growing speculation that, despite having a large majority inherited from the Harold Holt landslide in 1966, he would seek his own mandate by calling an election for the House of Representatives.

The speculation was so strong that the ALP decided to pre-select candidates for all federal electorates in anticipation of an election in the spring of 1968. It was against this background that Mick Young, the State Secretary, and David Combe, the State Organiser, arrived in Mount Gambier and offered me a deal that could see me elected to the Senate in 1970. However, conditions applied. First I would have to run for the federal seat of Barker in John Gorton's early election for the House of Representatives. The electorate of Barker was one of the safest conservative seats in Australia and there was no suggestion that Labor could win it but if I proved my commitment by running a competent campaign I would have the support of the Party machine for pre-selection at number three on the ALP ticket for the Senate election due two years later. At a time when the Whitlam-Dunstan forces were actively broadening the base of the Party to attract middle class professionals as well as blue collar voters, country as well as city, the wise men thought that a country veterinarian in his mid-thirties would make an attractive Senate candidate.

The special conference to preselect all candidates for the House of Representative seats in South Australia was scheduled within three weeks so a decision was required immediately. Gough Whitlam had replaced Arthur Calwell and there was general optimism about the future under his charismatic leadership. Patrice and I decided I should say yes; this was a once in a lifetime opportunity to secure a Senate seat and enter federal politics, from country vet to career politician.

I went to the conference and received endorsement as the ALP's candidate for Barker. However, contrary to all the speculation about an early election, John Gorton allowed the parliament to run its full term. The House of Representatives election was not held until 25 October 1969. Accordingly when pre-selections for the 1970 Senate election were conducted at the State Conference in June 1969 I was still the endorsed candidate for Barker and ineligible to nominate for the Senate under the Party rules. Geoff McLaren, a 49 year old poultry farmer from Murray Bridge, secured the number three position on the ALP ticket and was duly elected. When he retired in 1983 at the age of 62 he had been a South Australian Senator for 13 years. Had I secured that spot in 1970, at the age of 35, I may well have had a career in the federal parliament spanning more than 20 years, from Whitlam to Hawke and Keating.

Gorton's failure to call an early election proved to be a tactical error. By the middle of 1969 his unorthodox style and erratic behaviour had eroded his earlier popularity and he was now facing a much more formidable opponent in Edward Gough Whitlam. This was the 'Swing to Labor' election in which Labor won 59 of the 125 seats in the House of Representatives, an 18 seat swing from 1966 and just four seats short of a majority on the floor of the parliament.

Our Barker campaign was generally low profile but there was one high point. In June 1969 the Mount Gambier City Council, perhaps taking out insurance in anticipation of Labor's future munificence in government, invited the Leader of the Opposition to officially open the city's basketball stadium. Patrice and I took Gough and his alter ego Graham Freudenberg to dinner and afterwards she braved the Mount Gambier winter to attend the opening. Our 10 day old daughter Anna was left in the care of the mothercraft nurse who was living with us for six weeks after the birth. Lance Barnard, Gough's loyal deputy, spent a weekend with us and on the Sunday afternoon we took him to a public meeting in Tarpeena, a small timber town just north of Mount Gambier. He was introduced by Lively Burdon who assured us (as he almost always did in his opening remarks) that it was 'indeed a pleasure and a privilege for each and every one of us' to have Mr Barnard visit us. He then sat in the front row of the small hall and dozed during Lance's address.

The local commercial television station SES8 had no pre-recording or editing facilities in 1969 and the most harrowing part of the campaign for me was delivering 30 second political ads live to air – including four seconds for a top and tail: 'This is a political announcement' – 'Written and spoken by John Cornwall on behalf of the Australian Labor Party'. There was no room for spontaneity. I spent the day rehearsing my 26 second delivery, word perfect, then coped with the onset of nervous diarrhoea from around four o'clock. I was 'on' during the first commercial break in the local six o'clock news. There were no autocues at SES8 in 1969 so Patrice accompanied me to the studio with our 'cheat sheet', the message written in bold capitals on white butcher paper with a texta pen.

In 1969 there was a very big swing back to Labor in South Australia. In the Wilson family's conservative fiefdom of Sturt ex-wharfie and ALP firebrand Norm Foster captured the seat with a two party preferred swing of 16 per cent. Chris Hurford, Richie Gun and Laurie Wallis recaptured Adelaide, Kingston and Grey for Labor and Ralph Jacobi won Hawker, a new electorate created in a redistribution. The ALP won eight of the 12 South Australian seats. There was a 12.5 per cent swing in Barker but in the final count the dour incumbent Jim Forbes still had 57 per cent of the votes in a two horse race.

After 20 years in the political wilderness the ALP was now within striking distance of the victory that would be ours in 1972. However, I was not going to be one of the new members who would be sworn in when the 27th Parliament met on 25 November 1969 and I had missed my chance for the Senate in 1970. For any South Australian ALP member who aspired to enter federal politics there were no vacancy signs on the doors of both the House of Representatives and the Senate.

GEOFF MANEFIELD WAS THE FIRST qualified, registered veterinarian to practice in the Upper or Lower South East of South Australia, establishing a veterinary practice in Mount Gambier in the early 1950s. Alf Humble graduated from the Sydney Vet School around the same time and was posted to The Mount as the South Australian Department of Agriculture's government veterinarian. Geoff always claimed that Alf worked up a private practice on the side before leaving the Department to set up in direct competition. Alf counterclaimed that Geoff's irascibility upset clients to the extent that he was virtually drafted into private practice. Both sides had a point. Geoff was a competent, committed veterinarian but he could be less than affable.

The large animal practices were often absurdly busy at peak times of the year. It would have made good sense to amalgamate them and take on a third vet and after several years of cut throat competition I sounded Geoff out about this but he dismissed my proposal. When I raised the matter again the following year his response was more friendly but equally adamant. 'Partnership is like marriage John' he said. 'You shouldn't get involved if you don't think it'll work'.

I had employed Connor Jameson as an assistant in 1968 primarily because I was exhausted from being on call seven days a week with no back up and I was concerned that I had worked without day to day peer support throughout my professional career. With two vets available on a 24/7 roster the practice would be able to provide superior emergency services while having the professional depth to further develop beef and dairy herd health and production services. However, Geoff was quick to follow me and we now had an additional full time veterinarian in each practice. In the first full year after Connor joined the practice the clients enjoyed the enhanced service and the gross income increased by 15 per cent. However, the additional costs, including salary, motor vehicle expenses and insurance, increased by almost 30 per cent. It was time to rationalise and retreat.

Patrice and I agreed that we should leave Mount Gambier and move to Adelaide. An important consideration was the need to provide increased educational options for our 'seven little Australians' and the metropolitan area offered opportunities for an aspiring politician, now incurably addicted to politics, who was interested in a seat in the South Australian Parliament. Living in Adelaide I could personally foster and enhance contacts with the heavyweights and number crunchers in the Party machine who determined pre-selections. I approached Geoff and gave him first option to purchase the practice. He'd previously been dismissive of this alternative, describing the Humble practice as 'stolen goods' but this time, with Connor staying on long enough to provide a seamless transition, he quickly realised it was an offer he couldn't refuse.

I was unable to find a city practice for sale but during holidays in Adelaide in the previous two years I had been looking at suburbs where it might be possible to establish one. I elected to take a gamble, having convinced myself that this was hardly comparable to the Swan Hill debacle. I had 11 years of practice experience and enough money to meet set up costs, operating expenses and the household budget during the first 12 months.

On 1 July 1970 I opened the door of my clinic at Largs North in suburban Adelaide. The building was rough and ready – a mix of cement bricks and timber with a caneite ceiling and a rusting galvanised iron roof. But floor to ceiling partitions, additional plumbing and electrical work, painting, furniture and air conditioning transformed it into a respectable small animal clinic - office and waiting room, examination room, radiology, a small surgical suite (with an anaesthetic machine which delivered measured doses of fluothane) and two banks of new cages in the kennel room.

Patrice had stayed behind with the children in Mount Gambier to allow the older ones to complete the second school term and to sell the house. I was staying with Ray Gallagher, recently relocated from Mount Gambier, in the gracious 80 year old bluestone house he had purchased on the Esplanade in Largs Bay. I used to make a lightning round trip of almost 1,000 kilometres to The Mount and back every weekend, leaving Adelaide at midday on Saturday and departing from home at 4.30am on Monday morning.

I was driving a 1967 Dodge Phoenix that I bought in a moment of madness 12 months earlier, second hand and out of warranty. No other car ever built was less suited to farm work in a rural practice than this massive machine but between Mount Gambier and Adelaide it could cruise on the back road through the Coorong at speeds up to 150 kilometres an hour. However, on an early morning return 'flight' to Adelaide it had an engine meltdown just 60 kilometres short of my new practice and I missed the morning consulting hours. Ted, the barber in the complex, didn't do much for my spirits when he told me that a local dog trainer (who never returned) had been waiting impatiently for me with four greyhounds. No clients came for the rest of the day or for the evening consulting. My family was 500 kilometres away and my car was in the hands of a mechanic in the Adelaide Hills awaiting major engine repairs. On a cold, dark night I sat on the edge of the examination table in the clinic and sobbed quietly.

By early August our house had still not been sold and there was an increasingly urgent need to relocate the family. I abandoned the search for an ideal residence in Adelaide and looked for a house large enough to accommodate the family but cheap enough to be purchased without waiting for the Mount Gambier sale. I found a large turn-of-the-century villa in Largs Bay and a sympathetic bank manager who arranged the finance. On 26 August the furniture from the Mount Gambier house was loaded onto a removalist's van and Patrice, brave and determined, boarded the overnight train to Adelaide with our seven children. The villa in Adelaide was in a poor state of repair but fortunately the previous owner hadn't attempted to 'modernise' it. We eventually restored it to its former glory from the proceeds of the Mount Gambier sale and added a 12 metre swimming pool.

DEVELOPING A VIABLE PRACTICE by word of mouth was a frustrating business. The advertising restrictions imposed on the professions in the 1970s were a remnant of standards inherited from Mother England. Virtually any marketing or promotion was not only unethical but illegal. When I began practice I was permitted to insert a notice measuring two column inches in the local paper once a week for three weeks. It gave my name, qualifications, address, telephone number, consulting hours but nothing more. No further advertising was permitted. The blue and white illuminated Veterinary Surgeon sign at the front of the premises was not allowed to exceed 12 x 15 inches and at one point the South Australian

Veterinary Surgeons Board actually sent a clerk with a step ladder to measure it.

Fortunately we managed to attract some well known local identities as clients soon after we opened the clinic. They included Roy and Merle Marten, the long term Mayor and Mayoress of Port Adelaide. Regrettably I have long forgotten the name of their British Bulldog bitch but I have remained forever grateful to her. She was their only child and had virtually all the many problems associated with the breed but invariably showed remarkable resilience on the many occasions when I treated her. Roy and Merle took their mayoral duties very seriously. They were active members and patrons of many clubs in the area and visited everything from kindergartens to nursing homes on a regular basis. Whenever the bulldog came up in conversation (as she often did) they were generous in their praise of the vet on Strathfield Terrace.

I had set myself some modest growth targets for the practice. When we met our first goal at the end of nine months Patrice and I declared it an important milestone and celebrated by dining at the elegant South Australian Hotel, just three months before it was demolished. In 1964 'The South', on North Terrace opposite Parliament House, had added The Beatles to the countless visiting celebrities it hosted during its 92 years. The hotel's dining room had served discriminating diners since 1879 and for almost 40 years prior to its demise it was presided over by the legendary head waiter Louie. He insisted on the highest standards of dress and decorum, defying any compromise that challenged tradition. He gained national notoriety during the 1960s when he refused to allow a casually dressed Bob Dyer, host of the long running radio and television program *Pick a Box*, into the dining room without a tie. At the time Bob and his wife Dolly ranked with Prime Minister Sir Robert and Dame Pattie Menzies as Australia's most recognised couple.

We had hoped for a more civilised life in small animal practice but in many ways trying to develop it into a viable enterprise was just as stressful as rural practice. In addition to her multiple duties as wife and mother, Patrice doubled as the morning receptionist and practice manager. The only other staff member in the early days worked as the veterinary nurse, 'kennel maid' and evening receptionist. For the first three years I was still consulting seven days a week and taking emergency calls out of hours.

Lona Paddon was a woman in the tough, male oriented world of harness racing. I met her when she brought the stable dog to the practice and within a few months I was doing her stable work. In Australia the legendary Sydney vet Percy Sykes led the field in introducing science into horse training. Heart scores, improved exercise regimens, feed supplements, vitamin injections and blood counts became an integral part of the trainer's repertoire and in the 1970s anabolic steroid injections were still part of the vet's routine stable visits.[8]

In the Paddon stable I had found a supplementary income and a hobby. At one point Lona introduced me to Garrison Lad, an eight year old pacer who had gone sour, refusing to do his best when the pressure was on in a race. She convinced me that working close to the margins but within the rules of racing we could fire him up to change his mind set. I leased a half share in the horse and we set out to prove our point. At his first outing in our colours Garrison Lad drew the outside of the second row. The old Adelaide Showgrounds track at Wayville was only two and a half furlongs (500 metres) in circumference so that horses that drew 'the pole' (the inside position on the front row) at the start had a huge advantage over the rest of the field. The horse had been doing well but a potential young champion had drawn the pole and all the advice was that we couldn't possibly win. The bookmakers confirmed this, sending him out at 66/1. The trots at Wayville were held on Friday night and in those early days I still consulted at a branch practice each week night between 7.00pm and 8.00pm. I decided it would be business as usual for me. I wouldn't go to Wayville and I certainly wouldn't waste any money betting on our horse.

I finished consulting just in time to turn on the car radio and hear the race broadcast. From a standing start the even money favourite jumped in front, stumbled in its hobbles and fell, bringing down half the field. Garrison Lad avoided the scrimmage; racing out wide he breezed past the fallen horses, went to the front 'on the bit', led all the way and won easily. Perhaps science, pharmaceuticals and patience had changed his mind set. The following week when he drew number three on the front row I broke out and had more of my 'hard earned' on him than I could afford but he dogged it and finished second last. So much for Lona and John's magic mind therapy. He never finished in a place in four more races and we sent him home.

During my second year with the stable Lona started to complain to me about team driving in which the horse selected to win was given a dream run in the field by other reinsmen. She alleged that it involved several successful stables and a rather sinister hard man. Lona told me she had been approached but refused to be part of the set up and asked me if I could help. I told the story to Jeff Martin whom I had first met when he was working as a regional ABC journalist in Mount Gambier. He was now the Deputy Premier's press secretary but in a private capacity he put me in touch with a journalist at Adelaide's *Sunday Mail* which ran the story without naming the source of the allegations but attributing several quotes to me. It was hardly a coincidence that when I arrived at my Strathfield Terrace clinic for the 11.00am consulting hour that Sunday I found a house brick had been thrown through the large plate glass front window. Someone had obviously read the early edition of the paper. I got the message but so did the stewards. No one was ever charged but Lona assured me in the months that followed that they had virtually eliminated team driving at Globe Derby Park.

Early in 1975 Lona asked me if I would be interested in buying an interest in a promising young colt they were buying in New Zealand, the price for a half share a modest $4,000. I gave the offer serious consideration but decided that family financial commitments ruled it out. The colt turned out to be Markovina which became something of a sensation as he went through his classes at Globe Derby Park, Adelaide's new harness racing headquarters. Lona's husband Murray drove Markovina rather like a V8 motor car, often accelerating from virtually impossible places in the field to thrill the crowd as he strode to the front four bikes wide on the home turn. Family loyalty kept him in the driver's seat but once the horse reached free-for-all class Murray sometimes set him impossible tasks and he was eventually sold to Victorian interests. In 1978 Brian Gath piloted him to victory in both the Inter Dominion final and the first Australian Pacing Championship.

With Chris Sumner and Roy Abbot at the Trades Hall Club celebrating our pre-selection at the State Conference, June 1974, all later joining the short-lived Corcoran Cabinet for five months in May 1979.

CHAPTER EIGHT

It's time

The Dunstan Labor Government won the 1970 state election a month before I opened the Largs North veterinary practice. Don Dunstan had campaigned tirelessly for electoral fairness during the two years from March 1968 when Labor lost the election by one seat under the distorted electoral distribution in South Australia that had operated since 1936. Responding to irresistible community pressure, Steele Hall's Liberal Country League (LCL) Government had implemented partial reform of the system in 1969. The lower house was expanded from 39 to 47 seats, 28 in Adelaide and 19 in the country. The state election, conducted on these new boundaries in May 1970, resulted in a comfortable win for the ALP which won 27 of the 47 seats. South Australia was entering the Dunstan decade.

There was a spirit of generosity abroad as the government set about bringing progressive social reforms and community services to South Australia. But my political activities for the first 18 months in Adelaide were largely limited to having an occasional Friday lunch with some of the Dunstan Government press secretaries. I was too preoccupied, consulting at my surgery during extended hours every evening and on weekends, to take any part in the activities of my local sub-branch. Nevertheless, the State Executive asked me to contest the federal seat of Barker again in 1972 and I accepted on the understanding that as winnable seats in the South Australian Parliament became available, my name would be on the short list.

This was the famous 'It's Time' campaign which returned federal Labor to government after 23 years in the political wilderness. I recruited three journalists from those Friday lunches to my campaign committee: Peter Eltham, the *Australian Financial Review*'s South Australian correspondent, for whom the Union Hotel in Weymouth Street was his second home,

Phil Robins, a journalist at *The Advertiser* who two years later married the Union's publican, the vibrant Shirley Robins, and Jeff Martin, Deputy Premier Des Corcoran's press secretary. As much of our campaign planning was done over long Friday lunches at the Union Hotel I cancelled consulting on Friday evenings indefinitely.

The highlight of our Barker campaign was undoubtedly the visit by Bob Hawke, then President of the Australian Council of Trade Unions. David Combe suggested we might fly him to Bordertown, a small town in the heart of the Barker electorate where Bob was born in 1929. Hawkey was such a popular, high profile public figure that David believed the visit could draw national media coverage. We flew Bob from Adelaide in a chartered Cessna Skymaster, the 'push pull' model with a propeller at the front and rear of the fuselage. The visit was a huge success. Bob charmed the golden oldies, quite a few of whom knew his father Clem who had been the Congregational Minister in the town at the time Bob was born, and his mother Ellie. Some even claimed to remember Bob as a little boy. The visit was scheduled for mid-morning in anticipation that there would be crews from the metropolitan news services wanting to get back to Adelaide in good time for the evening bulletins. All the Adelaide television stations were there and the story ran nationally.

We drove to Naracoorte for an afternoon meeting with local dignitaries and the party faithful, then to Mount Gambier for our town hall meeting. Television, with its 15 second grabs, 30 second political commercials and 80 second news items, had already largely replaced the traditional public meeting of the Menzies era. However, that night a crowd filled the Mount Gambier Town Hall and spilled out into the foyer.

This was very much a presidential style campaign, Labor focusing all its efforts on the charismatic, erudite and articulate Gough Whitlam: 'Men and women of Australia, it's time…'. This contrasted with the performance of Prime Minister McMahon whose tremulous voice, slight speech impediment ('Biddy' McMahon) and inept use of autocues were playing very badly on television. To avoid distractions from the national strategy focusing on Gough and 'The Program', several prominent members of Labor's front bench were sent to campaign in regional Australia. We took Lance Barnard, Whitlam's loyal deputy and soon to be Australia's Deputy Prime Minister, to Victor Harbour where he was supported by Premier

Dunstan and, despite being in a conservative heartland, they drew a surprisingly good crowd to the Town Hall. Don was anxious to ensure that the meeting didn't drag on for too long, keen to get back to Adelaide little more than an hour's drive away. We negotiated a format in advance with Lance's press secretary Clem Lloyd in which I was to speak briefly to identify myself and introduce Don. He would use his short speech to energise the crowd and introduce Lance for what we agreed would be around 20 minutes, followed by a brief question time.

Lance was the opposition spokesman on defence. He stuck with the agreed format until we got to question time when he still had a lot of policy detail he was keen to share with the good folk of the South Coast. He was a little deaf which ensured that his answers were not necessarily related to the questions - the defence message was central and he was leaving no detail unspoken. Much to Don's chagrin the Mayor seemed delighted that the man who was soon to become Australia's Deputy Prime Minister was so generous with his time. He repeatedly urged the crowd to use this unique opportunity to glean every detail.

During the campaign we also hosted a visit from Tom Uren. Tom made a brief sortie into Barker and addressed a meeting organised by the ALP sub-branch at Tailem Bend, a railway town on the Murray River about 110 kilometres from Adelaide. He had a well deserved reputation for integrity, an activist who was a leading figure in opposing the Vietnam War, conscription and nuclear testing. He had been sitting on the opposition benches as the member for the Western Sydney seat of Reid since 1958 but was now only weeks away from the new portfolio of Urban and Regional Development. At Tailem Bend he spoke with passion about Labor's ambitious plans for regional cities, urban consolidation and built heritage. The audience wasn't a collection of aesthetes but an enthusiastic group of railway workers and other true believers. Within weeks he would be sworn in as a member of the first federal Labor cabinet in 23 years where he proved to be a highly competent minister and emerged from the Whitlam Government with his reputation enhanced.

Many of Australia's best known television performers who featured in the 'It's Time' commercial also campaigned actively on the ground for Labor. Members of the Barker campaign committee were very excited when they heard that Terry Norris (Joe Turner) and Lynette Curran (Rhoda

Lang), two of the stars of *Bellbird*, had volunteered to make a fly in-fly out Sunday visit to the electorate. *Bellbird*, set in a fictional township in Victoria, was one of Australia's first soap operas. It screened in the 15 minute time slot each week night, immediately prior to the ABC's 7 o'clock news, and was particularly popular in rural Australia. The Barker campaign committee hired the Naracoorte racecourse and organised a 'great big ALP barbecue' in one of the most conservative towns in South Australia. The crowd roared with delight when the two actors arrived, dressed in character, looking as though they had just stepped out of a television screen.

Friday night at the Trades Hall Club was the time to have a drink with Party people and influential trade union officials like Jack Nyland, the state secretary of the Transport Workers Union. Jack was as tough as they come, with a larrikin sense of humour typical of the workers and battlers of his generation. He was the workers' friend from central casting - well creased face, horn rimmed glasses and grey hair cut short back and sides. I was a friend and a fan.

Jack had heard about the enthusiastic campaign we were conducting in Barker and during one of my Friday night sessions at the club he asked me why we were spending so much time and effort. 'What the hell makes you think you can win' he asked, foxing me. 'Because I've got charisma Jack' I shot back, fortified by a few drinks. He jumped back two paces, feigned terror at the prospect of contagion and asked in a loud voice 'Is it catching?' The drinkers in our school had a great laugh at my expense and Jeff Martin immediately dubbed me 'the charisma kid'. This was later shortened to Charisma and used derisively by close friends whenever they thought I might be getting carried away with myself.

By 1972 there was a widespread feeling in the Australian community that it was time for a change after 23 years of conservative government. Public opinion was turning strongly against Australia's involvement in the Vietnam War and conscription. Prime Minister McMahon, who established a reputation as a competent economic manager during his years as the federal Treasurer, was now dogged by rising inflation and he made a serious political error when he attacked Gough Whitlam over Labor's policy of recognising the People's Republic of China. He had to make a humiliating back down at the height of the controversy he had created when President Nixon announced that he was to visit China. Ultimately the swing to Labor was a relatively modest 2.5 per cent. However, with 52.7 per cent of the two party preferred vote Labor won 67 seats, a comfortable nine seat majority in the 125 seat House of Representatives.

THE DUNSTAN GOVERMENT was returned in 1973 with a five seat majority in the House of Assembly. Having successfully achieved reform of the Lower House, Premier Dunstan now turned his political skills to reform of the Legislative Council. For decades members of the Upper House had been elected on five grossly distorted multi-member electoral districts. The boundaries of the two metropolitan districts ensured that the LCL and Labor shared one each (on either side of the River Torrens). In the country, however, the LCL won all three districts with an electoral weighting of 2:1 against Labor. The result had been consistently 16 to 4 in a 20 member Council. Many of the older members of the LCL in the Upper House not only saw the Council as a house of review but as representing what one member described as 'the permanent will of the people'.

Despite the old guard (derisively dubbed the troglodytes by Dunstan) several LCL members supported passage of the Bill, acknowledging the overwhelming case for a system based on the principle of one vote-one value. Eleven members of the 22 member Council were to be elected for eight year terms every four years on a statewide 'list system' of voting. My turn had come. At the preselection ballot held soon after the legislation was proclaimed I secured fifth position on the ALP ticket for the next Legislative Council election. In a period prior to the proliferation of minor parties and independents the fifth position was safe for Labor.

GOUGH WHITLAM WAS AN active Prime Minister like no other, pursuing a sweeping reform agenda, but his government was being consistently frustrated in the Senate by the combined opposition of the Liberal and Country Parties and the Democratic Labor Party (DLP). Meanwhile his Senate colleagues in the DLP had become disillusioned with their leader, Senator Vince Gair, particularly over his persistence in opposing recognition of the People's Republic of China which by now was recognised by the Australian Government and more importantly, in international terms, by US President Richard Nixon. Gair was forced to resign as DLP leader and his disillusionment (or worse) with his colleagues was common knowledge.

A half Senate election was due in 1974 and Prime Minster Whitlam saw an opportunity to create an additional Senate vacancy in Queensland if he could persuade the disaffected Gair to resign by offering him the diplomatic post of Ambassador to Ireland. If six Senate positions in Queensland were contested at the half Senate election instead of five, Labor would almost certainly win three. Gair would effectively be replaced by a Labor senator, giving the government control of the Senate. Gair accepted the offer and the stage was set for a clever political ploy. However, on 2 April the Prime Minister made an enormous tactical blunder when he announced the date for the half Senate election before Gair had formally resigned. Premier Bjelke Petersen's Queensland cabinet met within hours and recommended to the Governor that writs be issued for the election of five Queensland senators. The writs were issued at 11.00pm and 'the wily Gair', with his appointment already secured, waited until the following day before submitting his resignation, too late for Whitlam and the Labor Party.

Ostensibly outraged by this attempted manipulation of the Senate numbers, the Leader of the Opposition, Billy Snedden, announced that the opposition would take the extraordinary step of blocking the government's supply bills in the Senate, denying Treasury the funds necessary for the government to function. Prime Minister Whitlam responded by going to the Governor-General and seeking a double dissolution, triggered by several bills that had previously been defeated twice in the Upper House. On 18 May the Whitlam Government was returned to office with the loss of two seats. It still lacked a clear majority in the Senate but the bills on which the double dissolution had been based were passed at a joint sitting of both houses of parliament held on 7 August 1974. They included the legislation to establish Medibank, the universal health insurance scheme which had been twice previously rejected.

The government had an unparalleled record of social and legislative innovation and reform, despite a vehemently hostile Senate. Achievements included universal health insurance, abolition of the death penalty for federal offences, the Schools Commission, consumer protection legislation, the Family Law Act (introducing no fault divorce), the Family Court, the supporting mothers' benefit, equal rights and pay for women, Aboriginal land rights and abolition of university fees. The government also removed the last vestiges of the White Australia Policy, fostered cultural diversity and defined Australia's role in the world as a modern and independent nation.

On the other hand the Prime Minister's apparent inability to control or discipline several prominent cabinet ministers and an increasingly vituperative but effective Liberal-Country Party Opposition were creating a public perception that the Whitlam Government was losing control of the economy. For Australia's political commentariat, obsessed with the drama occurring in domestic politics, the global impact of the Organisation of Petroleum Exporting Countries (OPEC) oil embargo and the collapse of the Bretton-Woods financial system were not significant parts of their equation.[9] When Gough Whitlam died in 2014 it was finally acknowledged that 'the Australian economy under Whitlam actually did better than the United States and the United Kingdom during one of the most turbulent periods in modern economic history, a global recession that marked the end of the post-war boom'. Between 1973 and 1975 America endured its worst recession since the Great Depression and inflation in the United Kingdom grew from 7.4 per cent to 24.9 per cent, 'much higher than anything experienced in Australia'.[10]

By the end of 1974 cabinet was planning to bypass the Loans Council in a bid to raise a loan of $4 billion from unidentified oil sheikhs to 'buy back the farm'. Cabinet was concerned that most of Australia's abundant mineral and energy resources were being exploited by foreign owned companies who were paying relatively minute amounts in royalties or taxation to the state and federal treasuries.

On Friday 13 December 1974 the Prime Minister Gough Whitlam, Treasurer Jim Cairns (who had replaced Frank Crean as Treasurer) , Minerals and Energy Minister Rex Connor and other members of the Executive Council met and authorised Connor to borrow up to $4 billion 'for temporary purposes'. The Governor-General who normally presides over Executive Council meetings was attending the ballet in Sydney but signed the Executive Council minute the next day. Rex Connor immediately began the search for the petro-dollars using Tirath Khemlani, a mysterious Pakistani dealer who claimed to have contacts with the right people in the Middle East, as his broker. Connor always claimed he made it clear to Khemlani that once the contacts had been established he would have to look to them for any recompense for his services.[11]

On 27 January 1975 Connor's authority was reduced to $2 billion and cabinet revoked the authority altogether on 20 May, just five months after the original authority had been endorsed by the Executive Council. But by this time there was a widespread perception in the cabinet and in the community that the Treasurer, Jim Cairns, had lost his grip on the economy. On 5 June the Prime Minister moved him to the Environment portfolio and appointed Bill Hayden as Treasurer. It was subsequently revealed that Cairns had been freelancing without the Prime Minister's knowledge, attempting to raise overseas funds through George Harris, a Melbourne dentist turned businessman. Cairns provided Harris with a letter authorising him to raise $2 billion and promised him a 2.5 percent brokerage fee. On 4 June when the Deputy Leader of the Liberal Party, Phillip Lynch, raised the issue in the House of Representatives Cairns denied the existence of the letter but Lynch was being well briefed by a mole in Treasury. When he produced a copy of the letter Cairns denied having ever signed it but it was clear that he had misled Parliament. Whitlam sacked him from the ministry on 2 July.

In the meantime John Menadue, the Head of the Department of Prime Minister and Cabinet, had meticulously compiled a dossier that focused on the question of whether in dealing with Khemlani or anyone else, anything had been said or inferred that could provide grounds for a legal claim against the government. As a result the Prime Minister was able to report to Parliament on 9 July that not a cent had been paid or would be paid or was liable to be paid to the intermediary.[12]

Nevertheless the events had created a climate which helped a determined opposition to successfully promote the view that the government was losing control. This had been reinforced in the previous month by the debacle that was the Bass by-election. Following the double dissolution election in 1974 Lance Barnard had lost the Deputy Leadership to Jim Cairns. In May 1975 Gough Whitlam appointed him Ambassador to Sweden, Norway and Finland and he resigned as the Member for Bass, a Tasmanian seat that had been held by Labor for 60 years. In an exquisitely ill timed by-election held on 28 June the Liberal Party's Kevin Newman won the seat with a 17 per cent swing against the government.

Earlier that month Mick Young, now the Federal Member for Port Adelaide, had led a delegation of 12 rank and file Australian Worker's Union (AWU) and ALP members to the People's Republic of China (PRC). As the ALP's Federal Secretary Mick had played an important role with Gough Whitlam in establishing diplomatic relations with China in the lead up to and immediately after Labor's 1972 federal election victory and was a welcome visitor. I was a member of the delegation which included the South Australian Secretary of the AWU, Jim Dunford, and a young Adelaide lawyer, Chris Sumner. Although each member of the delegation had to meet their own travel and accommodation expenses to and from Hong Kong, the PRC was meeting all other expenses for the three week tour. However, my excitement about visiting this ancient and fascinating nation was short lived. On arrival at the Sheraton Hotel in Kowloon on the Friday evening Dunford, Sumner and I, who were all endorsed candidates for the South Australian Legislative Council, received individual but identical cablegrams: 'Return immediately. Election 12 July. George Whitten, State Secretary'. We flew home on Monday after what turned out to be no more than an expensive weekend in Hong Kong.

By June 1975 Don Dunstan was leading the only Labor government in mainland Australia. Fifteen months into their second term our federal colleagues were being buffeted by the ongoing world recession, a continuously hostile Senate and some notable examples of poor political judgment and timing. Although there is a degree to which the electorate can distinguish between state and federal government performance, the polls were starting to show that voter disapproval of the Whitlam Government was having an impact at state level. The question now being canvassed openly within the Party and in the local media was whether the South Australian Government should go to an election to escape the full effect of the turmoil in Canberra. The political reality, however, was that an election couldn't be called early without a substantial reason. Between them the government in Canberra and Dunstan's troglodytes in South Australia's Legislative Council were about to provide one.

Despite the political turbulence the Whitlam Government was still pressing on with its radical reform agenda. In a bold initiative to standardise rail transport nationally they now proposed that the states transfer their country railways to the Commonwealth. The capital value of rolling stock, land and buildings was substantial but the operating deficits were large, recurrent cost burdens on state budgets. Premier Dunstan described the offer as 'a very good deal for South Australia' and introduced enabling legislation. When a recalcitrant Legislative Council continued to oppose the *Railways Transfer (South Australia) Bill*, the Premier took a calculated gamble. On 20 June 1975 he called a snap election.

When I arrived back from my three day visit to Hong Kong I was sent to the South East to assist with the organisation of local campaigns in Mount Gambier and Millicent. New boundaries established in the redistribution had made Millicent unwinnable for the ALP and Deputy Premier Corcoran had transferred to a safe metropolitan seat. In Mount Gambier, where several rural districts had been included within the new boundaries, the ALP was going to struggle.

On a Sunday some weeks prior to the election being called the local member, Lively Burdon, was apprehended by a local ranger carrying a rifle in a nature reserve. He was there to shoot rabbits but why he had chosen a nature reserve for his 'sport' remains a mystery. Carrying a firearm in a nature reserve or national park for any reason is an offence, discharging it is worse. The case was listed for hearing in the Mount Gambier Local Court just days after the election was called and the ranger's evidence was reported verbatim in the local paper:

> On Sunday 7 June I saw the accused carrying a .22 calibre rifle in the Carpenters Rocks Nature Reserve. When I approached he attempted to conceal himself by crouching behind one of the small shrubs that constitute the vegetation on that part of the coast. The accused is a tall, heavy man and his attempt to hide was futile.

The thought of big Allan crouching behind a sparse three foot shrub on the windswept coast, rifle in hand, was a source of great amusement for the locals and dismay for his campaign team.

Much more damaging, however, was the 'March against Socialism' promoted by Allan Scott, the trucking magnate who by now had acquired both the *Border Watch* and SES8 television. His forays into local politics, based on his 'run over the bastards' business model, were erratic and, unlike his business activities, largely unsuccessful. But on this occasion he had the assistance of an astute Liberal candidate, Harold Allison, and the Liberal Party branch that Allison had rejuvenated. Scott's primary target was Don Dunstan. Don was a remarkably successful social reformer, by any objective measure a social democrat from the centre-left of the political spectrum, hardly a big 'S' socialist. However, in political matters Scott was not a man to be deflected by logic. The stunning result in Bass on 28 June and the sacking of Jim Cairns, a failed Treasurer who had attempted to negotiate unauthorised Middle East loans, just 10 days before polling day provided a colourful backdrop.

The march was scheduled for lunch time on Friday 4 July, just eight days before the election and I stood on the main corner to watch it. Having lived in Mount Gambier for almost 10 years I thought the prevailing mood was one of concern but I didn't detect a revolution. I reckoned that we would see about 200 diehards, headed by the local chapter of the League of Rights, straggling down Commercial Street. But I was seriously wrong. A crowd closer to 1,000 filed through the intersection and eight days later Harold Allison claimed the seat for the Liberal Party.

This was supposed to be a single issue election: the transfer of South Australia's country rail network to the Commonwealth, a very good financial deal for South Australia and the beginning of the transition to a national rail system. But the single issue was soon subsumed by numerous other state issues, overshadowed by events in Canberra and the annihilation of federal Labor in Bass. The Dunstan Government was fighting for its life. In the last week of the election campaign Dunstan distanced himself from the Whitlam administration:

> My government is being smeared and it hurts. They want you to think we are to blame for Canberra's mistakes. The vote on Saturday is not for Canberra, not for Australia, but for South Australia.

The result of the election was desperately close. Labor won 23 seats, the Liberal Party 20, Steele Hall's breakaway Liberal Movement (later the nucleus of the Australian Democrats) two seats and the National Party one. The count stood at 23:23 with the Independent Ted Connelly holding the 47th seat. Ted had been a popular Mayor of Port Pirie and a long time member of the ALP. When Labor's Dave 'Boxer' McKee announced in 1974 that he would retire at the next election Ted nominated for the Port Pirie pre-selection and should have been a shoo-in. However, the heavies of the AWU ran a strong campaign for their man, the Port Pirie based union organiser. Connelly was understandably outraged when he failed to gain Labor preselection and won the seat as an independent candidate. Premier Dunstan was on the phone as soon as the results were in. Not surprisingly Connelly, bargaining from a position of strength, secured the Speaker's job.

The upside of the election was in the Legislative Council. 1975 was the only year in which Labor won six of the 11 seats contested in the reconstituted Legislative Council. I came in at number five, as anticipated, and Chris Sumner surprised by winning the sixth Legislative Council spot for Labor. The newly constituted Liberal Movement had won two and with their support we would finally be able to pass full electoral reform for House of Assembly elections, based on one vote, one value.

Patrice and I had seven children in the education system, ranging from junior primary school to university at a time when parliamentary salaries were very modest. In real terms the basic salary of $16,500 was equivalent to approximately $75,000 in 2016, around half what backbenchers are currently paid. To supplement this base I had begun to explore ways to retain an interest in the practice without compromising my obligations to the parliament and the Party but I was caught out when the election was called eight months before the expiry of the normal three year term. After panicking briefly I met the immediate challenge of maintaining a viable practice by retaining the locum service (already in place for the ill fated trip to China). Then I persuaded Ben Benaradsky, my old friend and colleague from university days, to join us. Patrice retained her position as receptionist and financial manager.

THERE WERE FOUR NEW FACES in the 1975 Dunstan Government. Brian Chatterton, an agricultural science graduate from the University of Reading in the United Kingdom, had been appointed Minister of Agriculture just a month before the July election and retained that portfolio. Peter Duncan, at the age of 30 the youngest politician ever appointed as South Australia's Attorney-General, replaced Len King whose appointment to the Supreme Court had been announced as the Parliament was prorogued for the election. Ron Payne, the amiable Member for

Mitchell, replaced Len King in the Community Welfare portfolio and Don Simmons filled the vacancy in the Environment portfolio when Glen Broomhill resigned from the front bench soon after the election. Glen's wife had been diagnosed with multiple sclerosis and as her condition deteriorated without remission he took on the role of primary carer. He remained in the Parliament until 1979 when he retired to devote his time to her 24 hours a day.

During his time in the Environment portfolio Glen had introduced the beverage container legislation, despite the opposition of the powerful and politically ruthless packaging industry. More than 40 years later it still stands as a monument to his courage and integrity.

Don Simmons, Glen's replacement, was an intense, middle aged accountant with degrees in arts and economics and a distinguished flying cross awarded to him as a young pilot in the Second World War. Don was intelligent, diligent but inclined to get bogged down in detail. When everyone else had left and the office cleaners had come and gone Don would still be there, mulling over files, dockets, cabinet submissions, reports and briefing notes which were piled on the desk and spread around the floor. If the tasks couldn't be completed that night he would leave everything where it was and return early the next morning to complete unfinished business before starting another 12 hour day.

This was fine until one night when he left the office before the cleaners arrived. They were recent recruits who had not been well briefed on the fact that all paperwork in a minister's office was to be treated as 'very private and absolutely confidential' unless otherwise indicated: in other words do not touch. Nor were they as environmentally sensitive as one might have assumed. Recycling was not in their remit. More than a dozen folders and documents scattered on the floor were bundled into the general waste collection for transport to the Wingfield rubbish tip. Don was aghast when he arrived at the office at 7.30am the next morning and realised what had happened. Assuming full ministerial responsibility in the best Westminster tradition (and in his best suit) he set off for the tip with his driver to search through piles of assorted smelly garbage that had been tipped at first light. He never found a single file - the bulldozer had already worked over much of the area - but at least he could rest secure in the knowledge that the evidence had been buried.

THE LOANS AFFAIR DOGGED THE Whitlam government throughout 1975. By July it had destroyed the political career of the Deputy Prime Minister and Treasurer Jim Cairns. By October it would bring down the Minister for Minerals and Energy, Rex Connor, and become the basis for one of the most turbulent times in the history of Australian politics. This was despite not one dollar of loan money having been raised nor one cent paid as a commission to anyone.

From January Khemlani had sent regular telexes to Connor assuring him he could secure the loan from his Middle Eastern sources but when nothing had happened by May, Whitlam turned instead to a major US investment bank. As part of their negotiations the bank insisted that the government should cease any other activities related to the loan and Connor's loan raising authority was withdrawn on 20 May, But the matter did not rest there. During the budget session of Parliament in August members of the opposition, led by the Deputy Leader of the Liberal Party, Phillip Lynch, pursued the issue further. When Lynch claimed that Connor had continued to communicate with Khemlani after the authority had been withdrawn he denied the accusation, both in Parliament and to the Prime Minister. However, Peter Game, a journalist at the Melbourne *Herald*, had located Khemlani who claimed in an interview that he and Connor were still in contact. When Connor denied these claims Khemlani flew to Australia and on 13 October he provided the journalist with copies of the telexes sent to him by Connor, accompanied by a statutory declaration. Whitlam was given copies of the documents and he had no option but to demand Connor's resignation. Reviewing this sad ending to Connor's grand vision 20 years later Paul Kelly wrote that it was the national interest that drove him. As Kelly put it, 'he can be criticised for his naivety and poor judgement', but there was 'no charge against Connor's integrity'.[13]

Bill Hayden, who replaced Jim Cairns as Treasurer, had introduced a well crafted budget that responded to the turmoil created by the disastrous global recession. However, the opposition in the Senate seized the moment to announce the next day that it would take the unprecedented step of voting against the *Loan Bill 1975, Appropriation Bill (No. 1) 1975-76*, and *Appropriation Bill (No. 2) 1975-76*: in other words vote to deny supply. The motion for the second reading of these bills would be amended to the effect that the legislation 'be not further proceeded with until the government agrees to submit itself to the judgment of the people, the Senate being of the opinion that the Prime Minister and his government no longer have the trust and confidence of the Australian people.' Intense debate about the rights of the Senate and the House of Representatives and a series of tactical political manoeuvers followed. Then in a dramatic coup on Tuesday 11 November the Governor-General Sir John Kerr dismissed Gough Whitlam and appointed Malcolm Fraser as a caretaker Prime Minister.

In the double dissolution election held on 13 December the ALP lost 30 of the 66 seats it won in 1974. The Liberal-National Party Coalition formed government with 91 seats in the House of Representatives.

I HAD A STATEWIDE BRIEF as a backbench member of the Legislative Council and was allocated specific responsibility for three country electorates - Chaffey, Millicent and Mount Gambier - all three now held by the opposition. Against the odds one of the Party's 'horses for courses', Reg Curran, held the Riverland seat of Chaffey for three parliamentary terms (1962-65, 1965-68 and 1970-73) and Millicent had been the fiefdom of Jim and Des Corcoran, father and son, for 20 years. Successive redistributions took these electorates outside the ALP's reach from 1975. However, they had been important in gaining the numbers for the return of Labor to government in 1965 and 1970 and Premier Dunstan never let a seat get out of the 'possible' range on the electoral pendulum without fighting the good fight. Between 1975 and 1977 he visited Chaffey on a number of occasions and I worked with his personal staff in organising the itineraries.

Few of his parliamentary colleagues could ever claim that they knew Don well and despite travelling with him to marginal country seats on many occasions I am unable to say I ever did. However, there was one occasion when travelling with him and his wife Adele Koh that I was admitted into their personal lives. When he remarried critics claimed that his marriage to Adele was one of convenience, an arrangement without intimacy. But on one of the Riverland trips we were driving to our first appointment of the day when Adele suddenly expressed concern that she had left a thermometer behind at the motel where we stayed overnight. As they dispatched me with the Premier's driver to retrieve it their conversation made it clear that Adele was using it to assist with the prediction of ovulation: they were both keen to have a child. Soon afterwards Adele was diagnosed with cancer and Don nursed her through a harrowing terminal illness.

Chaffey was a long shot and on the new boundaries Millicent would become no more than a trip down memory lane, remembering the epic battles of the election and by-election in 1968.[14] However, Premier Dunstan regarded Mount Gambier as a demonstration model of social democracy in action and despite the new boundaries which gave the Liberal Party a considerable advantage, he wanted it back. The city had a diverse and balanced economy. The timber industry encompassed all aspects of production from plantation forests to sawn timber, paper milling and particle board manufacture. Primary production included dairying, beef, sheep, potato and canola crops. By 1975 Mount Gambier's Allan Scott was the biggest private transport operator in the southern hemisphere and in the mid-1970s Premier Dunstan offered generous incentives for Fletcher Jones and staff to establish a factory which provided 100 jobs for machinists and support staff. 'The Mount' had a good mix of private and social housing, school, vocational and continuing education facilities, health (including a new hospital) and welfare services. Premier Dunstan would later add the performing arts to the repertoire when he commissioned planning for the Sir Robert Helpman Theatre in the year before he resigned.

Between 1975 and 1977 I spent a lot of time in the electorate as 'Don's Man', much of it spent as a go between for the many individuals and organisations wanting to lobby the Premier for their projects. They had a great record of success. Project funding was not committed indiscriminately but between 1975 and 1977 a submission that had merit probably had more chance of success in Mount Gambier than in any other electorate in South Australia. We ran strong candidates against the sitting Liberal member Harold Allison in 1977 and 1979 but eventually had to concede that neither good administration nor pork barreling would ever retrieve the seat for the ALP on the new boundaries.

Patrice and I enjoying a restaurant dinner in 1972 before our social life became dominated by political commitments.

CHAPTER NINE

A waiting game

During 1977 the South Australian Electoral Commission completed a redistribution based on a maximum tolerance of 10 per cent between the highest and lowest number of enrolled voters in any House of Assembly electorate. The demise of the Whitlam Government, a modest improvement in local economic indicators, continuing domination of local politics by the charismatic Dunstan and a lacklustre opposition had combined to rebuild Labor's electoral stocks. Ostensibly because Premier Dunstan wanted 'to eliminate the difficulties of providing strong and stable direction with a minority government', he took South Australia to another early election. Parliament was prorogued in August and writs were issued for an election to be held on 17 September.

I had served a little over two years of my backbench apprenticeship as we approached the election. The campaign was going well and we appeared to be heading for a comfortable victory. On the Monday before the poll I was in Mount Gambier with the Premier and as we walked to the dining room at the Travelodge Motel that evening I told him I intended to run for cabinet at the first caucus meeting to be held after the election. I asked for his support and he agreed with quiet enthusiasm.

The Dunstan Government won 27 of the 47 seats in the House of Assembly with a two party preferred vote of 53.4 per cent, its fourth successive election victory. Now I turned to soliciting caucus support for the only place to be contested in the 13 member post-election cabinet. Des Corcoran had become my de facto campaign manager, supported by Geoff Virgo, a senior member of cabinet, a former ALP state secretary and still one of the heavies in the party machine. With Don Dunstan's support I was at unbackable odds.

Tom Casey had won the seat of Frome in 1960 and transferred to the Legislative Council in 1970 when the new boundaries set by the electoral redistribution that year made the seat unwinnable for Labor. He was half way through his last term and was the minister for me to beat in the ballot. However, as heads were counted it became clear that, although the old guard in caucus was prepared to support me, it would not be at Casey's expense. Brian Chatterton was the minister likely to go. When this emerged as the probable outcome Premier Dunstan rang me at home and asked me to withdraw, to wait for 18 months when Casey and Don Banfield, the Minister of Health, would retire. It was implicit in our discussion that I would be a front runner for the health portfolio in a Dunstan Cabinet early in 1979.

Having acceded to Don's request I got on with the diverse duties of the back bench, including membership of the caucus and ALP policy committees, the Council of the South Australian Institute of Technology (later the University of South Australia) and the Board of the Botanic Gardens.

WHEN PARLIAMENT WAS SITTING members on the government backbench were largely there for the numbers. Dorothy Dix questions, distributed to the backbench before question time each day, were used to give ministers the opportunity to indulge in a piece of puffery about something clever they had done or were about to do. Raising issues 'without notice' which might have the potential to embarrass a minister or the government was naturally taboo but networking could pay dividends. Soon after we moved to Adelaide I made the Union Hotel in Weymouth Street the place for a drink with a circle of friends whom I had met through the Party; it was a place to meet and greet and had a regular band playing trad jazz on Friday nights. In the 1970s it was also the regular watering hole for journalists from *The Advertiser* and the publican Shirley Robins was already something of a legend. Her husband Phil first made her acquaintance when drinking after hours with colleagues from the paper when it had been put to bed each night.

Patrice and I were pleased to count Phil and Shirley among our good friends. Early in 1978 she told me of her concerns that Sydney's notorious 'Mr Sin', Abe Saffron, was moving into the hotel scene in Adelaide. Shirley got her information from Bob Whitington, *The Advertiser*'s respected, veteran police roundsman who was a regular at the Union. She gave me considerable detail about how Saffron was involved directly and through third parties. I spoke to Attorney-General Peter Duncan about the issue and he agreed that I should raise it during question time in the Legislative Council. He would then respond the following day through a ministerial statement in the House of Assembly. I gave a detailed account of Saffron's growing influence in Adelaide and asked a series of questions of the minister representing the Attorney-General.

Abe was a very litigious character, using defamation law throughout his life to defend his 'good name', so my statement and questions had to be made under parliamentary privilege to provide immunity for me and media outlets that chose to report them. The story ran nationally and Saffron's usual rebuttal was immediate: 'I am a business man and a family man'. But the subject had been broached and it gave the Attorney-General the opportunity to pursue it in a way that none of his counterparts in New South Wales had ever done. Saffron never got off the ground in any serious way in South Australia.

DR RICHIE GUN WAS ONE OF the new members who had been elected to the federal Parliament in 1969 when Labor began its comeback from the 1966 disaster. An anaesthetist with a passionate commitment to human rights and an impressive intellect he was tipped to have a promising future in federal politics. However, he lost his seat of Kingston when the Whitlam Government was swept from office in 1975. In 1977 I was his campaign director in a bid to recapture the seat and Bob Hawke, still the charismatic President of the Australian Council of Trade Unions, joined the campaign. We took him on the obligatory shopping centre walk for the media and visited three of the most popular pubs in the electorate to share a drink with locals, including assembly line workers from Mitsubishi's Tonsley Park factory. In the evening we held a public meeting at Christies Beach. A young Paul Keating also spent a day in the electorate and spoke to a packed house at a fundraising dinner.

Each Saturday we toured the shopping centres with a jazz band on a tray truck, campaign volunteers distributing balloons to the shoppers' children and pamphlets to voters while Richie and local state MPs addressed the crowd from the back of the truck. We then moved on from the car park to the next shopping centre before the management became concerned about politics distracting the spending public.

Richie was an early and keen supporter of Fretilin and independence for East Timor and used to raise the issue whenever there was an opportunity. During his three terms as the Member for Kingston he pursued his issues in federal caucus meetings with passion and in detail, sometimes exhausting Whitlam's patience. On one occasion after Richie led one of one of these lengthy caucus debates Gough caught up with him in the corridor of the Old Parliament House, glowering and towering over him (Richie was about 166 centimetres tall with his shoes on). When roused in private discussions the great man was well known for his liberal use of expletives to give greater force to his maxims: 'Gun, you're the greatest fucking know all I have ever met'. Richie used to tell this story with wry amusement and I decided to tidy it up a little and give it a positive spin. We used it in the text for his campaign pamphlet: 'Gough Whitlam said of Richie Gun that he has the greatest all round knowledge of anyone he has ever met'.

However, our efforts were in vain. The electorate would not be ready to return to Labor until Bob Hawke led the party to victory in March 1983. Richie never returned to anaesthetics. His commitment to the greater good saw him spend the rest of his professional life in public and environmental health.

IN 1978 I WAS NOMINATED by my parliamentary colleagues for the study tour that was available in alternate years to a government or opposition backbencher in the Upper House of the South Australian Parliament. It was usually awarded to a promising member on the way up the ladder to cabinet, sometimes as a trade off for ambitions thwarted or occasionally to a member about to retire after 20 years of dedicated but undistinguished service.

In May that year Patrice and I left Adelaide on the three month study tour, leaving a live-in housekeeper with the challenging task of caring for our children. The itinerary and the appointments schedule were framed around a comparative appraisal of health care delivery and finance in western democracies of differing political complexions as well as the USSR (Russia) and Yugoslavia. The trip began in President Jimmy Carter's America and finished in the Soviet Union of Leonid Brezhnev, already in his 14th year as General Secretary and by then also Chair of the Presidium of the Supreme Soviet.

On the first leg of our tour, Sydney to Los Angeles, we cleared customs and immigration in Hawaii for an overnight stay before flying on a domestic service to Los Angeles. On arrival in Hawaii at 4.00am local time we were met personally by the Australian Consul General who drove us to our hotel. This was really impressive; clearly the diplomatic service knew of the importance of my fleeting visit! However, it was soon apparent that he had come to welcome Sir Percy Spender.[15] Informed on arrival at the airport terminal that Sir Percy was not on the flight and having been out of bed since 2.30am, he made the best of a dramatically downgraded mission.

Our first interviews were in Los Angeles, then on to San Francisco, a side trip to Portland, Oregon, then Chicago and Washington DC where we were taken on a private tour of Capitol Hill and given a front row seat in the gallery of the United States Senate. Top level medical and hospital care for insured patients (health insurance provided in most cases as part of a single or family salary or wage package) was impressive but the American version of free enterprise as it related to health care was fundamentally flawed. America, the richest of nations, was spending a higher percentage of its gross domestic product on health and hospital services than any other country in the world. Yet one in five American men, women and children had no private health insurance nor were they covered by health maintenance organisations or government programs. An estimated 50 per cent of all people filing for personal bankruptcy did so because of medical and hospital expenses.

In London I watched a relaxed, confident James Callaghan responding to the new Leader of the Opposition, Margaret Thatcher, during Prime Minister's question time in the House of Commons. It was just four months after she had wrested the leadership from Edward Heath and Prime Minister Callaghan seemed to have her measure. He referred to her in a dismissive way as 'the good lady', treating her with patronising avuncularity, but the lady was 'not for turning'. Within four years the grocer's daughter had become Prime Minister and pursued a ruthless course of economic rationalism based on the philosophy of Milton Freidman and Frederich von Hayek. She was Britain's Prime Minister for 11 controversial years.

During our time in London I was briefed by officials from Britain's National Health Service (NHS). The NHS was supported by both major parties when it was introduced by the Atlee Labour Government in postwar Britain, its objective 'to deliver comprehensive health and hospital care to residents of the United Kingdom on an equitable basis'. There was no direct cost to patients at the point of service and it was a basic tenet that health services were based on need, not the ability to pay. There had been some inevitable problems with both management and quality of care but in the 1970s it was largely meeting its objectives and being delivered at about half the comparable per capita cost of care in the United States, expressed as a percentage of gross domestic product.

When we left Britain we visited Amsterdam and Brussels, both brief tourist stops, then on to Paris, the city that never disappoints. I didn't absorb a lot of detail about the French health system, except that it was a costly mix which seemed to be generous to both providers and consumers. But I was delighted to absorb a lot of boulevard culture as our allocated *bureaucrate de sante* chose to talk us through heath care delivery, management and finance over drinks at charming sidewalk cafés.

From Paris we took an overnight train to Milan, via Switzerland, waking at dawn to marvel at *la neige eternelle*, the Alpine snow that never melts. Italy was our indulgence. Having decided against trying to comprehend the wonders of the Italian bureaucracy we were unashamedly tourists in this most fascinating but frustrating country. In more than a dozen subsequent visits during our life after politics we would get to know and appreciate Rome better than any other city outside Australia as Patrice embraced Italian language and culture with remarkable enthusiasm. We would also learn that the Italian health system is widely recognised as among the best in the world. On this first visit, however, I was a provincial innocent from the new world, inclined initially to think that some of Rome's Centro Storico might benefit from an urban renewal program.

We visited the Amalfi Coast and Venice briefly before travelling by train to Marshall Tito's Yugoslavia, a country that held special interest for me. Tito's socialist model, although based on tight central control, provided an interesting contrast with the extremes of Soviet authoritarianism. He supported a policy of nonalignment between the two hostile blocs in the Cold War and his successful diplomatic and economic policies allowed him to preside over Yugoslavia's economic boom and expansion in the 1960s and 1970s. The health professionals whom we met in Belgrade were generous hosts. Apart from the scheduled meetings and visits to hospitals and polyclinics they entertained us with a barbecue in the summer sunshine and spoke freely about their health system, a centralised communist model but with touches of humanity. Following my visit, just two years before Tito's death in 1980, I wrote in my report to the South Australian Parliament that I believed the federation was being held together more by the force of Tito's personality and central control than by any real desire for unity among the ethnically diverse population.

We travelled on to Bonn, the seat of the West German Government prior to re-unification, and to Stockholm where there were more interviews, more contrasts but health care delivery within the broad context of a social democratic model.

ON OUR ARRIVAL IN LENINGRAD (St Petersburg) we had our first brush with the repressive Soviet bureaucracy. Our Intourist guide was late arriving at the airport and officials were confused and agitated. How could two foreigners travel in the Soviet Union unaccompanied? They went through our luggage, presents purchased during the previous 10 weeks, souvenirs given to us by our hosts in countries we had visited officially and all our clothes and toiletries. There were also books, papers and a hand written preliminary draft of the report on which I was working. In a display of ideological zeal they confiscated a copy of *Time* magazine with a photo of Zbigniew Brzezinski (the United States National Security Advisor to President Jimmy Carter between 1977 and 1981) on the front cover. We were left to repack our belongings which had been strewn over the length of a long trestle table.

Things improved considerably when we located our guide who drove us to an Intourist hotel where we were accommodated in a large suite overlooking the Neva River. Fortuitously we had arrived during the last week of the White Nights. St Petersburg is situated at such a high latitude that for a period during the summer the dusk meets the dawn as the sun doesn't go under the horizon deeply enough for the sky to get dark. Each night around midnight I used to sit at a desk near the window watching the cargo ships and tankers passing under the many drawbridges of the river as they sailed to and from the Baltic Sea.

The Intourist guide was a pleasant woman in early middle age whose English and social skills were impeccable. She was our interpreter during hospital and polyclinic visits and took us on several personal tours which included the Hermitage Museum. There she narrated the story of the storming of the Winter Palace in 1917 by a detachment of Red Army soldiers and sailors and described it as a 'defining moment in the birth of the Soviet state'. Regrettably the Marinsky Theatre, home of the Kirov ballet, was closed for the summer. Most compelling were the stories and memorials of the 900 day siege during the 'Great Patriotic War'. The German army laid siege to the city awaiting its surrender but despite terrible hardship, starvation and suffering, the inhabitants refused to give up, displaying extraordinary heroism. During the siege at least 600,000 people died from disease and starvation, others froze to death. Some estimates put the figure at 800,000. The Piskaryovsky Memorial Cemetery alone holds half a million civilian victims of the siege.

Overall the visit to Leningrad was fascinating, although we had begun to understand that 'nyet' was the most widely used word in the Soviet Union. At Leningrad Airport we were herded onto the tarmac with all the other passengers and marched as a group to the waiting plane, one of the early Tupolev Tu-154s. Two large stewardesses stood at the foot of the aircraft stairs and issued orders to the compliant passengers who were summoned to board in some pre-ordained order. When we moved a little anxiously towards the stairs an angry stewardess waved us back to the end of the line.

Despite some interesting sidelights, the Moscow visit was seriously disappointing and stressful. We were left stranded at our hotel several times when appointments were cancelled at the last minute. When I did get to talk to health care professionals many of their responses, filtered through interpreters, were guarded to the point of farce. It was impossible to get frank comments or accurate assessments of the quality of care from those I interviewed and public health issues were effectively off limits. The official version was that there were no problems with nutrition, alcoholism, smoking, illicit drugs, air and water pollution or housing. There were a few diversions, visits to the Red Square, Lenin's Tomb, the GUM department store and, of course, the Berioska shop for souvenirs, most notably a matryoshka doll and the mandatory small but very heavy cast iron statue of Lenin. There were no summer performances and no guided tours of the famous Bolshoi Theatre.

We boarded a Japan Air Lines DC8 at Moscow's Domodedovo Airport early in August bound for Tokyo, then home to Adelaide via a brief stopover in Hong Kong but not before a visit to the Australian Embassy. In 1978 it was a hardship post where a relatively small staff complement worked in conditions that reflected the mutual suspicion and tension between East and West. Russian intelligence had bugged Australia's Embassy in Moscow and there was concern about Soviet espionage in Australia. For its part, cabinet documents released under the 30 year rule in 2009 revealed that Australia collected intelligence from the Soviet Embassy in Canberra, routinely tapping all the official and private telephones of diplomats and using listening devices in their residences and within the Embassy itself. Working in these conditions staff in Moscow were always pleased to see an Australian face and happy to have the chance to offer hospitality as a form of relief from the grind of daily life at the Embassy.

Mark Harrison, a young career diplomat, was allocated to look after us and took the job seriously. Over an interesting lunch and at a dinner the following evening in one of the few upmarket restaurants in Moscow (much favoured by Party apparatchiks) he gave us an informed perspective on the Soviet system, the pervasive repression it created and the temperaments and personalities of the Russian people under Soviet rule.

One of the major recommendations I made in my report of the study tour, completed by early September 1978, was that health as an overall state of well being must be central to health policy development. Coincidentally the International Conference on Primary Health Care, held from 6 to 12 September 1978, issued what became known as the Alma Ata Declaration. This redefined health as 'a state of complete physical, mental and social wellbeing, and not merely the absence of disease or infirmity'. It was to underpin the State Labor Government's health strategy for South Australians during my tenure as Minister of Health.

THE RELENTLESS PURSUIT OF DUNSTAN that characterised the South Australian political landscape during the 1970s was typified by the so-called Salsibury Affair. Police Commissioner, Harold Salisbury, had been recruited from the United Kingdom in 1973. In September 1977 Peter Ward, formerly an executive assistant to Premier Dunstan, now the Adelaide Bureau Chief of *The Australian* newspaper, submitted a list of questions to the Premier's office regarding political surveillance by the South Australian Police Special Branch and dossiers they kept on unconvicted people. Before he received a response he wrote an article which ran under the headline 'Exposed . . . the Secret Police Dossiers on Demonstrations'. Ward followed up with another article which criticised Dunstan's alleged failure 'to ensure that such surveillance of political dissenters and political terrorists as is necessary is conducted under the right kind of supervision, with the correct degree of care'.[16]

In response cabinet established a judicial inquiry into the Special Branch, to be conducted by Acting Justice White of the South Australian Supreme Court. His report, submitted to the Premier on 21 December 1977, was extremely critical of the Special Branch, its activities, and its management. The report concluded that 'a great mass of irrelevant material (often potentially harmful, sometimes actually harmful) has accumulated'. Moreover, the report noted that the Commissioner of Police had failed to inform the government fully about the existence of sensitive files on matters relating to politics, trade unions and other affairs.

In January 1978 cabinet decided that the White Report should be published immediately, that the Premier should ask for Salisbury's resignation, and if that was not forthcoming the Commissioner should be dismissed from office. Salisbury refused to yield. He came into direct conflict with the Premier and with the tenets of democratic government when he claimed absolute independence. 'As I see it', he asserted, the police owed a duty 'to the Crown and not to any politically elected government or to any politician or to anyone else for that matter'.[17]

The notice of dismissal was delivered to him on 17 January. Controversy raged with South Australia's establishment loud in Salisbury's support. Stewart Cockburn, a senior journalist at *The Advertiser*, led the media charge. The opposition questioned the rigour of the White Report and the legality of the dismissal. The Premier continued to reaffirm the principles of responsible government and argued that he had clearly been misled by the former Commissioner of Police. On 10 February 1978 as the controversy continued the government appointed a Royal Commission and at the end of May the Royal Commissioner, Justice Roma Mitchell of the South Australian Supreme Court, presented her report.

In dismissing the former Police Commissioner's contention that he owed a duty to the Crown and not to any elected government Justice Mitchell said that this suggested 'an absence of understanding of the constitutional system of South Australia or, for that matter, of the United Kingdom'. She found that Premier Dunstan and cabinet had acted properly, if perhaps precipitately, in dismissing the Police Commissioner. The dismissal while not the only course open to the government had, in her opinion, been justifiable. However, even in the face of Justice Mitchell's findings, the dramatic way in which Salisbury had been dismissed provided fertile ground for conspiracy theorists. Liberal members reaffirmed their faith in Salisbury's integrity and hinted that the government had something to hide.

Then in May 1978 Don Dunstan's wife Adele who was not yet 40 years old was diagnosed with inoperable cancer. Don nursed her through five harrowing months until her death in October. Deeply affected by her death and increasingly troubled by hypertension and migraine he continued to lead the government, now dogged by a deteriorating state economy in the stagnation and inflation that was bedevilling the western world.

He was also dealing with the ongoing controversy caused by the dismissal of the Police Commissioner and striving to find middle ground in the uranium debate within the strictures of the ALP's anti-mining policy. The pro-uranium lobby was beginning to sell the proposed Roxby Downs mine as the cure for all South Australia's economic ills while the anti-uranium lobbyists were talking of the destruction of the planet. Some form of compromise had to be found between the cargo culters and the candles and caves brigade. About this time stories began to emerge that Adelaide journalists Des Ryan and Mike McEwen had obtained copies of some very personal letters he had written to John Ceruto between 1970 and 1974. According to the rumour mill they were writing a book in which they would allege that the Premier had been involved in improper and criminal conduct.

It was against this background that Dunstan flew to a bitter European winter to inspect nuclear power plants and obtain face-to-face briefings from representatives of the nuclear industry and the International Atomic Energy Agency (IAEA). The itinerary was unrelenting. The media reported that as he stepped off the plane on his return to Adelaide he was looking pale and exhausted but nothing could have prepared us for the shock of seeing the gaunt, grey and sometimes hesitant Premier who addressed the caucus meeting three days later. Soon afterwards Don collapsed and was admitted to Calvary Hospital. Within days, on 15 February 1979, he held a media conference at the hospital where, politician and thespian, he made the dramatic announcement of his resignation.

A decade of unparalleled reform was over. In a remarkable political career Don Dunstan had fought for and delivered electoral reform (one vote, one value), championed multiculturalism, Aboriginal land rights and consumer protection, delivered important changes to South Australia's education system, amended the State liquor licensing laws, introduced anti-discrimination legislation, homosexual law reform and equal opportunity for women, appointed the first woman to the Supreme Court (an Australian first), established the South Australian Film Commission, the State Theatre Company, the Community Welfare Department, the Department of Environment and taken a leading role in getting rid of the odious White Australia Policy. And he had reinvigorated the social, artistic and cultural life of South Australia.

Ultimately when the book was published it caused an intense but short lived frisson among the Dunstan haters. It took the high moral ground in a salacious exploration of Dunstan's sexual relationship with Ceruto, alleging it was in return for political favours. It also alleged misuse of government funds and even attempted to implicate him with organised crime figures and the illicit drug scene.[18] The revelation that Dunstan was bisexual hardly came as a surprise. As to the allegations of misconduct or malfeasance, none was ever substantiated and by the time the book was published in November 1979 Don Dunstan had retired and the Corcoran Government was out of office. He never sued for defamation but in his 1981 autobiography *Felicia*, he dismissed the allegations of impropriety and criminality as 'a farrago of lies'.

On the campaign trail, talking politics with rock lobster fishers at Carpenters Rocks, 1982

CHAPTER TEN

Follow the leader

Des Corcoran who had been the Deputy Premier since 1970 was elected unopposed to replace Don Dunstan when he retired in February 1979. The following month Tom Casey and Don Banfield foreshadowed their retirement from cabinet and Chris Sumner and I were elected by caucus to replace them. We were sworn in on 1 May, Chris the big winner appointed as Attorney-General to replace Peter Duncan who was moved to the health portfolio which I had coveted. I was given Environment and Lands.

During those brief heady days in the cabinet I flew to Wilpena Pound with senior Environment Department staff to inspect a McLachlan pastoral lease that the government proposed to buy out and add to the Flinders Ranges National Park. My two youngest daughters, 10 year old Anna and 13 year old Louise, accompanied me, excited young girls occupying the spare seats in a chartered twin engine Cessna.

The property had been overrun by feral goats which were destroying much of the native vegetation. The damage was spectacular and distressing. The goats could climb the steep ranges and graze on anything they could reach by standing on their hind legs, stripping shrubs and ring barking sapling trees up to a height of five or six feet. I sought urgent advice from the Lands Department as to how we could control or eliminate them. Their first suggestion was to put in a team of professional shooters but I recoiled from the spectre of perhaps 2,000 or more fly blown goat carcasses decomposing in the ranges and being pursued by animal welfare activists with allegations of cruelty.

I sent back the suggestions and asked for some lateral thinking. Did the goats have any commercial value? Yes Minister, the young goats could possibly end up on restaurant menus and the old goats could be used by the pet food industry. How could we get them out of the rugged ranges?

Within months they came up with a solution. On the first run 1,600 goats were forced out of this inaccessible terrain with a light aircraft and transferred to more open country. There the ground crew, on motorbikes and helped by dogs, mustered them through 13 kilometres to specially reinforced holding pens at the Umberatana shearing sheds. There was good vehicle access to this point and they were trucked out to an abattoir.

Another highlight of my brief incumbency was a trip into the north-west corner of South Australia. I was keen to learn more about the vast arid and semi-arid country and the Anangu Pitjantjatjara Lands. Legislation recognising the traditional rights of the Pitjantjatjara people to their lands had been introduced while Don Dunstan was Premier and was still on the Parliamentary notice paper when he retired.[19] I took officers from Lands and Environment Departments, keen to use the opportunity for them to exchange ideas and resolve any potential conflicts between the old guard in Lands and the young turks in Environment. In July we gathered in Coober Pedy and travelled overland in two Land Rovers and a tough Toyota Land Cruiser, complete with bull bars and winches.

After crossing the dog proof fence north of Coober Pedy, we drove to Marla and Fregon, then across country on the legendary Len Beadell's 'highways', bush tracks barely marked by two wheel ruts straddling low scrub. The country had recently had more than two inches of rain and the ephemeral plants had burst into life. Whenever we topped a rise the wild flowers formed an amazing carpet of bright colours as far as the eye could see. We drove all day, winding through the scrub, stopping whenever the botanists or the agristologists sighted plants, trees or land formations of special interest, and paying our respects to the Aboriginal people in the settlements along the way.

When we camped at sundown the experienced bushmen in the party lit the camp fire, carved the mutton chops for the evening meal on the tailgate of one of the Range Rovers and produced some very welcome cold cans of beer from the portable refrigerators. The winter days were clear and sunny with temperatures in the mid twenties but at night as they fell towards zero we slept snug in our sleeping bags under the stars, covered by small canvass tarpaulins, feet towards the camp fire. No pitching tents to slow us down on this trip. As we woke at first light the occasional dingo could be seen, shy, careful but interested in what we were up to. We had no water for washing and when we came upon a spring on the fifth day we stripped to our underpants (no further, in deference to the two women in the party) and bathed in the freezing water.

Now we turned left, scrub bashing our way south, traversing the Nullarbor Plain towards the Eyre Highway. Then for the first time in 10 days we drove on the bitumen highway to Cook, near the Western Australian border, where we took a light plane back to Adelaide. If there had been any friction between Lands and Environment at the beginning of the journey it had been well resolved along the way. It had been an incredible journey.

DES CORCORAN BECAME PREMIER in February 1979, half way through the three year parliamentary term we had won in the fourth consecutive state election victory. He was a no nonsense social conservative who had always been regarded as something of a counterfoil to the progressive and innovative Premier Dunstan. He now had 18 months in which to establish his leadership credentials.

In South Australia the manufacturing sector was struggling, particularly the motor vehicle industry and the prospect of a major copper-uranium mining development at Roxby Downs was increasingly attractive. The Liberal opposition, led by the affable and avuncular Dr David Tonkin, were supporting it enthusiastically but binding ALP policy meant that the government had to remain implacably opposed to it. And despite Don Dunstan's departure, ill based but carefully fostered unease about the Salisbury Affair persisted in the electorate.

In this climate Premier Corcoran's decision to call an election to seek a mandate in his own right just six months after he assumed the leadership was a terrible mistake. Was it hubris, panic or was the medication which the Premier had been prescribed for his progressive and very painful rheumatoid arthritis causing erratic mood swings? The folly of an early election should have been obvious to everyone yet new minister Chris Sumner was the only member of the cabinet to speak against it when we were called to a special meeting and told what Corcoran was proposing. We learned within days that he took the decision without consultation with the party office and apparently without strategic advice from Rod Cameron of Australian Nationwide Opinion Polls.[20]

It took more than a week after the election had been called to come up with one of the worst campaign slogans in modern history: 'Follow a Leader'. The media campaign developed in haste to give Corcoran his personal mandate was a disaster. We were nearing the end of the seventies during which polling, surveys and qualitative analyses of swinging voters were the basis of sophisticated campaigns in which, for better or worse, focus group responses were increasingly driving election policy launches.

The first week of the campaign was used very effectively by our many opponents to create resentment, increasing to hostility, about the decision to call an election 12 months before it was due. Our opponents included several captains of commerce and industry who conducted a high profile third party campaign against the government. Most devastating was the extraordinary campaign conducted by Rupert Murdoch's afternoon tabloid paper, *The News*. For three weeks during the campaign it conducted an anti-government blitz unprecedented in South Australia. We followed the leader over a cliff. Labor lost government in 1979 with an 8.5 per cent swing against it.

Immediately following the devastating election result and the handover to Premier Tonkin, Des Corcoran retreated to the office of the Leader of the Opposition to consider his position. However, it was clear that the size of the defeat made his continued leadership untenable. He announced his resignation as leader within the week and John Bannon was appointed unopposed at the next caucus meeting.

Until we recovered our equilibrium we decided to allocate shadow portfolio responsibilities rather than appoint a full shadow cabinet. I was given Environment and Planning. Then early in 1981, as we approached the mid-point in the parliamentary term, additional members were recruited to our front bench and we were designated as a full shadow cabinet. I had finally made it into health, albeit as a shadow. I was also appointed as convener of the State ALP's health policy committee and set about establishing a network of health professionals and working with members of the committee to develop a comprehensive set of policies.

It was my good fortune during that time to work closely with Neal Blewett, the Shadow Minister for Health in the federal opposition, a productive working relationship that endured when we were both in government. A Rhodes Scholar who combined keen political judgment with an impressive intellect, Blewett was destined to become one of the best performers in the Hawke-Keating Governments from March 1983 until his retirement from federal politics in 1994 to take up a four year term as Australia's High Commissioner in London.

DURING FOUR YEARS ON THE BACK BENCH (1975-1979) I had retained a direct financial interest in my veterinary practice. By the middle of 1976 my friend and full time locum Ben Benaradsky had decided to move on but not until I had recruited Ken Holds, a very competent but rather nervous young graduate to replace him. I spent some time with Ken who gained confidence quickly and established a very positive reputation with the clients.

It was always implicit in our arrangements that he would eventually take over the practice and soon after I was sworn in as South Australia's Minister of Environment in May 1979 I transferred it to him. The modest sale price acknowledged his valued contribution during the previous three years but also took account of the reality: by that time much of the goodwill of the practice belonged to him anyway. But by September, after just five months as a cabinet minister, I was back on the opposition benches. Mark had graduated but Deborah had recently enrolled for an arts degree at the University of Sydney and Amanda was studying law, much of her time and energy devoted to student politics as President of the Students Association of the University of Adelaide. The other four daughters were still at school, Jennifer about to finish her matriculation year. The Cornwalls were facing penury, trying to maintain a large and expensive family on a basic parliamentary salary.

I met with Ken soon after the election to explore the feasibility of rejoining him as an associate in the practice which was continuing to expand, helped by an upmarket housing development in the new suburb of North Haven. We agreed to explore how this might work on a three month trial basis. Patrice resumed her place at the reception desk, working part time on a regular schedule, and I worked on a flexible sessional basis, depending on my parliamentary and Party commitments. The arrangement proved to be mutually beneficial; Ken no longer had to work unreasonably long hours every week and the Cornwalls could meet their mortgage payments. It continued for the remainder of the parliamentary term.

RECAPTURING THE TREASURY benches in three years after an 8.5 per cent swing against Labor would be a formidable task. In addition to refreshing and revitalising the Parliamentary Labor Party we needed to destabilise the Tonkin Government, to dent its credibility. I adopted a little of the whatever it takes philosophy. To paraphrase Gough Whitlam in his landmark address to the Victorian ALP conference in June 1967, only the impotent are pure.

In 1979 the Liberals had been in office in South Australia for only two of the previous 14 years (1968-1970) since 1965. The overwhelming majority of ministers had no previous experience in government and it was inevitable that some would make errors of political judgment. The Liberal's Health Minister, Jennifer Cashmore, brought an above average degree of administrative flair to her portfolio but her high profile (and some bad advice from her ministerial staff) made her vulnerable. Early in her term she not infrequently got into the trite rather than the substantial. Keen to project a public image as a financial manager carefully husbanding taxpayers' health dollars, she claimed credit publicly for the cost savings being made following a review of catering in the public hospital system. The health sector unions quickly identified this with restrictions on the biscuits for patients with their morning and afternoon tea. 'Tea without bikkies for Cashmore's patients' was the headline in a page three story in *The News*.

I was not averse to using these missteps to embarrass the minister but more telling was the ability to identify organisational defects in systems and services. I had the South Australian branch of the Nurses Federation and other health sector unions onside. Key people from the community health sector were helping with health policy development and increasingly senior doctors who were otherwise above politics but had a genuine concern for the health system were talking to me in private. In June 1982, around the time of the ALP State Conference, we released the first of a series of health policy papers which would take us through the next five months until the election in November.

THROUGHOUT OUR THREE YEARS in opposition we led the Tonkin Government in most of the published polls. However, there was one issue that was increasingly a millstone around our political necks: Roxby

Downs. From the beginning of its term in office, the government was extremely bullish about the benefits of the Roxby Downs development. In a state deep in recession the rhetoric was seductive. It was claimed the project would create up to 18,000 jobs during the construction phase. It was described as another Mount Isa. How could the Labor opposition counter their arguments or raise doubts in the public mind?

Just two months after the new government was sworn in we moved to establish an all party Select Committee of the Legislative Council with broad terms of reference embracing 'Developments which have a bearing on the mining, development and further processing and sale of South Australian uranium resources and the safety of workers involved in its mining, milling, transport, further treatment and storage'. We were able to get the numbers to establish the Select Committee with the support of the lone Democrat member of the Upper House, Lance Milne. The government members were reluctant participants but rather than have us roam at large with the power to subpoena witnesses and call for papers and records they nominated three members, one of whom took the chair. Norm Foster and I were the opposition nominees.

The Select Committee was a purely political exercise. When the time came to write a report the Liberal members followed the government line. Milne, whose constituency was implacably opposed to uranium mining, produced a brief and predictable minority report. I wrote the opposition's dissenting report. The Select Committee report (or more accurately the government members' report, the Democrat's minority report and the opposition's dissenting report) was tabled in the Legislative Council in November 1981, two years after it was established.

The Roxby Downs Indenture agreement was signed by Premier Tonkin and representatives of the joint venture partners, Western Mining Corporation and British Petroleum, on 3 March 1982. The Bill to ratify the indenture was introduced into the House of Assembly the following day. Then, after referral to a Select Committee of the Lower House it was returned with the Committee's report and passed early in June. It was then sent to the Legislative Council.

A first year pass in physics at university had given me a very rudimentary knowledge of atomic physics. Far more important was my long and active political involvement on the Legislative Council's Select

Committee. I was now the Parliamentary Labor Party's 'technical expert'. Speaking in the Council on 9 June I said that Labor was:

> absolutely committed to the responsible exploitation of the state's resources for the maximum benefit of all South Australians. However, we do not believe that most of the decisions regarding Roxby Downs need to be taken or should be taken in 1982. We recognise that this is an ore body in world class which could eventually offer substantial benefits to South Australia. At the same time we acknowledge that there are very real problems, both economic and moral, which cast a shadow over its viability at this time. Government approval should be given at the time that the Joint Venturers make a commitment to commercial production whether it is in 1987 or 1997, not prematurely as a political gimmick in 1982.

Western Mining's Hugh Morgan was unimpressed. When I debated the issue with him on the ABC's *This Day Tonight* he said they would withdraw their people from the Roxby Downs project and spend the money elsewhere if the indenture legislation for the project was defeated. With Democrat Lance Milne's support the Labor opposition had the numbers to defeat the Bill which would give Premier Tonkin a legitimate reason to call a snap election in which Roxby Downs would be the centrepiece. A second term for the Liberal Government would be almost a certainty.

But there was a glimmer of hope for us. Under the political pressure Norm Foster had become increasingly erratic. Without ever giving a reason he had failed to turn up to work with me in drafting the opposition's dissenting report on the Uranium Select Committee. When he attended caucus meetings he often monopolised proceedings for an hour or more. Sometimes his arguments were almost incoherent. At other times they were well informed but poorly constructed. He would talk at length about fossil fuels, acid rain, the ozone layer and the greenhouse effect without developing a particular point or proposition.

Foster told the ALP's State Conference days before the Bill was to go to a vote that he was 'under great trauma and mental strain' because of the Party's policy. In the event that we defeated the Bill he would 'find it very difficult to see Tonkin make an announcement on Thursday night to push us to an election on this issue'.

I was a front runner among a number of senior members of the shadow cabinet who began to see Foster as our potential saviour. Expulsion from the ALP would be automatic if he crossed the floor and voted with the government to secure passage of the Bill. However, he was due to retire at the next election. Despite the difficulty he would have in temporarily abandoning his lifetime tribal loyalty, he might do what he believed with passion was in the long term interests of the Party.

On the following Wednesday night Foster gave a rambling, two hour speech in which his 'trauma and mental strain' were evident. By prearrangement I played the role of *agent provocateur* with considerable help from Chris Sumner. With Premier Bannon's knowledge and support we had resolved to goad Foster whenever possible. Ostensibly our 'anger' was because of our contempt for a colleague who was wavering on the hard line anti-uranium policy. In fact we had calculated that the more scorn and ridicule we heaped on Foster, the more we would reinforce the chances of his defection. We reasoned it would be easier for him to repudiate enemies than friends.

However, during the course of his marathon speech Foster said that he did 'not intend to give passage to the *Indenture Bill*' and at 1.37am on Thursday morning he voted with the Labor opposition and Lance Milne to defeat the Bill at its third reading. But that was not the end of the drama. At 10.00am he sent a telegram to the State ALP Secretary, Chris Schacht, with his resignation from the party. At 3.00 pm in a brief emotional speech in the Council he said that he had been amazed during his speech on the Bill that interjections had been made by members of his own party indicating that he was not wanted in caucus. He had been surprised at the response of Labor MLCs as he thought they had known his attitude.

Norm Foster reversed his vote when the Bill was recommitted on Friday morning and Labor was out of a very difficult political net. No incoming government in a responsible democracy could repudiate an indenture agreement. Premier Tonkin had lost the opportunity for a snap election which was to cost him his chance for re-election. As the former Liberal Leader in the Legislative Council, the wily Ren De Garis, pointed out in his regular newsletter, the biggest electoral advantage to the Liberal Party would have lain in the defeat of the Bill.

At the ALP National Conference the following month (July 1982) there was intense pre-conference lobbying of delegates concerning a possible change to uranium policy and the opposition to Roxby Downs was virtually reversed by the so-called Hogg amendment. This recommitted the Party to oppose any new uranium mines but to phase out rather than repudiate Australia's existing involvement in the uranium industry. Most importantly from South Australia's perspective the amendment allowed consideration of the export of uranium mined incidentally to other minerals on a case-by-case basis. This enabled John Bannon to announce our commitment to Roxby Downs (as a major copper deposit) in his election policy speech delivered in October 1982.[21] At the state election held on 6 November 1982 Labor was returned to government with a three seat majority after just one term in opposition.

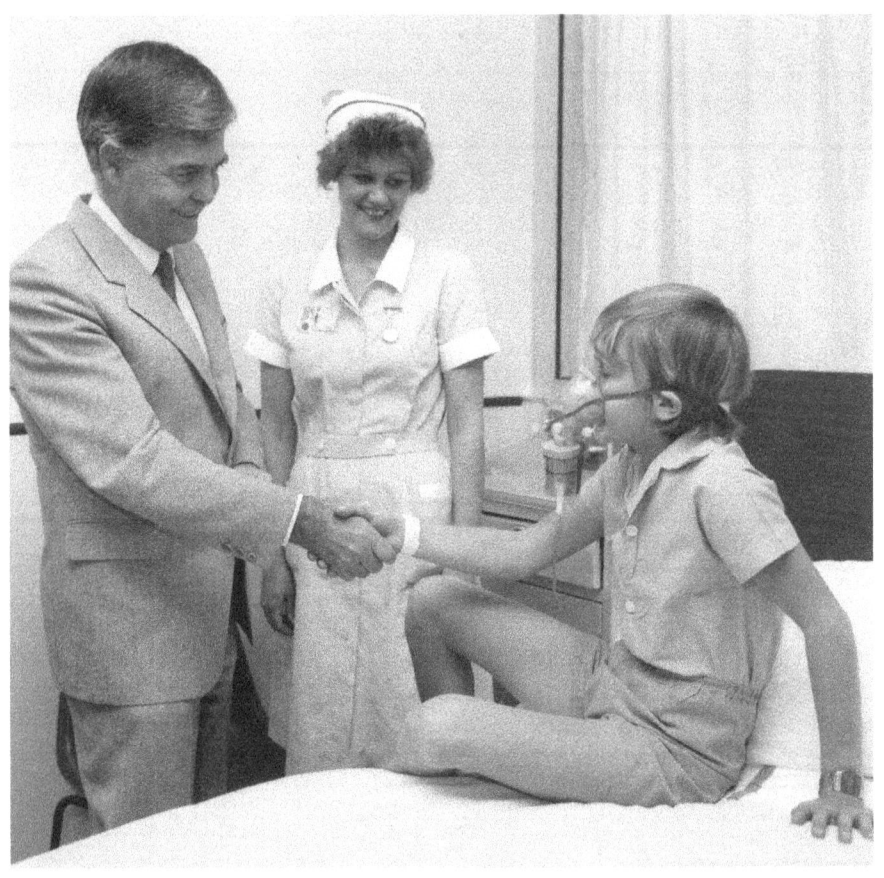
Visiting the Adelaide Children's Hospital as Health Minister, August 1983.

CHAPTER ELEVEN

Minister of Health

I was sworn in as the South Australian Minister of Health on 15 November 1982 and immediately began the task of translating promises into detailed programs. During the next six months I sought and obtained my cabinet colleagues' support to establish more than a dozen enquiries to review existing health services and provide recommendations that incorporated our policies.

For years much of the public debate about health in Australia was largely limited to issues around disease and disability, hospital funding and private health insurance. I was anxious to broaden public discussion in order to foster community involvement in a system that redefined health as a state of physical, emotional and social well being, not just as the absence of disease. However, I was keenly aware that community and preventive health programs would only attract popular support when constituents were not distracted by concerns about hospital services that failed to meet realistic expectations.

THE ENQUIRY INTO HOSPITAL SERVICES in South Australia was therefore a priority. It was chaired by Dr Sidney Sax who was eminent in the field of public health and health service reform in Australia. In the early 1970s he had published a report which analysed the ills of Australia's health system titled *Medical Care in the Melting Pot*. He had also chaired the Hospital and Health Services Commission, a Whitlam initiative set up in April 1974 (and dismantled by the Fraser Government four years later).

In the introduction to their 400 page report on South Australia's hospital services, released in September 1983, the Sax Committee noted that 'it appears to be without precedent for an Enquiry to have an explicit brief to report on Quality of Care and we are aware of the path finding role this imposes on us'. The Sax Report made 224 recommendations covering quality of care, hospital facilities, hospital administration and care of the aged and disabled. It was the blueprint that would guide us in moving the South Australian hospital system to pre-eminence over the next five years. Formal quality assurance protocols and programs were developed in all hospitals with more than 100 beds and patient care committees were established in all South Australian hospitals. In addition the Royal Adelaide Hospital, the state's largest teaching hospital, was funded to pilot a Medical Management Analysis project to review the clinical care of patients during their time in hospital rather than after they had been discharged. South Australia was also a pioneer with Victoria in refining Diagnosis Related Groups and case mix for use in the Australian hospital system. This provided a clinically meaningful way of relating the number and type of patients treated in a hospital to the resources required by the hospital.

Productivity and management in the hospital system were upgraded in tandem with improved clinical care. The average length of time that acute care patients spent in our major metropolitan hospitals was reduced from 5.9 to 5.4 days by a combination of better clinical management and improved administration. In addition the successful introduction of integrated hospital computer systems resulted in major improvements in patient and management information systems. Annual recurrent hospital costs were reduced statewide from 72.4 to 69.3 per cent of the total health budget. These productivity savings were reallocated to teaching, technology, research and community health projects. By the financial year 1987-88 funding for community health had been increased by 25 per cent. Over the same five year period we had also been able to fund new appointments at professorial level in palliative care, reproductive medicine, orthopaedics and trauma, child psychiatry, occupational and environmental health, anaesthesia and intensive care.

THE MENTAL HEALTH SERVICES enquiry was conducted by Dr Stanley Smith, a British based psychiatrist with an international reputation for his understanding and commitment to community mental health services. He examined the availability and quality of institutional and community based mental health services in South Australia and how well (or otherwise) they met patient needs. His report highlighted the urgent need for major organisational changes to the delivery of these services (with a shift from institutional to community care) and the lack of adequate child and adolescent psychiatric services. Other issues canvassed in the report included the formation of crisis intervention teams, an increase in outreach facilities and an expansion in the number and type of community services, including hostels. Dr Smith also highlighted the need to escalate the integration of mental health services into the general health care system.

Following the enquiry we established the Child and Adolescent Mental Health Service, a community-based service for infants, children and adolescents. However, our proposals to upgrade and provide statewide community services for adults met strong resistance from the mental health professionals. During the clinical revolution of the 1960s and 1970s 'the walls came down' at Glenside and Hillcrest, Adelaide's two major public psychiatric hospitals, resulting in a significant reduction in the number of long term inpatients. New psychotropic drugs made it possible to discharge many of them into community accommodation, mostly in private boarding houses. This proved to be a cheap but unsatisfactory arrangement with neither funding nor services following the patients. The Smith Report highlighted the fact that in 1983 more than 90 per cent of the mental health budget was still allocated to Glenside and Hillcrest, despite the serious gaps in community mental health programs for patients with chronic long term mental illness.

Early in 1986 Dr Bill McCoy, at that time the Director of the Central Sector of the Health Commission (later Chair and Chief Executive Officer) and Allan Swinstead, Chair of the Hillcrest Hospital board, developed a strategy to begin implementation of Stanley Smith's recommendations. They proposed that a central coordinating and planning body be established to take an overview of statewide mental health services; that as an interim arrangement the Hillcrest and Glenside Hospital boards be amalgamated to operate as a twin campus hospital with a single management structure; and that in the second stage of the transition the amalgamated psychiatric hospital service be consolidated onto one campus, based at Hillcrest. In the proposal the heritage listed buildings at Glenside were to be preserved and the capital funding from the sale of the enormously valuable 130 acre property in a prime inner suburban location used to provide flexible mental health units located strategically in the community.

I gave the proposals my enthusiastic support. However, both the psychiatrists and the psychiatric nurses were quick to mount a concerted campaign in opposition to them and although a central planning unit was eventually established, many of the responses to the Smith Report were suspended. On 1 April 1989, two months after I had resigned from the South Australian Parliament, the Health Minister announced that any plans to amalgamate the hospitals or their boards had been abandoned.

THE JULIA FARR CENTRE was originally called the Home for Incurables when it was established in 1879. By the 1970s it was a very large supported accommodation facility for 600 people with physical disabilities or debilitating long term illnesses. In 1981 the State Liberal Government renamed it the Julia Farr Centre, honouring the name of its founder and reflecting community standards and sensitivities. Regrettably, however, the board of management resisted the many other necessary changes that were identified in areas ranging from resident care to administration and financial management. It retained its autonomy and the board mounted a stubborn resistance to change, even though by now governments, state and federal, were providing virtually all of its recurrent annual funding.

The Centre had come to my attention during our period in opposition when documents leaked to me showed that their principal charity fund-raising event had reached a point where the costs of promotion equalled (and in one year even exceeded) the gross amount raised each year. More importantly, the Centre was being managed on a long term basis by a firm of accountants from their city office. Under these arrangements there was no identifiable general manager or chief executive officer.

Early in March 1983, less than four months after I was given the health portfolio, *The Advertiser* reported that while the dedication and loyalty of staff at the Centre was unquestioned, there was 'a volcano of dissatisfaction, a mountain of unrest spread by intrigue and misunderstanding'. Management had 'come down with a bad case of communication breakdown'. The story had been precipitated when the management circulated a letter, dated 2 March, revealing that it intended to relocate most of the 600 residents around the Centre in a massive one day shift. The letter did not reveal the day on which this was to occur but the date, Tuesday 8 March, had already been chosen without any prior consultation with the residents..

Until the letter appeared the Director of Nursing, board members and a handful of supervisors were the only ones with any knowledge of the move. It was traumatic news for the long term residents for whom the Centre was their home. They were to be moved from their rooms, friends and favourite staff at a moment's notice. Some of the proposed new groupings had a sound clinical basis and even some social advantages but the authoritarian way in which they were to be implemented was extraordinary.

After consulting the Chair of the Health Commission I formed the view that the levels of incompetence and insensitivity were such that ministerial intervention was warranted. I contacted the chair of the board and demanded, in plain and uncomplimentary terms, that the proposed resident moves be stopped, pending the appointment of a Health Commission administrator and a review of the management, role and function of the Centre.

I informed him that conditions would be imposed on Health Commission funding immediately and that an examination of the role and function of Julia Farr would be referred to the Sax Committee as an additional term of reference. An interim administrator from the Health Commission moved in the next day and announced that no residents would be moving for at least a month: 'Their bags have been unpacked'. A chief executive officer was appointed and began work within a month while Dr Peter Last was appointed as Director of Clinical Services.

Dr Last brought great energy and enthusiasm to the new position. Records were updated and residents reassessed, in some cases for the first time in more than 10 years. New admission criteria were developed. Under the old guidelines many residents had been admitted primarily because of the breakdown of social and family supports. On some occasions relatives had placed them on the Centre's waiting list without their knowledge. The reassessment conducted by Dr Last and staff at the Centre showed that there were at least 80 residents who required no more than basic supervision.

Under the new regime applicants would have to meet two important admission criteria. It had to be established that they wanted to come into the Centre, rather than being moved in by what Dr Last described as 'paternalistic manipulation'. And there had to be a demonstrated need for full time physical nursing in an institutional setting. Dr Last also established a slow stream rehabilitation facility for young brain injured patients, mostly the victims of motor vehicle accidents, and embarked on a campaign to highlight the deficiencies in state and federal government services for the young disabled.

The review proved to be an important first step in what would become a virtual revolution in disability services. Over the next 25 years the face of supported care changed remarkably. Home and community based disability services were established statewide and community housing for the disabled replaced large institutions.

THE ADELAIDE CHILDREN'S HOSPITAL was originally a charity cottage hospital, established a century earlier through the generosity of the wealthy citizens of South Australia. It was a response to the many needs of the sick waifs of the city, the young children of the poor who were so vulnerable to the epidemics of the time. Over the years it grew into the state's paediatric teaching hospital in association with the Adelaide University Medical School. The Children's was later adopted as a people's charity and members of the general public were involved through the Good Friday Appeal, sponsored by *The Advertiser* and radio station 5AD. High profile media personalities, sports stars and many other celebrities urged the public to support the appeal and acknowledged their donations on air. With the advent of television this was expanded into the Easter Appeal in association with ADS7 TV. Donations were tax deductible and money raised by the appeal was subsidised by the state government on a $2 for $1 basis. These funds, combined with bequests and a sophisticated year round fundraising program meant that the hospital's research, equipment and technology were among the best endowed, pro rata, in the country.

However, by the beginning of the 1980s the cost per patient, which was fully met by the state government through the hospital's annual operating budget, had become very high by national and international standards. This was despite better clinical management and changes in the philosophy and practice of patient care which resulted in a marked reduction in the average length of time children spent in hospital.

As the Commission began to push the hospital towards better management and cost containment, the old guard and the medical establishment began to appeal to the public to protect the status quo. On Friday 7 October 1983 *The Advertiser* published a highly emotional letter from a Dr Graham Dutton, a senior staff specialist at the hospital, in which he claimed that 'the Minister of Health's most recent attack on the staff and board of management at the Adelaide Children's Hospital' displayed my ignorance of the system. He wished to defend 'all those dedicated people who are struggling with ill-informed bureaucrats to maintain the high standard of care that the children of South Australia deserve'. He further asserted that a 'dangerous shortage of hospital and nursing staff is rampant throughout the public hospital system' based on 'inaccurately collected data' and that 'only hospital staff with years of experience can understand how hospitals run'. Then he moved to his own department: 'At times our intensive care unit is three or four beds over their bed capacity and, as such, is unsafe'. *The News* followed this up, calling it 'this potentially dangerous situation' and demanding 'an end to this unhealthy disquiet'.

I called an urgent meeting with the hospital's chief executive officer and board members the same afternoon to investigate the situation personally. When asked by journalists for follow up interviews to the story my press secretary made the mistake of telling them that I would be at the hospital at 2.00pm. When I arrived journalists from every media outlet, electronic and print, were waiting in the hospital foyer with a very excited Dr Dutton. He stepped forward and introduced himself and I told him immediately that I didn't think he had raised the alleged problems in a responsible way. Despite the highly personal attack he had made on me in his letter, however, he said disingenuously that he did 'not wish to argue with a politician or to politicise the issue'. In response I called him a 'maverick' and, in a hastily coined tautology, 'an unhappy malcontent'.

At that point Dutton challenged me to go directly to the Intensive Care Unit. When I declined, wishing to end the melodrama into which I had been drawn, he retreated to his unit and paged me repeatedly on the hospital's public address system. He subsequently joined the meeting which I held with board members and Dr Bill McCoy from the Health Commission.

In the early hours of Saturday morning Dr McCoy visited intensive care to quietly assess the situation. He indicated to me in a preliminary verbal report that staffing levels in the Intensive Care Unit were very tight but pointed out that the allocation of funding and resources between the hospital's departments and units was the responsibility of the clinicians, the administration and the hospital board, not the Health Commission. But this was a technicality that was never going to be grasped by the public: Dr Dutton's complaints were rectified at a cost to the taxpayers of $500,000.

However, having lost the battle through a flawed strategy I was not about to lose the war. On Monday, the Labour Day holiday, I called a press conference at my home which I used to apologise to Dr Dutton and announce that I was establishing an inquiry to examine the hospital's administration and management. I said that it could not operate in splendid isolation from the rest of the system or continue as though 'it's still funded by charity and chook raffles'. I made it clear that I could not carry the burden of ministerial responsibility when the hospital board was not accountable to the minister. The committee of inquiry would look 'very seriously at incorporating the hospital under the South Australian *Health Commission Act* to redress this anomaly'.

Following the committee's report and recommendations the Adelaide Children's Hospital was incorporated, replete with an updated constitution and a new hospital board with a considerably different membership and attitude. The chair retired and was 'honoured for his services over the years' but not before he had arranged the bequests and donor trust accounts to ensure they remained beyond the legal reach of the Health Commission. With Mrs Beverley Perrett as the new chair, the hospital was now a paediatric centre of excellence with a constitution and board structure to match its status. During her incumbency she was also one of the principal architects of the Child Health Research Institute, established in 1988 as a joint initiative between the South Australian Government (through the Health Commission), the trusts of the Adelaide Children's and the Queen Victoria Hospitals and the Variety Club of Australia.

MERGING THE QUEEN VICTORIA maternity hospital with the Adelaide Children's and consolidating them on a single campus was first canvassed early in 1981 by my predecessor Jennifer Cashmore, Minister of Health in the Tonkin Liberal Government. The logic was irrefutable but the public reaction to the proposal seemed to present insurmountable political problems. Many of the people who were prominent and influential in the professional and cultural life of Adelaide had been born at the Queen Vic and loss of its identity was unthinkable. John Bannon, then Leader of the Opposition, was among those active in the Save the Queen Vic campaign.

In 1984 I went to cabinet with a composite of the various studies that had been conducted over several years and a summary of the preferred alternatives. I sought approval to pursue them further but was refused, the only big issue on which I was defeated outright in cabinet in six years. I decided to recast my strategy, bide my time and make a political virtue of having 'saved' the hospital, repeating it frequently in the following months. At the annual general meeting in September 1985, just three months before the state election, I announced a $7 million proposal to upgrade the hospital. *The Advertiser* reported next morning that the hospital was now 'assured of a community role into the next century'.

The hospital board had originally sought almost three times that amount but Dr McCoy and I were of the view that to accede to this would be a terrible mistake. Amalgamation with consolidation onto a single campus, with all the advantages of the joint use of facilities and assured long term viability, was inevitable. But funding the board's original $20 million proposal would have ensured it would be deferred until the 21st century. The $7 million for a 'facelift' would provide some political respite but more importantly it would force the administration and the board to go through a thorough examination of the pros and cons of the proposal with the Parliamentary Public Works Committee with membership from both major political parties.

The chair of the hospital at this time was Judith Roberts. During the 1970s she had been a prominent and effective member of the Liberal Party, regarded as a woman likely to make her mark in conservative politics at either state or federal level. Judith had a keen interest in health, welfare, education and particularly women's issues and equal opportunity. It was the Liberal Party's loss when she ultimately resigned over their equal opportunity policy. In addition to the hospital board she chaired the South Australian Council of Social Services and South Australia's Home and Community Care Program.

Judith had originally been at the forefront of the Save the Queen Vic campaign. However, Dr McCoy and I believed that when she had to look objectively at the long term prospects of the hospital as an isolated maternity hospital when preparing the formal submission and her subsequent appearance before the Public Works Standing Committee, her better judgment would prevail. Our strategy worked. On 26 March 1987 *The Advertiser* reported that negotiations had begun on a possible amalgamation of the two hospitals. A special meeting of the Queen Victoria board was to decide its attitude to a range of options, including a merger and a move to the Children's site in North Adelaide.

Towards the end of 1988 the two hospitals were amalgamated to form the Adelaide Women's and Children's Hospital, Australia's first combined women's and children's hospital. Pending construction of the new facilities they continued to operate from the two campuses until 1993 when the maternity and all related services, including neo-natal intensive care, were relocated to the new building on the Children's site. Much of the project funding came from the sale of the Queen Vic building (redeveloped privately as apartments) and the $7 million in capital funding that was originally to be used for the facelift.

UPGRADING THE EDUCATION AND TRAINING of nurses to tertiary level and improving their clinical career structures were major issues in the 1980s. Prior to this time the medical specialist was the deity in the public hospital system and nurses were the hand maidens. For more than 100 years they had trained in the hospital wards, were paid a modest stipend for their full time hospital work, lived in supervised nurses' quarters in the hospital grounds during their training and were given rostered time off for lectures. During the 1970s some Australian states established a small number of formal nurse training courses and by the early 1980s the Sturt campus of the South Australian College of Advanced Education was producing 80 graduates a year.

In 1984 the Hawke-Keating Government made a formal commitment to support the transfer of all registered nurse training to the tertiary sector by 1993. There were varying degrees of enthusiasm for the change and disputes about the levels of funding the states would have to provide to support the transfer. Premier Bjelke-Petersen's Queensland Government led the opposition but I quickly came to the view that the transfer was not only desirable but irresistible.

Also contentious were the nurses' claims lodged at about the same time for a 38 hour week (configured as a 19 day month) and significant upgrading of their clinical career structures. The state treasurers, among others, were deeply concerned about the financial implications but a committed nursing profession was threatening industrial action in support of their claims. In Victoria Irene Bolger, the militant State Secretary of the Nurses Federation, led the profession into and through an unprecedented seven week strike. She was ultimately defeated by moderate elements in the Federation but radicalised the nursing profession in a way that few had thought possible. In South Australia the Secretary of the Nurses Federation through the period was Marilyn Beaumont. Despite her occasional public sabre rattling we spoke informally by phone on several occasions while I was negotiating an agreement with the nurses that would not only satisfy them but gain the endorsement of Treasury, the Public Service Board and the Premier's Department. Ultimately both the new clinical career structures and the 19 day month were achieved by South Australian nurses with little more than one or two stop work meetings.

THE FIRST CASES OF ACQUIRED immune deficiency syndrome (AIDS), diagnosed in Australia in 1983, posed a major public health challenge. All that was known about AIDS was that it was caused by an unidentified infectious agent, was transmitted through contact with the blood or other body fluids of an infected person and was prevalent in male homosexuals and intravenous drug users. In those early days some haemophiliacs and other recipients of contaminated blood used in transfusions also contracted the disease. A blood test to detect infection in symptomless carriers once seroconversion had occurred became available soon afterwards. Isolation of a retrovirus that would become known as HIV by a team of French scientists led by Luc Montagnier, was reported in the journal *Science* in 1983. The following year Dr Robert Gallo and his American team published their work in the same journal confirming its role as the cause of AIDS.

We knew enough to implement strategies to control its spread but this had to be communicated to the groups most at risk - people in the drug injecting culture and male homosexuals. And it had to be done without being interpreted as scapegoating while gaining their confidence and cooperation. In the climate of fear that had developed in the community, ignorance and victim blaming sometimes got out of hand. At one point a member of the opposition in the South Australian Legislative Council urged me during question time to set aside a wing of the Royal Adelaide Hospital where anyone diagnosed with AIDS could be forcibly detained.

One of the obstacles to a national strategy was the lack of uniform state legislation and policy about homosexuality. In South Australia homosexual acts between consulting adults in private had been decriminalised for almost a decade whereas in Queensland they remained a criminal offence. The notification requirements also differed between states. In South Australia only clinical cases of AIDS had to be notified to the public health authorities whereas in New South Wales, which had the highest incidence of AIDS, all positive blood tests had to be compulsorily notified. It is probable that this pushed significant numbers of symptomless HIV carriers out of testing.

From the outset and to his great credit Federal Health Minister Neal Blewett supported rational strategies at a national level, based on the best available evidence. He was instrumental in ensuring that the gay community took a leading role in AIDS awareness and safe sex practices. Despite some resistance, needle exchange programs, condom distribution, frank advertising and public education programs were all prominent weapons in Australia's armamentarium. Public health concerns had to take precedence over short term politics. We quickly moved ahead of the USA where the religious right preferred a failed morals crusade, urging abstinence rather than best practice in public health.

By 1987 when it had become apparent that the disease was not confined to gay men the message was delivered dramatically in the Grim Reaper television ads. The campaign featured a hooded, bowling ball-wielding Reaper knocking down men, women and children in a bowling alley. It was one of the most effective public health education campaigns ever launched in Australia, although for some the Reaper represented those people infected with HIV rather than the Grim Reaper harvesting the dead and was interpreted as reflecting adversely on the gay community. Nevertheless, Dr Ron Penny, Head of Immunology at St Vincent's Hospital in Sydney described the ad's impact as a wake-up call to Australia as 'astounding'.

AS A CONCOMITANT TO THE INTRODUCTION of Medicare, hospitals were improving their patient and management information systems quite dramatically. Accurate statistics on the number of patients booked on lists for elective surgery were available from individual hospitals and statewide for the first time. Of course, counting the total number of patients at any moment on what became known as the waiting lists without an analysis of patients listed by procedure and mean waiting times for those procedures was a very blunt instrument. Nevertheless it was being used by critics of Medicare to claim that the public hospital system was unable to cope with the demands being placed on it.

Early in 1988 I asked Professor Doug Coster, Head of the Ophthalmology Department at Flinders Medical Centre, to undertake a review of the highly political issue of 'waiting lists' and the management of elective surgery at Adelaide's public hospitals. He was assisted by Peter Agars, a management consultant at Touche Ross Services and Keith Bennetts, a solicitor with Finlaysons and Senior Lecturer in Health Services and Commercial Law at the South Australian Institute of Technology.

In his report Professor Coster referred to the misuse of the term 'waiting lists' to describe what were in fact booking lists. He pointed out that the total numbers on booking lists alone were 'an inappropriate measure of the effectiveness of surgical services because they merely reflect the turnover of elective surgery.'[22] Many of the patients on the lists were not waiting as they had already been given an appropriate date or opportunity for admission on an earlier occasion but had refused it for personal reasons. Moreover, a significant number of patients, particularly those who had been on lists for a long time, had already accepted treatment from other public or private hospitals. Professor Coster explained that 'the limitations of placing an importance on the number of patients on booking lists cannot be overstated' As the total number of patients on booking lists is a reflection of the turnover in the system, 'large lists can be seen to represent a busy and effective surgical service'. In other words, the more effective and active hospital services were, the more their booking lists would grow, but such an increase would not imply an increased waiting time for surgery generally. Of much greater importance was the proportion of patients who had to wait an unacceptable time for admission for elective procedures in specific areas such as orthopaedics.

Professor Coster found that there was no conclusive evidence of any major adverse medical or social consequences generated by the system but that the opposite view was often conveyed to the public. As he noted:

> This erodes the confidence of the public and discourages them from using public hospitals. Booking lists for elective surgery have become an issue of public concern and the media has a serious responsibility in the public interest to ensure an objective analysis is published.

THE SOUTH AUSTRALIAN BRANCH of the Australian Medical Association maintained its belligerent opposition to many significant initiatives in Labor's health reform agenda well into the 1980s. However, I was aware that there were senior specialists in South Australia who were keen to offer candid assessments and constructive advice about the health system. It was my good fortune to enjoy their support, their advice and often their friendship. Each month committed members of the public health movement gathered in the meeting room of a suburban community health centre on a Friday evening to discuss their issues: at about the same time I was meeting a dozen or more leaders of the medical profession, members of what my staff called the Eminent Doctors Group. We held frank and friendly discussions, always conducted under the Chatham House Rule. I know that they appreciated the opportunity to talk directly to me and I certainly valued their opinions.

Discussing the Nganampa Health Service with two visiting Pitjantjatjara men, 1988.

CHAPTER TWELVE

Social health, social justice

From 1984 the philosophy that health is a state of physical, mental and social well being and not merely the absence of disease or infirmity underpinned health planning in South Australia. In the five years between 1984 and 1988 we demonstrated that a social health model, based on inter-departmental cooperation and cabinet coordination, is compatible with and complementary to traditional models of health care.

The social determinants of health include affordable housing, equity and access to education, employment and training programs and satisfactory environments – at home, in the workplace and in local communities. Reliable public transport can make an important contribution to the quality of suburban life. Community services for children, families, the aged and the disabled help to maintain cohesive neighbourhoods. Individuals and families need ready access to treatment services in times of illness. Adequate nutrition is directly related to community education as well as incomes. A reasonable income within the framework of a social wage ought to be at the heart of any long term commitment to social justice. For social democrats these fundamental pillars are just as valid now as they were 30 years ago.

THE PORT PIRIE LEAD SMELTER is one of the largest in the world. In its first 90 years of operation between 1889 and 1979 an estimated 160,000 tons of lead escaped the smelter by a variety of routes. In the 1980s it was operated by the Broken Hill Associated Smelters Pty Ltd (BHAS), a subsidiary of Conzinc Rio Tinto Australia and was the city's major employer.

Port Pirie is a small provincial city on South Australia's Spencer Gulf with a population of around 15,000. The terrain is flat, the climate semi-arid and the summers are long, dry and dusty. Early in 1982 the South

Australian Health Commission conducted a city wide survey of blood lead levels in Port Pirie children. Of the 1,239 children tested 87 (seven per cent) had blood lead levels at or above 30 micrograms per 100 mls of blood (30 ugm/dl), the concentration which was at that time considered to represent a 'level of concern'. The worst single case was 54 ugm/dl. More detailed analysis of the results showed that the blood lead levels in three to five year old children were three times higher than in the older groups and the prevalence of elevated blood levels was estimated to be 10 to 15 times higher among children living in the most heavily polluted areas of the city. In the suburbs of Solomontown and Pirie West and the central area of Pirie the percentage of pre-school children with blood lead levels exceeding 30 ugm/dl ranged from 31.8 per cent to 46.7 per cent. The benchmark set by the National Health and Medical Research Council as the level of concern has been progressively reduced over the past 30 years. Most recently (May 2015) it was further amended to 5 ugm/dl, reflecting the global view that there is no safe level of exposure. However, even using the 30ugm/dl benchmark current in 1983, it was estimated that two pre-school children in five in those areas had blood lead levels which were causing subtle but marked and irreversible brain damage. One of my first tasks as the South Australian Health Minister was to initiate action to protect the community from this environmental health disaster.

A ten year slump in world metal prices had already generated considerable pessimism about the smelter's future. The plant was old and much of it was nearing the end of its useful life. BHAS and its parent company Conzinc Rio Tinto Australia were considering a number of options for its future, ranging from rehabilitating the plant at an estimated cost of up to $100 million to running it down and ultimately closing it. As they saw the viability of their city under threat Port Pirie residents reacted in predictable ways: some called for urgent action to protect their children, many denied there was a problem. Across the community there was deep concern, mixed with anger, that any intervention we planned to confront the problem would act as a catalyst in hastening the smelter's demise. With the Mayor Bill Jones leading the charge I was being cast as 'an enemy of the people'.[23]

On 6 May 1983 I announced the membership and terms of reference of a task force which had been established to examine the environmental lead problem and make recommendations concerning its amelioration. At the same time I said that Dr Philip Landrigan would visit South Australia in September to review their work and recommendations and provide the government with an expert second opinion. Dr Landrigan was a graduate of the Harvard Medical School with post-graduate qualifications in occupational medicine and industrial health. Since 1975 he had led research demonstrating the connection between blood lead levels and cognitive impairment in children. In 1983 he was a Divisional Director of the United States National Institute for Occupational Safety and Health based in Cincinnati, Ohio.

Mayor Jones had been employed by BHAS as their corporate affairs officer prior to his retirement and had previously been investigated by the South Australian ombudsman following allegations that positions he held could have led to a conflict of interest in the lead levels controversy. At a joint press conference I held with Jones to announce his membership of the task force he was asked by a journalist for his view on what blood lead level should be considered a problem. He confidently asserted that 'the real level of concern accepted by many countries is 60 ugm/dl'. A month later he was quoted in a report in *The Australian* as saying that 'there is no real lead problem in Port Pirie'. In my view these public statements should have resulted in his automatic removal from the task force. But Premier Bannon's politics of pragmatism prevailed, concerned that his dismissal might prompt Jones to run as an independent candidate against the sitting Labor member at the next State election. The other members of the task force would have to work around him.

Meanwhile the Health Commission had devised and mounted a modest public information display in a local shopping centre in Port Pirie. I agreed to speak at the opening of the display which was the beginning of an ongoing public education program about environmental lead contamination, its effects and things householders could do to reduce exposure to it. It was to be a low key affair – no stage, no amplification, no prepared speech, just some friendly words of encouragement.

The Mayor was there with several councillors and soon after I began to speak he launched into a tirade of abuse. 'A health minister. What a joke! A cabinet minister. What a joke! A minister of the crown. What an idiot!' Encouraged by the fact that this extraordinary mayoral behavior had me visibly riled, several of Bill's fellow councillors joined in the chorus. When I ultimately decided that it was better to give than to receive I showed what I believe was considerably more flair than the Mayor, describing him, among other things, as a 'middle aged ocker larrikin'. The local television station GTS4, there to film the launch, captured the incident and distributed the film to every metropolitan Adelaide television channel in time for their evening news bulletins. For the next 12 months the file film was available whenever television news services wanted to tag me as 'irascible'.

Mayor Jones had always cultivated an image as a popular knockabout character. He had now moved to a public position as defender of the status quo at the smelter. By implication he was protecting the jobs of the smelter workers who believed they were being threatened by the adverse publicity. Nor was BHAS above playing a tough game in those early days. At one point the managing director was reported as saying that the alleged association between lead levels and an intelligence deficiency was 'nonsense and totally unsupported by scientific finding'. On the other hand Conzinc Rio Tinto, the parent company, played a straight bat in making it clear that the future of the smelter would be based on purely financial considerations.

Dr Landrigan arrived in early September and three weeks later presented his report *Lead Exposure, Lead Absorption and Lead Toxicity in the Children of Port Pirie: A Second Opinion*. He confirmed the finding of the task force of an urgent need to devise a major decontamination and rehabilitation program, posing the question: 'Can Port Pirie afford the permanent, albeit invisible loss of one child in 20 with truly superior intelligence; and can Port Pirie afford a concomitant quadrupling in the number of children there with intellectual impairment'?

The report's recommendations were in many important respects identical or close to those of the task force. However, his preferred option was much more radical in one respect: he recommended that all residents from the worst areas of the city be relocated into new housing outside the contaminated zone and duly compensated.

This would have been clearly the preferred option. However, the central government agencies, especially Treasury, were aghast at the estimated cost for a government still struggling with the financial aftermath of the worst bushfires in South Australia's history which had occurred during the previous autumn. In a compromise balancing health, economic and social factors the Health Commission's implementation group developed a major decontamination strategy. Ceiling dust and lead paint were to be removed from houses, schools, kindergartens, public buildings and other contaminated premises. Soil testing was conducted and a major greening program was planned with the professional staff of the city council to reduce the dust problem. Many of the cottages were very modest and in a poor state of repair. Where rehabilitation costs were excessive compared to their value they were to be demolished and rebuilt in safer areas. The budget for social housing in the city was to be doubled over a five year period. An environmental health centre was established to provide special counselling and follow up testing, initially to all children and their parents where blood lead levels exceeded 30 ugm/dl. The BHAS undertook to improve management of the slag and ore heaps and provided new facilities at the smelter to ensure clothing was changed on entering and leaving the work area. Later they announced that they would spend $60 million upgrading the smelter.

Despite the continuing struggle for resources we began to see tangible results. In January 1987 I released figures showing that in the most recent round of testing the percentage of children with blood levels exceeding 30 ugm/dl had decreased from seven to four per cent. Community sentiment had also shifted, with an editorial in the *Port Pirie Recorder* boasting that 'we are showing the world that our city and our state can take on a major problem and deal with it successfully'. It was the end of the beginning.

WOMEN HAVE MANY HEALTH ISSUES that lie outside traditional services They include poverty, domestic violence, dependency, child care and lifestyle issues such as the double burden of paid and unpaid work. Women's basic physiology and their social and cultural positions mean that good health and opportunity are very closely linked. In the 1980s the women's health movement was increasingly seeking a role in mainstream policy, planning and resource allocation decisions as a more effective way of ensuring that health services were provided in a way that met their expressed needs. This view was supported in the South Australian Government's Policy on Women and Health. Our stated aim was to increase women's influence on the health system commensurate with their numbers in society and their many social roles. To ensure that their voices were heard by members of the Heath Commission I created the position of Women's Adviser on Health, at executive officer level, an Australian first.

My predecessor, Jennifer Cashmore, had established South Australia's first Women's Health Centre in North Adelaide in 1981. From 1985 through 1987 I gave my enthusiastic support to the addition of three more centres in suburban Noarlunga, Port Adelaide and Elizabeth as the North Adelaide service morphed progressively into a statewide service. The services were provided from an explicit feminist philosophy.

ABORIGINAL HEALTH SERVICES in South Australia were among my highest priorities. In August 1983 I invited Gary Foley, who was at the forefront of the National Aboriginal and Islander Health Organisation, to chair a committee to review them. To gain a better personal understanding of the many problems confronting members of the small Aboriginal communities in the remote areas of South Australia I asked him to join me on a journey to the north west corner of the state and in early October we flew out of Adelaide to spend five very busy days bumping through turbulence in an aging Beechcraft Queen Air aircraft. The nine member party included the Director and Chair of the South Australian Aboriginal Health Organisation, the State Secretary of the Nurses Federation, three staff members from the South Australian Health Commission, including a senior medical officer, and my executive assistant, Christine Giles. The visits to Indulkana and Ernabella were unique experiences for me. We sat in the red dirt in the shade of the eucalypts listening to the elders, many speaking in Anangu Pitjantjatjara, as they told us through interpreters about their problems and the communities' needs. We also visited Oodnadatta, Nepabunna, Davenport and Port Augusta.

During the trip we met the chair, Yami Lester, and the members of the Pitjantjatjara Council and reached agreement in principle about state government funding for the Nganampa Health Service which would become the first community controlled Aboriginal health service established in South Australia.

The Foley Report, completed in 1984, highlighted the disastrous state of health in Aboriginal communities across urban, regional and remote areas of South Australia. They included very high levels of infectious disease, poor diet and substance abuse, especially alcohol. Foley listed some of the more important underlying causes which included low levels of education linked to poor school attendance, very high unemployment, poverty, inadequate housing, lack of clean water, poor sanitation, rates of incarceration (which were up to 10 times higher than the general community) and paternalism in the provision of services. This was all deeply disturbing but there was little that was new in this part of the report. The solutions it recommended, on the other hand, were quite radical: Aboriginal community control and self determination.

Working with the Aboriginal Health Organisation and local Aboriginal communities through 1985 and 1986 the Health Commission supported the establishment of community controlled Aboriginal health services at Yalata and Ceduna-Koonibba and the Pika Wiya Health Service to serve the Aboriginal communities in Port Augusta and Davenport. Numerous other Aboriginal support services were developed. Aboriginal representatives were elected or appointed to several hospital boards and Aboriginal liaison officers were appointed in the Queen Elizabeth and Adelaide Children's Hospitals as well as in several country hospitals.

However, the transition was not without its problems. Decades of disadvantage had created a serious lack of social cohesion, exacerbated by a high incidence of alcoholism. Small communities, some in the most remote areas of South Australia, were moving from decades of white paternalism to community controlled programs based on the social determinants of health. In many cases this meant dealing directly or indirectly with more than a dozen commonwealth and state government agencies. In addition to the Commonwealth Department of Aboriginal Affairs they were involved with health, education, employment and training, housing, social security, water, sewerage, electricity, road maintenance, community welfare, police and legal services. At the same time the wide range of different but firmly held opinions in and between the Aboriginal communities often made life difficult even for a most committed politician. I sometimes felt that the number of faxes sent to my office from the Pitjantjatjara Council criticising our initiatives (and sent by press release to the Adelaide media) were in direct proportion to the support I was giving them.

Notwithstanding these problems, self determination and community control continued to underpin successful programs. In 1987 the Healthy Aboriginal Lifestyle Team was established to provide counselling and support to combat substance abuse, especially petrol sniffing. The program was based on elements of traditional Aboriginal culture and family identity. In 1988 the Public and Environmental Health Division of the South Australian Health Commission, working with the Nganampa Health Service, completed a major environmental health study. In the same year the Pika Wiya community controlled service was able to demonstrate improvements in Aboriginal health using several major indicators, including reductions in hospital admissions, sexually transmitted diseases, trauma and gastroenteritis. Finally, in 1988 I secured a multi-million dollar allocation of money from the newly established social justice budget for some additional or complementary Aboriginal programs, ranging from the provision of essential services to employment and training.

DURING MY FIRST MINISTERIAL TRIP to the United States in 1984 my itinerary included a visit to the Mount Sinai Beth Israel Medical Center in New York. The heart of the Center was a 1,300 bed tertiary level teaching hospital but it also had one of the nation's largest networks of methadone treatment clinics. I had come to talk to staff specifically about their methadone maintenance program which was still quite a controversial area in Australia. During our meeting the conversation turned to adolescent health and they urged us to visit The Door, a centre providing a wide range of services to meet the needs of young people between 12 to 21 years of age. The services were delivered in an informal, friendly environment by non-judgmental staff. Apart from medical and dental health services the centre provided mental health support, advice on sexual health and contraception (including gender identity and anger management), legal services and free classes in performing and visual arts, music and dance.

I decided that Adelaide must have a service based on this model. Dr McCoy was given the task of planning and establishing the service, supported by a youth ambassador to liaise with potential clients. To ensure that we incorporated its spirit, we brought one of the senior staff members from The Door to Adelaide to act as an adviser during the establishment phase.

The Second Storey was opened by the Premier in the run up to the 1985 state election and very quickly attracted young people from street kids to students. It was originally located on the second storey of a building just a few metres from Rundle Mall, Adelaide's main shopping precinct. In a play on words I dubbed it The Second Storey, a reference to both its location and the ways in which we hoped it could help our clients. Later the service became so popular that it had to be relocated three blocks away at the insistence of the good burghers of Rundle Mall who claimed that the kids using the service were 'frightening the shoppers'. The 'e' was dropped from the Storey but the enthusiasm and commitment were undiminished. The Second Story Youth Health Service is still going, now operating from two additional sites in the northern suburb of Elizabeth and in the south at Christies Beach.

IN DECEMBER 1985 THE GOVERNMENT was returned with a further 2.3 per cent swing, giving it 29 seats in a 47 seat chamber. I was given the additional portfolio of Community Welfare and appointed as Chairman of the Human Services and Social Justice Cabinet Committees. In addition to my own portfolios I now had a general, overarching view of portfolios from Housing to Recreation and Sport, from Education and Vocational Training to Juvenile Justice. South Australia was adopting a social health infrastructure as an integral part of the social justice strategy.

During 1985 we had established Noarlunga Health Services in Adelaide's southern suburbs as a model for delivering health care and support within a social health framework. The services included the Noarlunga Health Village, the Morphett Vale and Southern Vale Community Health Centres and the Southern Women's Community Health Centre. At the same time the Parks Community Health Centre was established at Angle Park. In addition to clinical services, the community health centres conducted disease prevention and health promotion programs, developed user friendly client services that offered social support programs to reduce domestic violence and acted as advocates for their clients in gaining access to legal aid, welfare payments and housing.

In 1987 Noarlunga (with Canberra and Illawarra) was chosen to participate in the federal government's *Healthy Cities* project and in 1988 Adelaide hosted the World Health Organisation's (WHO) Second

International Conference on Healthy Public Policy. It was co-sponsored by the WHO and the federal Department of Community Services & Health. The quality, innovation and effectiveness of the community health centres in Adelaide were acknowledged by the WHO as being as good as any in the world. The community health research funded by the Health Commission during this period would earn South Australia an international reputation for its work on social health. It was also partly responsible for Professor Fran Baum of Flinders University being appointed as a Commissioner on the WHO's Commission on the Social Determinants of Health from 2005 to 2008. This was a global network of policy makers, researchers and civil society organisations brought together by the WHO to give support in tackling the social causes of poor health and avoidable health inequalities and inequities.

Health Minister's Conference, Hobart 1983 with Neal Blewett on my left and New South Wales Minister Laurie Brereton at the other end of the group.

CHAPTER THIRTEEN

Tobacco, alcohol and other drugs

The Sackville Royal Commission into the non-medical use of drugs, chaired by Commissioner Ronald Sackville AO, released its report early in 1979. It was the most comprehensive report on substance abuse that had ever been completed in Australia. Media attention inevitably focused on the recommendation that possession or cultivation of marijuana in small quantities for personal use should be decriminalised but there was much more. Commissioner Sackville outlined a comprehensive strategy to reduce and control abuse of both legal and illegal drugs. The report said:

> Hard as it may be for some people to accept, effective social policy on drugs cannot be guided by absolutes. The use of almost all drugs can be beneficial in some circumstances and harmful in others and it is clear that policy, to be effective, must be guided by the concept of relative risks of different kinds of drug use.

The Dunstan Government had established the Royal Commission in 1978 but by the time it reported Don Dunstan had retired. It took Premier Corcoran less than 10 minutes to get cabinet support for shelving it. The report was archived for almost four years until I retrieved it soon after I was given the health portfolio.

BY 1983 MARIJUANA LAW REFORM had emerged as an issue within the South Australian Branch of the ALP. Several motions concerning decriminalisation appeared on the agenda for the State ALP Conference in June that year. It was declared a conscience issue which meant that any motion passed by the Conference would not be binding on the Parliamentary Labor Party but it seemed an ideal forum in which to test the attitudes of the Party and to launch discussion in the general community. I informed John Bannon that I intended to lead the debate.

The composite resolution put to the Conference recommended the decriminalisation of personal possession and cultivation of marijuana and the expunging of existing criminal records for personal possession. Existing penalties for commercial growing and trafficking were to be maintained. Following a spirited debate, in which my old friend Jack Nyland from the Transport Workers Union led the opposition forces, the motion was passed by 135 votes to 55.

Following the Conference I took the marijuana debate into the community, often facing hostile audiences at public gatherings. After one meeting of parents and friends at Saint Michael's College in suburban Henley Beach I described myself as having been the main grill at the barbecue. However, over the following months I continued to explain why it was preferable to pursuing an unwinnable war which criminalised users and created a credibility gap between generations. In July 1983 Cabinet had endorsed my submission which sought approval to draft a *Controlled Substances Bill* to control the licit and illicit use of drugs in South Australia. By 1984 I had Cabinet approval to introduce the Bill into the Legislative Council and I had done enough work to know that I had the numbers to ensure its passage through both houses of the parliament.

The Controlled Substances Act 1984 repealed several Acts including the *Food and Drugs Act* and consolidated controls over legal and illegal drugs, poisons and 'therapeutic substances'. The legislation established the Drug Assessment and Aid Panels recommended by Sackville: adults charged with a simple possession offence for illicit drugs (other than marijuana) could opt to be diverted out of the court system to a panel which determined whether they should be referred for rehabilitation or prosecuted. Each panel consisted of a lawyer and two people with extensive knowledge of the problems and treatment of drug abuse. Given community attitudes, drug law reform had to be necessarily incremental. Although personal possession and cultivation of marijuana for personal use was not yet decriminalised, the maximum penalties were reduced from a $2,000 fine or two years imprisonment to a maximum penalty of $500. There was a trade off: the legislation increased the penalties for trading and trafficking in commercial quantities of illicit drugs. In 1986, two years and one election later, a further amendment reduced the maximum penalty for personal possession of marijuana to $150 which attracted no criminal record and could be paid as an expiation fee if the charge was uncontested.

DRUG AND ALCOHOL SERVICES in South Australia had been delivered within the framework of the *Alcohol and Drug Addicts Treatment Act* for almost 30 years. The legislation reinforced the authoritarian and institutional approach adopted by the Alcohol and Drug Addicts Treatment Board which under the legislation operated at arm's length from the Health Commission. The Board worked in isolation with their executive officer, overseeing the delivery of services which were largely based on 'treatment and discipline'. Prevention and education programs in both schools and the general community were at best rudimentary.

One of the principal treatment centres was based in the grounds of Hillcrest, a large public psychiatric hospital. Basic facilities were provided for inpatients ranging from 18 year olds with a heroin addiction to aging alcoholics. They shared a common room and group activities. The authorities were ambivalent about the methadone treatment program and the criteria for admission to it changed as often as clinical directors. A major policy shift at one stage resulted in 160 of 200 participants being removed as malingerers with no follow up program.

Several programs for alcohol addiction were outsourced to the Salvation Army and the Adelaide Central Mission. The Salvos were responsible for rehabilitation through The Bridge program but many of their facilities and services were dedicated to the care and support of end stage alcoholics. The Mission had for many years conducted a 'rehabilitation' program at Kuitpo Colony, south of Adelaide where the male clients were accommodated in basic quarters and encouraged to reform through a 'manual labour in athletic singlets' approach. In most cases the exercise was a program for resting the liver prior to the next drinking bout.

In 1983 I introduced the *Public Intoxication Bill* which repealed the offence of public drunkenness more than four years before it was recommended by Justice Muirhead in the first report of the federal Royal Commission into Aboriginal Deaths in Custody. Under the legislation anyone found drunk in a public place could be apprehended without being charged and taken home, to a sobering up centre or to a police station where they could be detained for up to 10 hours.

The *Controlled Substances Act 1984* repealed the *Alcohol and Drug Addicts Treatment Act*, abolished the Alcohol and Drug Addicts Treatment Board and replaced it with the Drug and Alcohol Services Council (DASC). The stage was now set for the development of what was to become the most comprehensive strategy in Australia to combat drug and alcohol abuse. In mid-1984 members of the Drug and Alcohol Services Council were charged with developing a comprehensive three year program and implementation strategy to combat substance abuse and to radically improve services. I received and endorsed their proposals towards the end of the year. All I needed was the funding to implement them. In April 1985 Prime Minister Bob Hawke called a special Premiers Conference on drugs, the so-called Drug Summit, which led directly to the National Campaign Against Drug Abuse (NCADA). South Australia was in a unique position in already having a detailed program that met the NCADA guidelines. During the initial three financial years of the campaign (1985-86 through 1987-88) federal funding for South Australian drug and alcohol programs was increased by 50 per cent.

DASC provided clinical services to patients, clients and their families through its own units and funded services delivered by other health and welfare agencies. It provided consultancy services to doctors, nurses and other health professionals, welfare workers, legal practitioners and correctional services personnel. It supported the Salvation Army and The Mission whose new funding guidelines reflected government policy and facilitated relevant research by outside bodies, in addition to its own research and evaluation programs.

It provided community education programs on substance abuse; prisoner assessment and rehabilitation services through the Prison Drug Unit; residential facilities including a dedicated alcohol services unit, a drug services unit and methadone program; a drug free therapeutic community at The Woolshed; and half way houses for clients recovering from addiction. DASC also funded the Drug and Alcohol Resource Unit at the Royal Adelaide Hospital and the Drug and Alcohol Service at Flinders Medical Centre. It was a major source of funding for The Second Storey adolescent health service and the Learning for Life program conducted in primary schools. And it was a partner with the Education Department in developing preventive drug education programs in secondary schools.

CONTROLS ON TOBACCO SPONSORSHIP and advertising were given a very high priority. In April 1983, a little more than a month after the election of the Hawke Labor Government, I attended my first Health Ministers Conference. The Conference passed a three part motion on tobacco and smoking, the first part calling on the federal government to increase tobacco excise and allocate at least part of the additional revenue to smoking control programs; the second declared that sponsorship of sport was a definite form of tobacco advertising and promotion and contrary to a national anti-smoking policy; the third agreed to explore the possibility of establishing pilot schemes to assist sporting bodies to obtain alternative sponsorship.

By the early 1980s smoking and health had become a high priority community health issue. However, through 1983 into 1985 my opportunity to take a prominent role in what was becoming a national movement against tobacco was limited by the Premier's reluctance to make it an issue for the South Australian government. Initially he was opposed to government interference with the tobacco-sport-performing arts alliance, ostensibly based on the civil liberties argument that tobacco was a legal drug. It was clear I would have to be careful not to over commit and underachieve.

This was an issue, on the other hand, where I could always rely on the support of the Democrats. In May 1983 Democrat Lance Milne fired the first shot with a Bill to prohibit the advertising and promotion of tobacco products. Eventually I would be able to use the Democrats' initiatives as a catalyst to push cabinet collectively to show political courage but meanwhile I had to be uncharacteristically patient. The Milne Bill lapsed when the parliament rose for the winter recess. When he reintroduced it in the spring session my response, acting under cabinet instruction, was timid and cynical. I moved an amendment to ensure that if the Bill was passed it could not be proclaimed unless similar legislation had already been brought into law or commitments made to introduce it from the Australian Capital Territory and three other states. As a further safeguard, it could only come into operation after the Commonwealth had acted to ban the televising of events where tobacco brand names were displayed.

The Bill had been amended to the point where it was simply an exercise in semantics. When it got to the House of Assembly for consideration no member of the government or the opposition sponsored it and it lapsed. Tobacco was still too hot to handle, the tobacco companies holding the sporting and arts organisations that they sponsored in their thrall. Everyone, ranging from the South Australian Jockey Club to the football codes and the South Australian Theatre Company were adamant in declaring that they could not survive without tobacco sponsorship and for the first time the Liberals declared the opposition's position. They vigorously opposed any move to limit or ban advertising and sponsorship, a position they were to pursue consistently for the next five years.

It was a difficult political environment for me. Many of my cabinet and caucus colleagues were initially less than enthusiastic about the proposed ban on sponsorship while the Premier and the Minister of Recreation and Sport had actively resisted it. As late as October 1987 when he launched the State Theatre Company's program for 1988 the Premier made 'appropriate acknowledgement of the support that the Benson and Hedges Company has made to the State Theatre Company'.[24]

But the pressure from the anti-smoking movement continued to grow. In October 1984 the Democrats had introduced the *Tobacco Sales to Children (Prohibition) Bill*. It increased the penalties for selling cigarettes to children under sixteen and placed greater emphasis on the prohibition of tobacco sales to minors by enshrining it in its own Act. Lance Milne had consulted my staff during the drafting of the Bill which was picked up and supported by the government when it reached the Lower House.

Seven months later the Health Ministers' Conference in Brisbane (May 1985) unanimously supported a proposal that 20 per cent of the front and back panels of cigarette packets should carry one of four mandatory warnings to be used in rotation. This was to be effective from July 1986 but extensive inter-government and industry-government negotiations about the space (eventually 15 per cent) and colour contrasts delayed its implementation until 1987. It was hardly a landmark or a turning point in the smoking or health debate but the result was a uniform national approach to labelling in an inherently cumbersome federal system.

In the spring session of 1985 the harmful effects of passive smoking were addressed in the South Australian Parliament when Lance Milne moved a motion requesting the Minister of Health to introduce legislation to prohibit smoking in confined work and public places. In addition he moved for the provision of non-smoking areas in all recreational, retail and restaurant premises to counteract 'the harmful effects of sidestream tobacco smoke on non-smokers in the community'. In response I foreshadowed several initiatives which I intended to put together as a package for adoption by the Bannon Government early in its second term in office.

During 1985 I had anticipated that the real game would be on if we were returned to government at the end of that year and appointed Dr Simon Chapman on a contract basis to head the South Australian Health Promotion Unit. In August 1986 my *Tobacco Products Control Bill* passed both Houses of Parliament. South Australia now had health related controls over the sale, packaging, advertising and use of tobacco products together in one piece of legislation. Public opinion was moving in our favour but most sponsored sporting bodies and sports commentators were still vociferous supporters of tobacco sponsorship. It would be another 12 months before we reached the major legislative turning point in the debate.

In September 1987 Mike Elliot MLC, who was now pushing the issue for the Democrats, introduced the *Tobacco Advertising (Prohibition) Bill* with the intention of banning advertising on billboards, promotional giveaways of tobacco products and newspaper advertising. It banned sponsorship by tobacco companies 'where it is used as an advertising tool', although it allowed for exemptions in the short term for national or international events like the Formula One Grand Prix which was held on the Adelaide Street Circuit for 11 years from 1985. Because it was a Private Member's Bill it could not encompass financial matters. Accordingly, Elliot urged the government to insert a money clause and proposed a small increase of two or three per cent in the tobacco franchise to set up a fund to replace tobacco sponsorship.

On this occasion the Democrats were not prepared to allow a phony war to be conducted in the Legislative Council only to have the Bill lapse for want of a sponsor in the Lower House. On the next private members day Martyn Evans, who had been elected as an Independent Labor member in 1985, introduced the same Bill in the House of Assembly. It was now in the people's house where it was deferred by the government 'for further consideration'.

Meanwhile the Victorian Health Minister, David White had secured the support of Premier John Cain and his Cabinet to introduce legislation to ban sponsorship of sport and the arts by tobacco companies. Under the legislation the sponsorships would be replaced, funded instead by an increase in the tobacco franchise to be paid into the Victorian Health Promotion Foundation (VicHealth). The Foundation would also provide an increase in funding for health promotion and research.

During 1987 we had continued to emphasise the dangers of side stream smoke and highlighted the statistics that showed that increasing numbers of school children, especially young girls, were becoming addicted to cigarettes. Despite a marginal decrease overall in tobacco consumption, the estimates of new recruits among 10 to 15 year olds were alarming. By now adroit management of the public debate had us in front of our opponents. However, Premier Bannon was still cautious and concerned about taking on the tobacco-sports axis. Drawing once more on the Whitlam dictum that only the impotent are pure I had to play a rather soiled ace to get him onside. As the Premier of Australia's most important wine producing state, Bannon had always been a major supporter of the wine industry. However, the issue of social and health problems caused by alcohol had been raised that year at the Ministerial Council on Drug Strategy. It was referred to a committee which produced and circulated a draft national volumetric pricing policy which would reflect the actual alcohol content of the beverage and would have a particular impact the prices of cask and cleanskin wine. It also canvassed a compulsory code of ethics for alcohol advertising and recommended that it should be phased out in the longer term.

The recommendations alarmed the wine industry which was actively opposing the proposals and lobbying the government for support. For my part I felt that for the time being I had enough on my plate with tobacco. Despite the real merit contained in the recommendations, alcohol would have to wait. In return for Premier Bannon's undertaking that he would support my anti-tobacco strategy I agreed to use my best efforts at the next Ministerial Committee on Drug Strategy meeting to have the alcohol draft policy amended to take a less radical approach.

In October 1987 I was able to announce at a media conference that cabinet had agreed in principle to follow Victoria in banning sponsorship of sporting and cultural events by tobacco companies and that their sponsorship would be replaced by public funding. The Elliott-Evans private members Bill would be replaced by the government legislation to be introduced early in 1988. Yet the ever cautious Bannon continued to be ambivalent and concerned. It was important that we maintain momentum during the Christmas-New Year period 1987-88. My office had established and maintained a close relationship with David White's Victorian office and we continually learned from their experience. Dr Nigel Gray, the talented and energetic executive director of the Victorian Anti-Cancer Council was another important ally and adviser. The South Australian Anti-Cancer Foundation had historically directed its resources to patient support and most of its considerable funding to research. It had never sought to play an entrepreneurial role and initially did not have a senior staff member who could head the campaign. However, the two professors on the Foundation's Executive Committee, Barry Vernon-Roberts and Tony McMichael, agreed to take the lead. Vernon-Roberts came to relish the role and led a well organised independent campaign throughout the summer.

At the Health Promotion Unit Simon Chapman, working with the epidemiology branch, developed a media package incorporating photos, statistical data and anecdotes illustrating the devastating effects of smoking. All electorate offices were sent epidemiological data with an estimate of how many smoking related deaths had occurred in their electorates over the previous 10 years. Opposition politicians in marginal seats were lobbied by members of the Public Health Association.

The Bill introduced in the autumn session of Parliament in 1988 prohibited tobacco sponsorship of sporting and cultural events and prohibited tobacco advertising in cinemas, on billboards and other external signs. The tobacco license fee was increased by three per cent to raise an estimated $5.2 million which funded Foundation South Australia, an independent trust to provide replacement funding for sporting and cultural groups and to promote good health.

The Liberals opposed it all the way. The Shadow Minister of Health, Martin Cameron, declared that it was 'the most cynical, hypocritical and farcical Bill that I have seen introduced into this Parliament in my 17 years as a member'. The Bill was 'all gesture and no guts, laudable in its aim but laughable in its application'. But they were on the wrong side.

Once the sporting bodies calculated the additional financial benefit that would accrue to them from Foundation South Australia their opposition collapsed. Speaking during debate on the Bill on 14 April 1988 I said rather prophetically:

> There is not the slightest doubt that, in public health terms, this will be the most significant piece of legislation that I am likely to be associated with.......it is the most significant public health initiative that has taken place in this state since the Jonas/Salk polio vaccines in the mid-1950s. I have the highest commitment to this legislation. I view it as the apex of my political career.

The Bill passed both Houses and was assented to on 5 May 1988. Print and electronic advertising were outside the state jurisdictions. However, this loophole was closed when the Keating Labor Government introduced the *Tobacco Advertising Prohibition Act*. More than 20 years later Australia again led the world when the Federal Health Minister, Nicola Roxon, introduced national legislation for plain packaging of cigarettes.

TOBACCO, ALCOHOL AND OTHER DRUGS

Signing the Commonwealth-State Medicare Agreement, January 1984.

CHAPTER FOURTEEN

Medicare

Designed to ensure that health care was available to everyone based on their need, not their ability to pay, Medicare was a major election commitment of federal Labor in the March 1983 election campaign. The policy was an important part of the Prices and Incomes Accord which had been negotiated with the Australian Council of Trade Unions and became law on 1 February 1984, just 11 months after Labor was elected to office.

Medicare provided universal health insurance cover and made fundamental changes to the funding and delivery of health care. Every Australian citizen was eligible for treatment as a public patient in the public hospital system free of charge and had access to primary health care at little or no cost. It was funded by a fair (progressive) tax system, supplemented by a Medicare levy. Public and private delivery of hospital care coexisted and health insurance continued to be available for those who opted to use the private hospital system and pay the private health insurers' premiums.

As Stephen Leeder has pointed out, it was much more than just a reorganisation of the funding and administration of the health system:

> It not only changed the way we pay for health care but challenged us to think about why as a society we provide health care and to whom – the equity question. We found ourselves thinking about health risk not only to us as individuals but as communities, the divide between private and public payment, what it is reasonable to expect from the health care system, our ideas about universality of benefits and payments, and much more besides.[25]

THE STATES HAD LITTLE DIRECT INPUT into the design of Medicare but played a central role in its implementation. The administration and management of the public hospital system was their responsibility and the cost sharing arrangements between the commonwealth and the states to fund those hospitals were set out in the Commonwealth-State Medicare Agreements. Doctors treating public patients in public hospitals were to be paid on a salaried or sessional basis. All other services provided by doctors, whether in hospital or in their private practices, would continue to be provided on a fee-for-service basis. Accordingly the Commonwealth developed the Medical Benefits Schedule (MBS), a comprehensive schedule of medical and surgical procedures and the patient rebates that they would attract. These rebates were provided to patients, at 85 per cent of the scheduled fee, for consultations and treatment services by GPs and specialists. Doctors had the option of bulk billing, sending their accounts directly to Medicare 'in bulk' and accepting the rebates for the scheduled fee in full payment.

Within this framework visiting specialists and salaried specialist staff had the right to treat and charge private patients in public hospitals. However, the contractual obligations which they were being asked to meet as a condition for payment of those services quickly emerged as a major area of contention. To contain costs the federal government had amended section 17 of the *Health Insurance Act* to compel doctors to charge those private patients fees at or below the MBS. Acting in accordance with the Commonwealth-State Medicare Agreement the South Australian Health Commission therefore instructed the chief executive officers in our public hospitals to send so-called section 17 contracts to specialists who treated private patients in their hospitals. The letters accompanying the contracts were to inform them that 'visiting medical specialists who wish to continue rights of private practice in or for patients of the hospital are to sign the relevant private practice agreement(s) and return them to the hospital before 29 February 1984'.

Not surprisingly the medical profession was angered and alarmed by what they saw as de facto price control. This became a central issue in the doctors' fight against Medicare and fuelled a bitter national dispute. The resistance was especially fierce in New South Wales where Premier Neville Wran and Health Minister Laurie Brereton conducted a very public and acrimonious battle with the Australian Medical Association (AMA) and the more radical specialists' groups. As the dispute in New South Wales escalated doctors began threatening to withdraw their services from the public hospital system and it became increasingly likely that those in the other states would follow.

I became deeply concerned about this possibility after seeing a copy of a letter sent to an Adelaide Radiologist from the national office of the Royal Australian College of Radiologists. It advised members to return their unsigned contracts to their hospitals with a letter explaining that signing it would be a tacit recognition of the federal minister's power to unilaterally impose conditions under section 17. The College recommended that members inform their hospitals that the contract contained unacceptable proposals and that 'the whole matter is not yet mutually agreed and resolved'. The letter further recommended that the radiologists ask hospital management whether the current agreement concerning the right to private practice would remain unchanged in the event that the contract was not signed. It concluded:

> Hopefully a negative answer to that last request would provide the excuse to no longer attend or to work to rules.... None of our medical organisations can out talk or out manoeuvre the dedicated full-time opposition. The only power we have is the provision of services.

This incitement to industrial action was by no means confined to the radiologists. Members of other medical and surgical specialist groups and associations, including the Australian College of Orthopaedic Surgeons and the Australian Society of Orthopaedic Surgeons (ASOS), were also threatening to withdraw from or restrict their services in the public hospital system.

By the beginning of the third week of February it was becoming clear to the state and federal governments that the contracts would have to be put on hold during further negotiations between the AMA and the federal minister. To facilitate these negotiations the Health Minister, Neal Blewett, appointed Professor David Pennington on Wednesday 22 February to chair an inquiry into the issues involved in the dispute. Two days later, acting on advice we received from Minister Blewett's office, the Health Commission directed Adelaide's public hospitals and our hospitals in regional South Australia to recall the contracts and ask the doctors to provide a 'letter of intent' as an interim measure. This was to indicate that the doctors agreed to charge the MBS fees pending the outcome of the Pennington Inquiry and a negotiated agreement between the federal minister and the AMA. I was optimistic that the immediate threat of industrial action had been averted.

Two weeks earlier Minister Blewett had asked his counterparts in the four state Labor governments to examine contingency plans or sanctions that might be available to them to force the doctors' compliance in the event that ongoing negotiations ultimately failed to resolve the dispute. The Policy and Projects Division of the South Australian Health Commission came up with a deceptively simple solution. Their advice was that if mediation and conciliation failed, the private patients of non-complying doctors in South Australia's public hospitals could be reclassified by hospital management as public patients under the regulation making powers of South Australia's *Health Commission Act*. The specialists would then forfeit entitlement to payment of a private fee: as a public patient the individual would receive both hospitalisation and treatment by the doctor free of charge.

I held a joint press conference with Dr Blewett on Friday 24 February to update the public about the doctors' dispute and the interim arrangements we had made, based on our request for a letter of intent from the doctors and Professor Pennington's inquiry. As the reclassification strategy had not yet received cabinet approval I simply foreshadowed it in very general outline but *The Advertiser* on Saturday morning labelled it as our 'secret strategy'.

On Monday 27 February, three days after Dr Blewett and I met the Adelaide media, cabinet endorsed the 'secret strategy'. The next day I called a press conference for 3.00 pm in the media room on the second floor at Parliament House to release the details of what could be a last resort for South Australia if Professor Pennington's recommendations failed to provide a basis for resolution of the impasse. By this time the doctors' dispute with the federal government was dominating the national headlines and television news bulletins around the country and media interest was intense. During a light lunch I 'rehearsed' the conference with personal staff and shortly before 2.00 pm I asked to see Ian Bidmeade, the Commission's legal officer. I wanted to go through the details with him so that I could handle any questions journalists might raise about the relevant sections of the *Health Commission Act*. To my horror he informed me that he had not been consulted when the strategy was devised and his legal advice, just confirmed by the Crown Solicitor, was that reclassification of patients, as proposed by the Policy and Projects Division, was not possible under the regulation making powers of the Act. The strategy had collapsed less than 30 minutes before the scheduled time of the press conference.

Cancelling it was not a political option. The press release to be handed out to the waiting media was shredded. I decided to meet the media pack, summarise the current state of play and appeal to South Australian doctors to sign the simple letter of intent as an interim measure to avoid disruption to our hospital services. I would use the letter to its members from the Royal Australian College of Radiologists to illustrate how serious the situation was and that I was seeking further advice about our legal options should we be forced to consider a patient reclassification strategy.

Just as I was about to leave for the short drive to Parliament House an officer at the Health Commission brought a copy of a letter to my office that had been written to five public patients in the Murray Bridge area by Dr Peter Humble, an Adelaide orthopaedic surgeon. In the letter Dr Humble, who was a visiting surgeon at the local hospital, informed them that he had cancelled their surgery 'due to government interference who (sic) expect me to sign a contract'. The letter was received on Monday 27 February, giving them just four days notice. He suggested that they arrange their transfer to an elective surgery list at an Adelaide public hospital and that the waiting time for their procedures would be an estimated six months.

Dr Humble had received a section 17 contract in the same week that hospitals were being advised to replace them with the letters of intent. He responded by cancelling the surgery for five of his public patients and became the first (and to the best of my now distant recollection the only) doctor in South Australia to withdraw his or her services.

Without the benefit of a press release, my opening statement to the press conference was completely off-the-cuff. I reiterated what Dr Blewett and I had announced four days earlier: as part of the interim arrangements no patient in South Australia would be denied admission to any public or recognised hospital or access to their doctor and no visiting doctor would be refused access to any of their patients in any of our hospitals. Doctors were being asked to provide a simple letter of intent to their hospital CEOs stating that they would charge the scheduled fee for private patients until Professor Pennington had completed his report and an agreement had been negotiated between the federal Health Minister and the AMA. I added that 'in the event that these [letters of intent] are not forthcoming a situation could arise where private patients would not be able to claim Medicare refunds [for their treatment]'.

The arrangements were to apply to all doctors previously asked to sign the formal contracts which had been sent out by the hospitals. I used the Humble letter to demonstrate my concern that patients should not be used as pawns in the dispute and used the letter from the College of Radiologists to illustrate my anxiety about Eastern States intervention in South Australia. Rick Burnett, a television news journalist, then led the media pack aggressively through a heated press conference during which I was under intense pressure and became visibly riled. The television news services that evening confirmed my fear that the press conference had not been the high point of my political career. But much more damaging was *The Advertiser*'s report the next morning which was virtually replicated in *The News*, at that time still Adelaide's afternoon tabloid, the same day.

I had been asked about doctors' fees and charges and the proposal in the section 17 contracts to remove the right of specialists treating private patients in public hospitals to set their own fees. This was a critical issue in the dispute. In the Eastern States allegations of excessive fees and overservicing had been a hot political issue in the debate leading up to the introduction of Medicare and were the rationale behind the section 17 contracts. In my response I referred to those specialists who charged their patients excessive fees (and were among those leading the charge interstate to defend their right to do so) as 'robber barons holding the nation to ransom'. However, *The Advertiser* reported that I had referred specifically to Dr Humble as a robber baron. The article further stated that I had called him a liar. What I had said was that any suggestion that we were forcing non-complying doctors out of public hospitals was 'a lie'. It was also reported that I had called Dr Humble a 'scurrilous fool', of which I had no recollection.

I had borrowed the expression 'robber baron' from a visiting American physician who had used it in a lecture delivered in Adelaide the previous year. Lamenting the ethics and behaviour of some high profile surgeons in the United States, he described them as 'the robber barons of the second half of the 20th century'. It was in the context of those specialists who charged exorbitant fees that I used the expression 'robber barons', the plural reflecting its intended application to this group generically and not to any particular individual. Prior to receipt of the letter I had never heard of Dr Humble and had no idea of his status within his specialty or the medical profession generally.

I knew that I had to obtain a correction and apology from the newspapers as a matter of urgency, with a full retraction which recognised that the respective reports were simply unfounded. My press secretary obtained a tape recording made by John Stanton, a reporter from *The Australian* who had been at the press conference. We listened to it carefully with senior members of my ministerial staff and felt confident that, despite some inevitable background noise on the tape and some indecipherable words as several journalists talked over each other jostling to ask questions, the recording would be sufficient to rebut *The Advertiser*'s report. A full transcript of the recording was also made and was checked thoroughly as to its accuracy. It confirmed my recollection that I had not called Dr Humble 'a liar', a 'scurrilous fool' or a 'robber baron'.

However, I suspected that the newspaper reports were defamatory as to what they claimed I had said about Dr Humble and there was a real possibility that he might consider legal action. Anxious to obtain advice about this, I spoke to my colleague Attorney-General Chris Sumner who recommended the industrial law firm Stanley and Partners, where he had previously worked as a solicitor. Eventually I would realise, far too late, that being represented by an industrial law firm rather than one with in-house expertise in defamation and media law (as Dr Humble had done) was akin to seeking advice from a dermatologist about coronary artery disease.

I contacted Stanley and Partners immediately and instructed them to write to *The Advertiser* on my behalf strenuously denying that I had called Dr Humble a 'scurrilous fool' and 'a liar'. The newspaper was requested to publish 'a full and complete' retraction and an apology in its next edition. Acting on my lawyer's advice I also sent a letter to Dr Humble, drafted for me by my solicitors. I said I was writing to him to correct the inaccuracies appearing in *The Advertiser* and *The News* articles in which it was reported that at the news conference held the previous day 'I called or referred to you as a 'liar' and a 'scurrilous fool'. It advised him that a reporter's tape recording of the proceedings confirmed that this was not the case and that I could only explain the words attributed to me as 'incorrectly reported'.

A week after the offending newspaper article had appeared *The Advertiser* published a retraction which acknowledged that I had not used the phrase 'a liar' but nothing more. I made a further request to both newspapers the following day to publish the full retraction and apology I had originally sought. *The News* responded several days later indicating that they would have but were no longer able to: they had since been advised by Dr Humble's solicitors that he was bringing a defamation action against the newspaper. As my solicitors explained to me, to do so might be considered an admission of liability by the paper. I received a similar letter at the same time informing me that Dr Humble would be bringing defamation proceedings against me concerning 'remarks reported to have been made' by me at the press conference. The letter was dated 13 March 1984, just two weeks after the press conference.

The Pennington inquiry's interim report in June 1984 found (among other things) that there was little evidence of over-servicing in public hospitals; supported the right of doctors to charge more than the scheduled fee for clinical services under certain conditions; and that doctors should have an important say in the administration of public hospitals. In South Australia this was seen as a victory for the doctors and a major step towards resolution of the dispute. As I had no more correspondence from Dr Humble's solicitors I assumed he was not pursuing further action in the matter. Then in December, nine months after the press conference, a letter was received from them demanding that I make an apology using the text they had drafted. My solicitors wrote to advise me of the demand, noting how surprised they were by this development so long after the event and concluded 'we presume that you are not prepared to make the statement requested'. I took this as virtual advice and so did not pursue the matter with them.

I cannot recall the wording of the proposed apology but presumably my solicitors considered the contents to be highly prejudicial to me and dismissed the demand as being part of some strategy to revive the issue. When they responded to Dr Humble's solicitors they queried the current status of the matters raised in the text of the prepared apology. They pointed out that Dr Humble 'had long since resumed surgery at the Murray Bridge Hospital' and as such they considered the matter had been resolved for some time. A month later when nothing further had been heard my solicitors interpreted it as an encouraging sign.

In the meantime the Medicare dispute had dragged on in New South Wales with the Australian Society of Orthopaedic Surgeons accusing the AMA of taking 'too soft a line'.[26] In January 1985 there was a meeting between Prime Minister Hawke, Minister Blewett, NSW Premier Neville Wran, ASOS representatives, the federal AMA and its state branches. Dr Blewett would later describe the offer made to the doctors at the meeting as 'a fairly abject surrender.' Following the meeting it became clear to other parties that further negotiations with ASOS would be pointless. The dispute was finally resolved in February 1985 when Bob Hawke, Neal Blewett, Neville Wran and the Federal President of the AMA, Lindsay Thompson, negotiated an agreement which was subsequently supported by 80 per cent of the AMA membership.

It was to be more than 12 months before I heard anything further about the matter. Immersed in the 70 to 80 hour working weeks involved in my portfolio responsibilities, I gave the matter little further thought until my solicitors informed me of their discussions with the other seven defendants from Adelaide's news media about a joint settlement proposal. Dr Humble subsequently settled with them for a total of $55,000 plus legal costs. However, he refused to even enter into settlement discussions with me, intent on having the matter go to court. Two years later, in December 1987, my solicitors confirmed that there was 'no prospect of Dr Humble agreeing to accept any reasonable amount in settlement of this action'.

Although we were headed for court, my solicitors were confident that Dr Humble would be unable to establish that I had described him as 'a liar' and a 'scurrilous fool'. Their assessment was that I had reasonable prospects of success in mounting a defence of fair comment as to the making of certain remarks on a matter of public interest. The only real concern they expressed was in relation to my description of Dr Humble's letter as 'a lie' and the contested reference to him as 'a robber baron'. In their opinion there was 'a definite chance' that I would be found liable. However, I took comfort from their view as to the amount of damages I would be faced with in this event. 'We suspect', they wrote, 'that in all the circumstances the damages awarded against you would be modest, perhaps not more than $5,000' and 'a portion of Dr Humble's legal costs of perhaps $3,000'. This was an amount I could manage to pay personally.

Cabinet had previously indemnified me for 'a reasonable out of court settlement and costs' but this had not yet been revisited when the matter was listed for hearing in the District Court on 13 June 1988. It was not until the morning I was due in court that the Premier took me aside after an Executive Council meeting and made it clear that the indemnity no longer applied. My only substantial asset was the family home so I had to hope that my solicitors would be proved right.

Entering the Supreme Court Building with Brian Martin QC, June 1988.

CHAPTER FIFTEEN

Dismissal

On 2 August 1988, four and a half years after the press conference, Acting Judge Bowen Pain in the District Court found that I had defamed Dr Humble's character; that I had referred to him as a 'scurrilous fool', 'bloody minded', 'a wild man', 'a robber baron holding the people of South Australia and the people of the nation to ransom' and 'totally irresponsible'. He further found that I had done so with malicious intent. The four legal precedents upon which he relied in finding my words were defamatory were English cases decided before 1840.

He rejected the defence of qualified privilege based on his extraordinary finding that the withdrawal of services by Dr Humble was 'entirely independent' of the other matters raised in the press conference. He found that they merely involved 'the cancellation of one operating schedule at the Murray Bridge Hospital'. There was 'no way in which it can be suggested', according to Bowen Pain, 'that the South Australian public had any interest in being told about Dr Humble's action or my statements in relation to this'. Any interest 'was confined to the five patients that Humble had written to'.

This was in the middle of a major national dispute in which doctors in the eastern states were already beginning to withdraw from or limit their services, with the potential to cause widespread disruption to public hospitals. Dr Humble had become the first specialist in South Australia to follow them and, based on the evidence he provided to the court, other orthopaedic surgeons visiting the Murray Bridge Hospital were intending to do the same. But Bowen Pain simply ignored or failed to grasp that this was the context within which Dr Humble had acted.

As to my defence of fair comment, that also failed. In his opinion, the only words I spoke that constituted comment were in my response after reading out Dr Humble's letter. Having advised the patients that he had cancelled their operations just four days before they were scheduled, he had informed them that they would now have to join the six month waiting list at another public hospital for the procedure. I said 'I don't think that is good enough and it's totally irresponsible'. However, Bowen Pain found that no fair-minded person would have formed that opinion.

The Acting Judge also considered that Dr Humble 'had been more deeply hurt by these events than could ever be adequately compensated by an award of damages'. But he made a valiant attempt. The amount that he considered might provide some solace and comfort to Dr Humble was $80,000, the largest amount ever previously awarded by the South Australian District Court in a defamation matter. It included exemplary (punitive) damages as he was of the view that my conduct warranted additional punishment. It was at that time one of the rare occasions on which a punitive component had been awarded in a defamation action in South Australia. When added to the $70,000 awarded to him in legal costs, the total bill was $150,000, about the median price of a family home in Adelaide in 1988.

It is clear from the judgment that the Acting Judge had taken it upon himself to rectify what he considered to be the low quantum of damages awarded in defamation actions in South Australia compared to the rest of the country. Accordingly, the amount was closer to the range awarded in bodily injury claims. Given the tenor of his judgment generally it was perhaps fortunate that Bowen Pain was constrained by the legal requirement to take account of the $55,000 already received from the media outlets and the jurisdictional limit of $100,000 imposed on South Australia's District Court in the 1980s.

Six weeks after the judgment was handed down the distinguished Australian human rights lawyer Geoffrey Robertson QC commented on it during a lecture on freedom of speech and defamation law reform at Flinders University. *Humble v Cornwall* was not 'some arcane history' he said but a recent decision of the South Australian District Court. According to Robertson it demonstrated just how outdated Australia's defamation laws were, based on a costly and ineffective remedy entailing a long and expensive trial several years later and available only to those with the means to pursue an action.

The idea of awarding large sums of money to remedy a damaged reputation was, he argued, a legal relic of the class system of nineteenth century England 'when social and political life was lived in the gentlemen's clubs and in Pall Mall, when escutcheons could be blotted and society scandals resolved by issuing writs for slander'. The leading cases that shaped the present law in defamation were decided at a time when 'it was a dreadful libel' to allege that someone had been cheating at cards or had 'shot at a fox rather than [having done] the decent thing and hunted it down with hounds'.

Robertson referred to the 'great exhumation of case law used in *Humble v Cornwall* to remove any defence of fair comment from adjectives like bloody minded, wild men or robber barons, even though it was 'the sort of language which is freely bandied about by both sides when politicians and doctors collide in other states and other countries'. This was in part a reference to the very public and acrimonious war that had broken out in New South Wales following Medicare's introduction in 1984 when members of the Wran Labor Government had levelled far more direct and explicit language at those doctors who were withdrawing their services.

He proposed a form of public correction as a more timely, meaningful and equitable remedy. This, he argued, would sufficiently redress any harm to an individual's reputation from falsehoods while not interfering with a person's fundamental right to express an opinion. The uniform defamation laws introduced in all the States and Territories in 2006 went some way towards achieving this balance. They included clear provisions for settlement of matters to avoid unnecessary litigation, a limitation period of 12 months for the commencement of proceedings and a cap on damages. The outcome of *Humble v Cornwall* would have been quite different had they applied at the time.

The archaic defamation law was not my only problem. I believe Bowen Pain displayed a pervasive bias and partiality throughout his judgment. He was excessive and unrelenting in his attack on my character and made no attempt to conceal his disdain for me. For example, the letter drafted by my solicitors which I sent to Dr Humble in the days following publication of *The Advertiser*'s report was described as 'arrogant and deceitful'. He said it indicated that I was 'in no way contrite' for what I had said at the press conference. The Acting Judge would have known that I had acted at all times on the advice of my solicitors, not in the wilful manner he suggested.

He found my demeanour to be contemptuous, stating that I had displayed 'an arrogant, deceitful and unrelenting attitude' and had shown 'little or no contrition' for my actions at the press conference. 'When pushed into a position where even he had to concede that he had erred', he continued, 'the defendant gave some limited apologies and retracted certain positions of the statements which he had made'. But I had done so, he wrote, 'without any apparent goodwill' and only because I felt I 'had no alternative.' He made much of the fact that at no time prior to the hearing had I offered an apology or a retraction 'in any form'. Other than the letter of apology drafted by Dr Humble's solicitors which I declined to sign on the advice of my solicitors, my legal team had never raised the matter of an apology with me. Had I known it was an option at any time following the press conference to keep the matter out of court I would have given it very serious consideration. It would then have been seen in perspective - a public apology for intemperate remarks about doctors who were leading the bitter opposition to section 17 contracts.

As for my evidence, Bowen Pain dismissed it variously as self-serving, unreliable or simply just false. He described me as a 'most unimpressive witness' and the manner in which I had given evidence as 'unsatisfactory', 'evasive', 'non-responsive' and 'defensive'. He said I had been 'guilty of prevarication' in answering questions and had used my appearance in the witness box as a forum to 'further [my] political ends by making political statements at every opportunity'. Accordingly, my evidence 'ought not to be accepted' and 'in some respects not believed' without being corroborated by an independent witness.

The reality was that in the unfamiliar and hostile court environment I had no real idea what to expect, even the type of questions I might be asked or the manner in which I should frame my responses. My experience of the courts was confined to television court room dramas. I may have rambled in response to questions posed by counsel for the plaintiff but I had spent the previous six years facing question time in the adversarial environment of the South Australian Parliament where I had been conditioned to give answers designed to cover all contingencies. Statements might otherwise be misconstrued by opponents and journalists to fit their own slant - the 'gotcha' syndrome.

Moreover, a last minute change of barristers was unhelpful. Over some weeks prior to the trial I had several meetings with the senior barrister who had accepted the brief for my defence. However, he was called to a case in the Supreme Court just days before my trial began. Brian Martin who replaced him at short notice came with an excellent reputation. He was later to become a Judge of the South Australian Supreme Court and Chief Justice of the Northern Territory Supreme Court. But he was faced with the daunting task of having to absorb the complex brief in a matter of days.

At no time did I give anything other than what I believed to be considered, detailed and truthful answers to questions put to me or knowingly engage in the political grandstanding of which I was accused. As far as I was concerned it was essential that the court be made aware of the anxiety and concern I felt in 1984 at the prospect of industrial action in the public hospital system and the impact that would have on patients. I attempted to convey to the court the genuine distress I felt on learning, minutes before the press conference began, that Dr Humble had withdrawn his services from patients at the Murray Bridge hospital. I viewed this development with alarm. It went against the spirit of the 'ceasefire' that had been put in place - the withdrawal of the section 17 contracts pending the Pennington Report and recommendations - and presaged the possibility that other surgeons in South Australia would follow Dr Humble's example.

It was on this issue that I think Bowen Pain provided an astonishing illustration of making the evidence fit the crime. At page 25 of the judgment he wrote:

> The only evidence which we have in relation to the proposition that as at 27 February 1984, when Mr Humble wrote and posted his letters to the patients, there was no longer any requirement that he should sign the contract, is the evidence of Dr Cornwall. He stated, not once but several times, that this decision had been made towards the end of the previous week. There is no support for that suggestion in any of the press reports or in the behaviour of the persons, other than Dr Cornwall, involved in this matter. This was the least convincing part of his evidence.

This was totally at odds with the facts which were clearly on the public record. It was during the week prior to the press conference that Federal Health Minister Blewett appointed Professor David Pennington to chair an inquiry into the issues involved in the dispute and section 17 contracts were put on hold pending the outcome of further negotiations between the Australian Medical Association (AMA) and the federal government. This initiative received national news coverage and the details were repeated for South Australians when Dr Blewett and I held the joint press conference in Adelaide on Friday 24 February.

Furthermore Bowen Pain's account of what led Dr Humble to withdraw his services reinforced the impression that the Acting Judge was quite confused (or worse) about the sequence of events leading to the introduction of Medicare. He wrote:

> During the course of 1983 it would seem that the administration of the Murray Bridge Hospital was approaching patients who had private cover and persuading them to be admitted as public patients. This practice caused Dr Humble concern that this may be an early indication of nationalisation of medical treatment.

These events could not have taken place during 1983 as Medicare was not introduced until 1 February 1984. Throughout 1983 the public hospital system continued to operate under the 'Fifth Fraser Scheme'. Patients who did not qualify for a means tested Health Benefit Card or an age or invalid pension were all billed by their hospital. As more than 10 per cent simply could not afford private health insurance or had decided to 'chance their arm', debt collection was a growth industry. Even after February 1984 there was no incentive to persuade privately insured patients to be admitted as public patients, quite the opposite. In the event they were admitted as private patients their private health insurer's rebates provided a financial benefit to the hospital. In addition, Bowen Pain's apparent acceptance of the legitimacy of Dr Humble's action, based on his assertion that the federal government was seeking to nationalise the health system, revealed the Acting Judge's fundamental misunderstanding as to how Medicare worked: a taxpayer funded universal health insurance scheme which preserved fee for service practice.

The character assassination in Bowen Pain's judgment, including that I was 'not to be believed' and, by implication, unfit to hold public office, left me in a state of shock and disbelief. He had set out to shred my integrity and professional reputation and left me fighting, unsuccessfully as it transpired, for my political career.

Premier Bannon was in Canberra on the morning the judgment was handed down. I expected him to phone me personally to express his dismay at the judgment's severity and begin a discussion about strategies we might consider to counter the immediate political damage. Instead, he simply instructed a member of his staff to call me later in the day to tell me that his boss was 'very concerned', clearly not a reference to my welfare.

When he flew into Adelaide the next day Bannon conducted a 'door stop' with the waiting media at the airport. In view of the malign ferocity of the judgment I anticipated that he would refrain from making any comment other than he wanted to give further consideration to the matter and would be meeting with me immediately to discuss a measured response. In the wake of the press conference in 1984 the Premier had been publicly supportive of me.[27] On this occasion, however, that support was not forthcoming. After making a series of complimentary remarks about my performance in the health portfolio (which sounded ominously like a political eulogy) he proceeded to distance himself from me. It was not for him 'to debate the legal principles or the judge's finding', he told the media pack. However, 'they do raise serious implications which will have to be considered'. It was becoming clear that he already had a preferred 'surgical option'.

I felt battered by the extraordinary hostility of Bowen Pain's judgment and now faced the real prospect that the Premier seemed to be considering me as a disposable asset. The continuous public support I had given him ever since caucus installed him as leader after the 1979 state election debacle did not appear to be part of the equation.

John Bannon did not speak to me either personally or by phone prior to our formal meeting at 11.00 am the following day. When we met he offered no words of commiseration or otherwise: he simply asked for my resignation. When I refused to resign on those terms he proposed that I stand aside pending the outcome of an appeal to the Supreme Court. But he gave me no undertakings about my political future, contingent on that outcome, and he made no commitment to covering the government's payment of the damages and court costs. I asked him to refer the matter to the full cabinet for consideration. The first option I canvassed was that I immediately announce an appeal to the Supreme Court and decline to comment until the appeal had been heard. The second was that he appoint an acting health minister while I stood aside, my future in either case pending the outcome of the Supreme Court appeal. His option was that I should simply resign, effectively sacked. Bannon agreed to refer the matter to cabinet but insisted that I should absent myself from the discussion. Denying me the opportunity to attend that cabinet meeting to canvass options with my colleagues and seek their support virtually ensured that his opinion would prevail.

The next morning I had to wait in the foyer adjacent to the cabinet room with the assembled journalists and television crews while my colleagues decided my fate. I met the Premier when cabinet adjourned and he simply told me that the government would indemnify me, including the cost of an appeal subject to my 'voluntary' resignation. As accepting personal liability for the legal costs and damages would require relinquishing the family home resignation was my only option. The question of indemnity, of course, should have been a given rather than a bargaining chip. In an editorial published on 3 August, the day before I announced my forced resignation, *The News* posed the following question: 'Is it fair that someone should be personally pauperised in such circumstances?' As it noted, 'most authors, broadcasters and journalists would be appalled at the thought of such strict accountability.'

In an otherwise cautious administration dedicated to keeping politics off the front page I had always been a source of discomfort for John Bannon. I served my political apprenticeship in the 1970s, a decade of innovation and reform under Don Dunstan's leadership. Bannon, on the other hand, was always cautious about pushing the boundaries of reform. As the *Sunday Mail*'s political correspondent Randall Ashbourne observed, in a cabinet of conservatives I 'did not fit'.[28]

I submitted my resignation that afternoon and announced it to a packed media conference with an unscripted statement:

> It's a very high, a very heavy price to pay. It is no secret that I have enormous affection for the health and welfare portfolios and I have

been the principal architect of the government's social justice strategy, the practical effects of which will begin to be seen in the next state budget. I have also been chairman of cabinet's human services committee. In those positions I believe I have been able to work with my cabinet colleagues to make a significant contribution to improving the quality of life of the people I am most concerned about, the 'ordinary' battlers. As I have said so often, I see the definition of social justice as being a very simple one. It's about a fair go and a fair share for everybody.

For the first time in more than nine years, in opposition and in government, I moved to the back bench. A little more than two months later, having seriously considered my future and my family, I decided I had had enough. Towards the end of October I announced that I would be resigning from the Legislative Council early in 1989 to seek a future outside politics.

I was deeply touched by the hundreds of spontaneous expressions of support I received, many offered immediately in the twenty four hours prior to my resignation, others in the days and weeks that followed. David Mercer, Chairman of the South Australian Public Service Board, sent me a hand written letter in which he wrote that 'I begrudge the loss to the community of your badly needed and rare administrative talents'. Many others came from the professional people with whom I had dealt in the health portfolio, including the Deans of the Medical Faculties at Adelaide and Flinders Universities, senior members in many disciplines across the medical spectrum and the allied health professions, hospital boards, professional registration boards, the Guardianship Board, the Mental Health Tribunal and the Community Health Association. I also received many from the government sector generally, from senior public servants in departments ranging from Education to Juvenile Justice. My detractors, of course, were smug in what they saw as a victory. The AMA's State President expressed his considerable satisfaction with my resignation and, in an unedifying display of triumphalism, the President of the South Australian Branch of the Australian Society of Orthopaedic Surgeons demanded that I apologise to every orthopaedic surgeon in the state.

I lost count of the hundreds of letters, faxes and phone calls from people in the wider community, including committed Liberal voters, who expressed their outrage at my demise. One that I particularly appreciated was from a Lutheran minister on the Yorke Peninsula who wrote to me offering his sympathy and support. He identified himself as a committed conservative voter but told me that when my name had come up at a recent meeting with his congregation there was a general view that I had been treated very unfairly. The other heartening aspect was the way I was offered spontaneous goodwill from passing strangers on Adelaide's streets. Less sensitive in the wake of the resignation was the response from the Premier's office. He had his staff send me the names and addresses of the 130 constituents (of 900,000 on the state electoral roll) who had written to him opposing the payment of my bill for damages and costs.

The appeal against the judgment had been lodged with the South Australian Supreme Court soon after my resignation but as the weeks passed I was troubled by the prospect of being subjected again to the vagaries of the defamation law. In the event that the Supreme Court failed to set aside or significantly ameliorate the judgment it would reinforce the damage to my reputation wrought by Bowen Pain. The judgment had already cost me my political career so I was increasingly inclined not to be involved in what I had come to see as little more than a game of chance. I had little understanding of the legal or evidentiary grounds of the appeal so even less about the chances of a success. My only recollection of any contact with my barrister is when he rang me with the very bad news on the morning the judgment was released and advised me not to make any public comment. As far as I recall there was no subsequent conference with my legal team to go through the judgment with them.

It seems that even Dr Humble and his legal advisers may have been surprised by the harshness of the judgment. My solicitor rang me on 4 December, a week before my appeal was due to be heard, to say there had been a tentative approach from Dr Humble's solicitors to accept a pre-appeal reduction in the amount of damages with the 'discounted' amount to be donated to charity. On the morning of the appeal his solicitors proposed that the original judgment be set aside to the extent that 'by consent' damages be reduced by $50,000 and the amount donated to the Bone and Joint Research Foundation. I accepted the offer in good faith, describing it to the chagrin of Dr Humble and his legal representatives as a 'gentlemen's agreement'. I then withdrew my appeal. No one had advised me that this had no effect on the judgment: it still stood.

As to allegations that I was at war with South Australia's orthopaedic surgeons in general, in negotiations for the 1988-89 State budget I had secured funding from the state and federal governments to endow a chair in orthopaedic surgery at the Adelaide University, located at the Royal Adelaide Hospital. At the same time more than $500,000 was allocated as a first step in establishing a national centre of excellence in joint replacement and research, hardly the actions of an aggressor.

NOW APPROACHING ITS THIRTY FOURTH anniversary, Medicare has the enthusiastic endorsement of the Australian people. It also enjoys the conditional but constructive support of the medical profession generally. Perhaps the most significant convert is the AMA, its office bearers now much more astute and rational than the spear carriers of a generation past. As a universal health insurance scheme, buttressing universal access to treatment services on the basis of need rather than ability to pay, it can fairly claim to be a world leader. The balance between public and private treatment services has long since reached a reasonable complementarity and claims that the system is too costly to survive come largely from right wing ideologues.

The long term sustainability of Medicare will not be achieved by freezing doctors' Medicare rebates, forcing them increasingly towards a user pays service that will ultimately strike at the heart of Medicare's universal cover. But it will require some amendments to take account of Australia's aging population. In their recent paper 'Chronic failure in primary care', Hal Swerissen and Stephen Duckett highlighted the fact that in 2016 three quarters of Australians over the age of 65 had at least one chronic condition that put them at risk of serious complications and premature death. They estimate that ineffective management of heart disease, asthma, diabetes and other chronic diseases 'costs the Australian health system more than $320 million each year in avoidable hospital admissions' and that 'each year there are more than a quarter of a million admissions to hospital for health problems that potentially could have been prevented'.[29]

While ensuring that the principle of Medicare's universal cover is not compromised, it will become increasingly important to develop a more efficient and cost effective way to deliver care for this cohort. Swerissen and Duckett propose a model that promotes social, economic and environmental changes as the best way to prevent these diseases in the longer term and make patients healthier for longer. They point out that the role of GPs is vital, that there are much better outcomes where good quality primary care services are in place but that to implement this model successfully 'the focus must move away from fee-for-service payments'.[30] This will be the next major challenge for governments, doctors and the health professions generally.

Media conference announcing resignation as Minister of Health and Community Welfare, 4 August 1988.

CHAPTER SIXTEEN

An enigmatic Premier

Close friends and family described him as lively, witty and animated in private but I was never in John Bannon's circle. Despite working with him on Labor's front bench for ten years, in opposition and government, he remained an enigma to me. I had many snapshots but no moving pictures. I had very early glimpses of the lively, animated Bannon, relaxing after a long day at a weekend seminar conducted by Young Labor, having a drink with comrades, mixing Gilbert and Sullivan with the *Internationale*, doing his favourite party routine as he mocked Herr Hitler's rants in fluent German. I have clear memories of Bannon almost 20 years later, the cautious Premier who was also Treasurer, lecturing cabinet on the need to shepherd the state's finances with care, the carousel on his projector always loaded with slides containing interminable statistics, bar charts and graphs to reinforce the need for austerity. Even at the annual cabinet planning retreat, held in February each year, the Premier spent most of the time on the state's budget rather than big picture policy issues. He did delegate discussions about coordination (between departments and portfolios) to cabinet committees, although on any contentious issue that came to cabinet his decision was rarely challenged. He consistently displayed what Mike Rann, his press secretary and *spinmeister* during his years as Leader of the Opposition and in his first term as Premier, called 'the courage to be cautious'.[31]

The 6 percent swing back to Labor in November 1982 was impressive and returned Labor to government with a three seat majority. But these were difficult times. There had been a worldwide double dip recession between 1980 and 1982 and the South Australian Treasury was coping with the aftermath of the disastrous Ash Wednesday bush fires that razed the state in February 1983. Ministers were advised that submissions brought to cabinet had to have a very modest price tag, identify savings from other areas in their budgets or access to program funding from their federal colleagues. Practical administration and sound financial management were the public face of government during this first term in office. John Bannon had captured the Spirit of South Australia and the marathon runner intended to be there for the long haul.

Bannon's political career had begun as an undergraduate at the Adelaide University. He was President of the Students Representative Council and the University Union and developed a national profile as President of the Australian Union of Students. He graduated with degrees in arts and law and was recruited to the South Australian Branch of the Australian Workers Union (AWU) as a research officer and industrial advocate. Clyde Cameron, the legendary AWU and Labor heavyweight, was an influential sponsor during this period and when Clyde became the Minister for Labour in the Whitlam Government in 1973 Bannon joined his ministerial staff as a senior policy advisor. Less than three years later he was Assistant Director of the South Australian Department of Labour and Industry and in 1977 was elected to the South Australian Parliament. Within a year Bannon was a minister in the Dunstan Labor Government, virtually anointed by Don Dunstan as a future leader. Following the defeat of the Corcoran Government in 1979 he was drafted to lead the Parliamentary Labor Party and within three years the clean cut 39 year old alumnus from St Peter's College led the Party back to government after just one term in opposition.

INDUSTRIAL DEVELOPMENT IN SOUTH AUSTRALIA after the Second World War was based principally on the motor vehicle industry and white goods production, built behind large tariff walls. This meant that from the 1970s, as successive federal governments dismantled that protection, South Australia was especially vulnerable to the evolving free markets in the global economy. Against this background the Premier's successful bid for the contract to build the Collins Class submarines and develop the related defence and high technology industries were important achievements. He was also a keen supporter of the Roxby Downs development, having played an important part in the Party's opposition to uranium mining being modified ('the Roxby Downs SA election clause') at the ALP's National Conference in July 1982. The relevant part of the lengthy amendment moved by Bob Hogg allowed Labor to consider the export of uranium mined incidentally to the mining of other minerals on a case-by-case basis (in this case copper). This enabled Bannon to pledge Labor's support for the Roxby Downs development in the lead up to the 1982 election.

The Premier gave his enthusiastic support to what was described as the crane led recovery. Deregulation of the financial system in 1983-84 was fuelling investment in property development, funded by superannuation funds and insurance companies and an influx of overseas banks. The lack of controls created a climate of unrestrained growth and speculative development that would eventually devastate South Australia's economy and much of Adelaide's built heritage.[32] However, what the public saw in December 1985 was a competent administration, balanced budgets and important achievements in school education and health which created the political climate for a further 2.3 per cent swing to the government at the state election.

With 29 of the 47 seats in the House of Assembly, a four year term and a stratospheric approval rating of 72 per cent I thought the Premier should use the authority the voters had given him to introduce some of the long term reform initiatives that required political courage. Against this background I sought advice from a senior economist in Treasury about the realistic options open to the government to implement its social justice commitment. His analysis reached two central conclusions: the provision of affordable housing was the most effective contribution a state government could make to reduce poverty and disadvantage and the most efficient and equitable means of securing additional finance for this would be a modest annual property tax. I believed we could promote it as a social justice levy, an equitable contribution based on the assessed market value of both residential and commercial properties. The money raised from the levy could be held in a community housing fund defined in legislation and used on a means and asset tested basis to augment the availability and affordability of housing for rental or purchase.

I took the idea to cabinet seeking approval in principle to develop a detailed proposal for further consideration. The idea of a levy, however equitable, was hardly likely to be universally popular in the first instance but given the Premier's standing in the community (and a seriously depleted opposition) I was confident we could manage the politics of a well crafted proposal. However, the Premier's initialled annotation on the submission was 'Return to Minister', usually a euphemism for submissions destined to disappear into the bottom drawer.

The other important aspect of the social justice strategy was the reallocation and coordination of resources within and across government agencies to promote access to community services. This was making limited progress but several departments were meeting notional targets by simply rebadging existing commitments rather than reallocation and in my assessment the strategy was in danger of stalling. I decided to float the idea of a social justice levy publicly to promote community discussion but I chose the wrong journalist and the wrong newspaper. The hostile beat up about 'the government's new tax grab' ran on the front page of *The News* which bucketed it in an editorial in the same issue. Self appointed voices of the state's taxpayers railed against it and radio's conservative talk back hosts bayed for blood. The Premier was so concerned to distance himself from the idea that he formally demanded (and received) a public retraction and apology from the Australian Broadcasting Corporation for even suggesting that he might consider the proposal.

As a Dunstan disciple it was always my view that progressive governments should try to lead public opinion and in matters of social justice should appeal to the better angels of our nature. Instead, in what had become a quest for perpetual popularity, the Premier was increasingly risk averse. The timidity grew to the extent that by early 1989, six months after my removal from cabinet, Adelaide journalists on state political rounds were beginning to run stories critical of what they perceived as a paralysis of government. An article in Adelaide's *Sunday Mail* in March 1989 was headed 'A tired government drifts on'.

This was reflected in deteriorating opinion polls and at the state election, held on 25 November that year, the government virtually stole re-election with only 48 per cent of the two party preferred vote. The result was Labor 22 seats, Independent Labor 2, Liberal 23. The government and opposition each had 23 seats on the floor of the parliament with the government relying on the casting vote of the Speaker. Ironically, the party of Don Dunstan who strived for so long to achieve electoral fairness had been returned by a de facto gerrymander - electorates distorted by population shifts between boundaries that had not been redrawn for more than four years.

THE STATE BANK OF SOUTH AUSTRALIA was established with some fanfare by legislation proclaimed in 1984. Described as the bank that 'had its heart in South Australia', it was created by merging the Savings Bank of South Australia with the State Bank and retaining the latter's name. But within seven years it had collapsed, forcing the government to commit $3.15 billion from the state's treasury under its legislated guarantee.

The history of the two banks is instructive. Sir Thomas Playford used financial support from both the Savings Bank and the State Bank to establish two of the state's most successful statutory authorities, the South Australian Electricity Trust and the South Australian Housing Trust. To further facilitate the role of the banks in fostering the state's development Don Dunstan floated the idea of a merger in the 1970s. However, the conservative trustees of the banks were strongly opposed to the idea and the matter rested there until Labor was returned to government in 1982.

The *State Bank of South Australia Act 1983 (SBSA Act)* reflected the Dunstan vision, enshrining an active role for government in the affairs of the bank. The legislation made it clear that the chairman, deputy chairman and directors of the Bank were to be appointed by cabinet. Further, the board was to enable 'true and fair accounts' of the bank to be prepared and have them 'conveniently and properly audited'. The Treasurer was to be given an annual report on the operations of the Bank and this, together with the audited accounts, were to be presented to both houses of parliament. Most significantly, as any liabilities of the bank were 'guaranteed by the Treasurer', the *SBSA Act* made it clear that the board was subject to 'the control and direction of the Treasurer'. How then did we reach a point where the Premier had to announce to a shocked South Australian public on Sunday 10 February 1991 that the state's taxpayers had to indemnify the Bank for losses of $970 million, a figure subsequently amended to $3.15 billion, the greatest financial disaster in the state's history?

Samuel Jacobs QC, a recently retired Supreme Court Judge, was appointed in March 1991 to conduct a Royal Commission with terms of reference to investigate the relationship between the Bank and the South

Australian Government and the arrangements under the *SBSA Act* for the governance of the bank. The Royal Commission was conducted over two years and produced three reports, published in 1992 and 1993, the first and second presented by Commissioner Jacobs while the final report was presented by John Mansfield QC when the Commissioner became ill.

In the first report Commissioner Jacobs rebutted the argument that commercial considerations meant that the bank operated at arm's length from the government. After examining the merger process and the provisions of the *SBSA Act* he found many clauses that conferred responsibility on the government to supervise the bank closely. He concluded that there was 'no reason to be found in the legislation why a commercially independent bank and a vigilant and well informed government cannot coexist'. He said that 'to describe the bank as "autonomous" is quite inconsistent with the tenor and purpose of the Act'.[33]

When considering the appointment of Tim Marcus Clark as the SBSA's chief executive, the board's chairman, Lew Barrett, had sought a background briefing from personnel consultants who cautioned that 'from time to time [he] needs a little bit of controlling but that can be supplied by the board'. They also reported that 'Clark has a very strong personality and he will quite often get his own way'. Clark demanded a place on the board as a precondition to his acceptance of the position which meant the appointment had to be formally endorsed by the Treasurer under the *SBSA Act*. Treasurer Bannon who, it seems, didn't see the consultant's warning met Marcus Clark on 30 November 1983 and recommended his appointment as managing director.[34]

'From the very beginning' the Commissioner's report said 'it was not properly understood that the government had a part to play in assessing the quality of its "investment" as owner, and the nature and extent of its potential liability as guarantor'. He also observed that the bank began its expansion overseas unquestioned. As he attempted to supercharge the institution and turn it into a major financial player Marcus Clark opened offices in London and New York. 'What is not acceptable' the Commissioner said 'is to observe the government in the comfort zone it had chosen by its policy of non-awareness'. He said 'the stated prospect of profit seems to have displaced or prevailed over any careful consideration of financial viability or the bank's charter'.

In 2009 Justice Jacobs, lucid and reflective in his 89th year, was interviewed by John Emerson for the South Australian Law Society's oral histories record.[35] Conventional wisdom in Australian politics is that you should never establish a Royal Commission unless you are reasonably confident of the outcome. However, the government underestimated Justice Jacobs. 'I think (members of) the government were a bit disappointed, I think they thought that a Royal Commissioner was going to come down on the government's side but they chose the wrong man'. He thought the Attorney-General Chris Sumner 'was disappointed that I didn't let the government off a little more easily'. In Justice Jacobs opinion John Bannon had 'complete trust in Marcus Clark and that was one of the problems'. He described Marcus Clark as a charismatic man who was very persuasive and said Bannon accepted his advice in preference to anyone else. He lamented the fact that the Treasurer did not have a stronger Under-Treasurer whom he described as very much a back room man without much political savvy. 'If he had thumped the table and been more emphatic, Bannon might have listened to him but he gave up advising Bannon because he took no notice of him'.

Justice Jacobs was also critical of the Reserve Bank. Although the State Bank was not subject to the oversight of the Reserve Bank as the trading banks were it nevertheless took an interest in its performance because it was seeking to operate in competition with them. 'The Reserve Bank knew how unwise some of its activities and procedures were, but it never alerted the Treasurer because it said it had nothing to do with the State'. He thought that was very wrong. 'If the Reserve Bank had gone to Bannon and said, look here, this bank is in trouble, Bannon might have taken a bit of notice, but they didn't do it'. Justice Jacobs said he found the board couldn't control Marcus Clark and in the end wanted to get rid of him but 'Bannon went to a board meeting, when they were going to terminate [his] appointment, and wouldn't let them do it'.

Marcus Clark was ultimately considered by the Commission to be more than any others legally responsible for the Bank's downfall but he nevertheless moved on without penalty. The second and third reports of the Royal Commission into the bank's collapse cleared John Bannon of any wrongdoing but as Justice Samuel Jacobs QC recalled in 2009: 'He knew as soon as the bank collapsed that his political career was at an end because he was the Treasurer and the buck stopped with him'.

Bannon resigned in September 1992, two months short of ten years as Premier of South Australia. The young man who had been destined for greatness in the Labor movement, identified by Don Dunstan as a future political prince, had become a political pariah. At the state election held 15 months later the government, led by the brave caretaker Premier Lynn Arnold, was overwhelmingly defeated, reduced to only 10 of the 47 seats in the House of Assembly.

THE CAREERS OF MANY HIGH profile politicians end in tears. The viability of parliamentary democracy is sustained by fluctuations in political fortune and changes of government. When Premier Bannon had to announce that the Bank had collapsed the responses varied across the spectrum from shock and disillusionment through anger to denial. Such was the size of the financial disaster that many lesser mortals might have resigned and retired to a life of seclusion. Michael Jacobs wrote at the time of his death in 2015 that John Bannon held on 'taking on all the blame and humiliation of the State Bank disaster without complaining about the injustice of it all'.[36] At the time of his resignation 23 years earlier others saw it from a quite different perspective. In *State of Denial*, published in 1993, Chris Kenny (at that time the political commentator for *The Adelaide Review*) wrote that politicians and the media sought to exonerate the Premier by interpreting the disaster as the 'result of a singularly devastating financial misadventure by executives at the bank'. South Australia' he said 'seems to be in a state of denial'.[37]

John Bannon never sought refuge in exile. After retiring from politics he completed a Doctorate in Australian political history at Flinders University. He was Master of St Mark's College at Adelaide University from 2000 to 2007 and an adjunct professor at the University's Law School. He was also a member of the Boards of the Australian Broadcasting Corporation and the South Australian Cricket Association and was appointed an Officer of the Order of Australia (AO) on Australia Day 2007.

When John Charles Bannon died in December 2015 after a harrowing eight year battle with cancer there was an outpouring of public grief and tributes. He was remembered as 'a man of fairness and foresight never to be forgotten'. *The Advertiser* reported that 'the legacy of John Bannon was evident in the love and respect shown by hundreds of mourners at his state funeral yesterday' and wrote of 'a man who had devoted his life to his people'. Mourners included former Prime Ministers Julia Gillard and Bob Hawke. In his tribute Hawke said that John Bannon 'would be remembered with affection and respect by the thousands of South Australians and the many who had the pleasure of working with him'. The Labor Party has a history of kindness to its fallen heroes.

Although I was a loyal colleague throughout his period as Opposition Leader and as Premier, we were never comfortable with each other. I was a radical reformer, impatient for change, challenging and confronting the system, practicing politics with passion. Bannon was the man for South Australia in the eighties, cautious and conservative, uniquely in tune with the state's free settler culture. He hated adversarial politics and saw the pursuit of perpetual popularity as a political imperative. Hence his reluctant support for some of my most important but controversial reforms in the health portfolio, including drug law reform, the ban on tobacco sponsorship of sport and the arts and the merger of the Queen Victoria and Adelaide Children's Hospitals. And his enthusiasm to clear me from his cabinet within 24 hours of Acting Judge Bowen Pain's judgment against me in *Humble v Cornwall*.

How can we reconcile this 'courage to be cautious' with the free rein given to Marcus Clark and to those whom Frank Blevins (appointed Treasurer when Bannon resigned) described as 'the bastards at the bank'? The original vision for the bank was to reinforce the traditional roles of support for families and small business, and to promote ambitious but prudent expansion of commerce and industry to a level from which there would be substantial profits returned to the state budget's bottom line. But when Marcus Clark captured John Bannon's imagination he raised the stakes to far greater heights - to finance enterprises 'off budget' nationally and internationally, to transform South Australia from a mendicant state into a financial hub with the best resourced community services and amenities in Australia. It was a grand but seriously delusional vision, truly a Greek tragedy in the city that Don Dunstan once described as the Athens of the South.

Holidaying with Patrice, Santorini, September 1991.

CHAPTER SEVENTEEN

Life after politics

Following what was effectively my summary dismissal I began to actively explore what I might do with the rest of my working life. I had been out of touch with important advances in veterinary medicine and surgery for a decade so I had neither the opportunity nor the motivation to return to practice. On the other hand I had gained a valuable insider's knowledge of the administration, management and small 'p' politics of the health sector during six years in the portfolio that could have served me well. There was a story circulating soon after my resignation that I was to be offered a management position in the Hawke Government's *Healthy Cities* program in Adelaide's southern suburbs but it was apparently vetoed by the Premier's office.

As a first step towards exploring the interstate market I lodged my curriculum vitae with three leading recruitment agencies and flew to Sydney to meet with them. They were helpful to the extent that they explained to me politely why I did not really fit in the corporate world. At the end of January 1989 I resigned from the Legislative Council and began a more targeted search for alternative employment. At the same time I decided to level the playing field a little by telling my side of the story, described by Hugh Stretton in the foreword of the book as 'an insider's account of South Australian politics, warts and all'. I completed the hand written draft of *Just for the Record* in five months, Wakefield Press agreed to publish it and my friend and colleague Neal Blewett launched the book in September.

From February through June I had applied unsuccessfully for several positions interstate. Then in early July, at the urging of some of my veterinary colleagues in Adelaide, I applied for the newly created position of National Veterinary Director of the Australian Veterinary Association (AVA), based in Sydney. The day after the shortlisted candidates were interviewed I was asked to start as soon as possible. On Sunday 27 August, as the notorious 1989 pilots' dispute worsened, Patrice and I flew to Sydney on one of the last flights out of Adelaide and I began work the following day.

The AVA board members, led by Dr Bob Kibble, were increasingly aware that some fundamental changes were needed in the Association. At the annual general meeting in May 1990, eight months after I was appointed as the veterinary director, I was upgraded to chief executive officer with a broad brief to examine virtually every aspect of the AVA's structure, management, culture and mission. At the same time Bob Kibble began his term as president and we replaced an elderly book keeper with Dan Hutchinson, a qualified accountant in his mid forties.

The Kibble-Cornwall partnership produced many important changes to the Association which are too numerous to detail in this memoir. At a personal level the two years as the AVA's CEO restored my confidence. I was back on top of my professional game, well satisfied with what we had been able to achieve as a team but I felt that it was a good time to move on, ostensibly to seek other challenges. Actually I was motivated by a desire to quit while I was in front, having decided that by virtue of its diverse membership and interests it was inevitable that the Association would always be a rather fractious animal. I left early in December 1991 with the AVA's Meritorious Service Award and an invitation to give a keynote address at the national conference in Adelaide in 1992.

THE AUSTRALIAN YOUTH FOUNDATION (AYF) was established in 1990 with a grant of $12.4 million, the surplus remaining when the Bicentennial Authority was wound up. Its mission was to help disadvantaged young Australians achieve their full potential. In March 1992, three months after I left the AVA, I had a chance meeting at Canberra Airport with Deidre Tedmanson, then deputy chair of the Foundation. Deidre was an old friend and an occasional adversary on policy issues in the forums of the South Australian Branch of the ALP. She asked me if I might be interested in taking a leadership role, working with the chair Brian Burdekin (at the time the high profile Human Rights Commissioner) and the board to ensure that the Foundation developed to meet its considerable potential. Within two months I was working at the AYF as the Executive Officer.

With a constitution that enshrined its autonomy and an assured income from its investments, the AYF was uniquely placed to act as an independent advocate for its constituency. To facilitate this the board decided early in 1993 that instead of simply receiving and considering random project submissions we should consult young people directly and listen to their stories and opinions about the support they believed they needed. Associate Professor Ann Daniel, Head of the Sociology School at the University of New South Wales, was contracted to design and supervise the project and I conducted the field work, speaking with 700 young Australians in focus groups in urban, regional, rural and remote communities. The opinions and aspirations of young people contained in our report *A Lost Generation?* were the pivot for the AFY board as it developed a strategy to move to a distinctly proactive policy. In addition to the $3.6 million previously distributed under the grant application system, including the establishment grant for the National Children's and Youth Law Centre, the chair announced in June 1994 that a further $4.5 million would be allocated over the next three years to projects that had been identified as high priorities. They included adolescent health, juvenile justice, access and equity in education, children's rights, youth employment, youth homelessness prevention and the National Aboriginal Youth Law Centre.

As I approached the end of my two year appointment and my 60th birthday I decided it was time to make way for a younger successor and did not apply for an extension of my contract.

PATRICE AND I LEFT FOR EUROPE in July 1994 for a three month motoring holiday, driving through France, Spain and Italy. I described the trip as a retirement bonus but I had always lived through and for my work and realised that it was not something I could easily relinquish. Besides, the European 'odyssey' had opened new travel horizons for us but I had resigned from the South Australian Parliament more than six years prior to the date on which I would have qualified for the maximum superannuation entitlement. Without a supplementary income my modest parliamentary pension would make it difficult to pay for little more than an annual 10 day holiday on Queensland's Sunshine Coast. However, job opportunities don't come easily for 60 year olds. I decided to explore a niche market as a private consultant and registered J & P Cornwall & Associates as our business name. My career over the next two and a half years was less than spectacular, although it did pay for two more overseas visits. The most complex and satisfying consultancy was the review of the New South Wales *Health Care Complaints Act*, reconciling the competing positions of the health professionals, insurance companies and patient advocates to reach a broad consensus.

By 1997 we were ready for what we believed would be the grand final overseas tour. We spent five months in Europe, initially living simply but very happily in a one room bed-sit in the Rome suburb of Testaccio. Patrice had been studying Italian intermittently for several years and having decided that she should take it seriously, took an Italian language course at Sapienza Universita di Roma, the beginning of her enduring love affair with the eternal city. At the end of June we relocated to Orvieto, where we had rented a little flat in the centre of the historic hill town for three months. Patrice spent the first month hosting visits from family members and friends and honing her conversational Italian with the locals. Having previously studied French to an intermediate level with the Alliance Francaise in Sydney, I took the opportunity to complete a four week course at Tours in the beautiful Loire Valley. When I returned from France we visited Verona to attend *Madama Butterfly* in the Arena di Verona, the ancient Roman amphitheatre in the Piazza Bra and used Orvieto as our base for the remainder of our time in Europe during which we visited Prague and the Amalfi Coast.

We were unaware at the time that a job opportunity was coming that would enable us to indulge our passion for overseas travel for many more years. Former AVA President Bob Kibble, now the founding chair of the recently established Delta Society Australia, rang me just three weeks after we returned to Australia and asked me to accept a six month contract as the Society's managing consultant. Delta had been established with a one-off interest free loan from the Animal Welfare League with a mission to promote positive interaction between people and companion animals. This was to be achieved by taking over and expanding two core programs, therapy dogs and a hobby course for pet dog trainers which had been developed by a small group of enthusiasts on Sydney's North Shore.

The six month consultancy turned out to be a 10 year appointment.

The trademarked Canine Good Citizen (CGC) pet dog training program was upgraded from a hobby course to a nationally accredited Certificate IV vocational training program and we graduated professional trainers in every state in Australia. The Delta Therapy Dogs program grew from 30 Sydney volunteers visiting local nursing homes with their temperament tested dogs to a program which by 2015 involved almost 1000 volunteers and their therapy dogs visiting more than 800 participating facilities around Australia. The facilities included residential aged care complexes, children's and adult hospitals, mental health centres, dementia specific units and prisons. Delta's dogs, with their volunteer owners, visit any facility where they can act as an adjunct to physical therapy or psychological well being.

I FINALLY RETIRED IN JULY 2007 and Patrice and I set out for another overseas trip. By the time we returned to Sydney in September I was just four months short of my 73rd birthday but within weeks I decided that retirement was not for me: I had simply given up working for money. The New South Wales Centre for Volunteering provided me with several leads and very soon I was spending 20 hours a week working in a voluntary capacity as the Executive Director of the Horn of Africa Relief and Development Agency (HARDA).

HARDA had been founded in 2003 by Hassan Omar, a charismatic Somali man who had come to Australia as a student in the late 1980s. Hassan worked across borders, tribes and religions for the refugees and their families from the countries of the Horn of Africa. Some years earlier he had become a friend of Phil Glendenning, the current President of the Refugee Council of Australia, who was working at Caritas, an international aid and development agency. By 2003 Phil was the Director of the Edmund Rice Centre (ERC) where his social justice activities nationally and internationally included support for asylum seekers and refugees. The ERC became HARDA's life support, providing the volunteers with work stations, a fully serviced computer network and office facilities free of charge: Muslims, Christians and others, all volunteers, working together for humanity.

Hassan literally gave his life to the cause, dedicating more than 30 hours of voluntary time over seven days each week while still maintaining a full time position at the Royal North Shore Hospital. Sixteen months after I joined HARDA he collapsed and died from a heart attack on the Gosford railway station while waiting for a train to work. He was only 50 years old.

During my six years at HARDA our volunteer staff, working with representatives of the African communities, developed and conducted numerous projects in the Sydney basin for adults and young people to foster integration and community participation. The projects were funded by a combination of grants hard won from government agencies as well as contributions from the philanthropic and corporate sectors and private donations. In Africa our flagship program was the cataract surgery and eye health project, organised by HARDA's Dr Mahmoud Sheikh and conducted in the field by a team of volunteer ophthalmologists and nurses from Doctors for Hope. Other achievements included funding the construction of a residential facility in Northern Kenya for 250 girls who are now able to attend a local school. Many of them are orphans whose families have been destroyed by years of vicious fighting in Somalia's civil war and by the jihadist Al-Shabaab. More recently Mahmoud Sheikh has played a prominent role in the development of a centre for maternal and child health in a remote tribal area adjacent to the Somalian border and hundreds of reconditioned computers and hospital beds have been donated and shipped to Ethiopia. It was challenging and rewarding work but by December 2013, three weeks before my 79th birthday, I was ready for full retirement and farewelled my colleagues at HARDA's Annual General Meeting.

I NEVER PARTICIPATED IN ACTIVE party politics again after I moved from South Australia although I have maintained a keen interest and will be a social democrat 'even unto death'. As I write the final paragraphs of this memoir in March 2017 I am horrified by the vicious cruelty that has replaced compassion in Australia's treatment of asylum seekers; dismayed by the persistent refusal of right wing politicians to move decisively towards a carbon free economy; ashamed that in a country formerly acknowledged as one of the fairest and most prosperous on earth, more than three million adults and children are living below the poverty line; deeply disappointed that the sector blind, needs based school funding recommended by the Gonski Committee, was corrupted by Labor ('no

Australian school will be worse off financially') and emasculated by the Abbott Government.

The surge of wealth created by 25 years of continuous economic growth should have been the basis for a visionary social contract between the government and the electorate. Instead it has been appropriated by the super rich while wage and salary earners cope with stagnant wage growth and the uncertainties of employment on a contract or casual basis. Abbott Government Treasurer Joe Hockey divided us into 'lifters and leaners', Prime Minister Turnbull's Treasurer Scott Morrison divides us derisively as 'the 'taxed and the taxed nots'. As to the debt and deficit disaster, the real disaster lies in a revenue shortfall, based on distorted tax concessions, omissions and avoidance.

Patrice and I have now lived in Sydney, Australia's global city, for 27 years, a fulfilling and happy period during which travel has continually expanded our horizons and broadened our interests. There have been many satisfying moments in my professional and political life, as well as some inevitable disappointments. I have often been impatient, sometimes impetuous, occasionally irascible but rarely irresolute. Love's been good to me. Patrice has loved me all her adult life and while our children have been variously sources of pride, anguish, despair and joy, loyalty and love have been constant components of our family life.

In January 2015 Patrice and I were joined by members of our extended family and some friends for dinner at a restaurant on Sydney Harbour to celebrate my 80th birthday. It was a very happy occasion, combined with some serious reflections on a long life. Then in May 2016 we gathered again, this time for an intimate family lunch at Sydney's Bathers Pavilion to celebrate our 60th wedding anniversary.

After work, after play, after all, it's been a fortunate and fascinating journey.

Edna Bilston and Joseph Cornwall, c1926.

APPENDIX

Ancestry

My mother's convict pedigree was impeccable. On 26 January 1788, six generations earlier, Ellen Wainwright arrived at Sydney Cove on the *Prince of Wales*, one of 11 vessels in the First Fleet. In January 1787 at Preston Quarter Sessions 17 year old Ellen, alias Esther Eccles of Rishton, was convicted of stealing a scarlet woollen cloak, a blue stuff quilted petticoat and a black silk hat. She was sentenced to seven years and transported.

In 1789 Ellen gave birth to a daughter Mary Ann at Port Jackson; her baptismal record shows 'father unknown'. In March the following year they were among 300 passengers, marines and convicts, who were sent to Norfolk Island on the *Sirius* and *Supply*. When the 540 ton *Sirius* was shipwrecked on the island's coral reef Ellen and her baby daughter were among the passengers and crew who were all rescued but the ship and most of its provisions were lost. In 1791 Ellen had a son Henry who died when he was very young and her three year old Mary Ann died in 1792. Then in 1795 Ellen gave birth to another daughter whom she also called Mary Ann. Like the first Mary Ann, the paternity of these two children is a matter for conjecture.

Thomas Guy, alias Thomas Gay, was arrested as a highwayman and sentenced to death at Gloucester on 14 June 1784 for 'assaulting one John Barnes and robbing him of two guineas in gold, 43 shillings in silver and a silver watch'. The sentence was later commuted to transportation for life and he was dispatched on the *Matilda*, one of 2,000 convicts to arrive at Port Jackson with the Third Fleet in 1791. From Port Jackson he was later sent to Norfolk Island.

Sometime before 1800 Ellen began to co-habit with Thomas and presented him with three daughters, Ann, Elizabeth and Frances, born between 1800 and 1805.

There are conflicting versions of life on Norfolk Island. Most describe the harsh conditions endured by the convicts, including the frequent use of the lash, although an early report claimed that 'despite initial setbacks soon after settlement, it began to flourish' as crops were planted and harvested and the settlement became a tiny township. However, the continuing arrival of convicts from Sydney during the following few years saw Norfolk Island become 'nothing more than a labour camp for Sydney's most difficult officers and least wanted felons'. By 1803 the cost of maintaining the civil administration, a military presence and providing stores and shipping for the island had become a burden and from 1805 onwards the population began to dwindle as people were withdrawn or forced to emigrate.

On balance it seems that for many of the convicts the only benign aspect of life on the island was the climate but it appears that Thomas and Ellen did quite well. By 1808 the records show that Thomas was classed as a 'second class settler' with 'a boarded and shingled house and three outhouses valued together at £40 as well as 11.25 acres of cleared land and 6.75 acres of uncleared land'. However, in September that year Thomas, Ellen, their three daughters and Ellen's Mary Ann were forced to move; they were one of the 28 convict families sent on the *City of Edinburgh* to New Norfolk on the Derwent River in Van Diemens Land. Today New Norfolk is described in the tourist brochures as 'Tasmania's Best Kept Secret, 30 minutes west of Hobart on the beautiful Derwent River, teeming with historic houses, magnificent rugged scenery, mountain views, valley views and the gateway to Mount Field National Park'. But in 1808 the Norfolk families were thrust into Tasmania with only the most meager shared housing to protect them.

Sometime after his arrival in New Norfolk Thomas was granted 14 acres of land on the Derwent River 'being in compensation for land relinquished by the grantee at Norfolk Island' and on 24 May 1812 in another notable event he finally married Ellen. The marriage certificate shows that Ellen was aged 42 and Thomas 53.

Thomas and Ellen's daughter Elizabeth married William Wheeler, a seaman, and they produced four sons and two daughters, including Ann who married Thomas Bilston in New Norfolk on 23 April 1835.

Thomas had arrived 11 years earlier in January 1824 on the convict ship *Asia*. On 19 April 1823 the *Warwick Advertiser* reported that William Dolman, Thomas Bilston, James Yates and Joseph White had been found guilty of 'burglariously breaking and entering the dwelling house of George Hewitt at Birmingham and stealing thereout one cloth coat and other articles'.

He was only 15 years old but such was the harsh penal code of the time that he was transported for life. Thomas and Ann moved to the new settlement at Port Phillip in 1837 just 18 months after John Batman had declared 'This will be the place for a village'. Their son, George Yarra Bilston, the first of nine children, was born there in August 1838, 'the first white child born in Melbourne'. Thomas was granted a conditional pardon in the same year (*Hobart Town Courier*, 23 March) and a full pardon two years later.

In 1839 Thomas was one of the men involved with a pastoral syndicate who walked a large flock of sheep west from Port Phillip to take up a new pastoral run. The records of the venture are uncertain but it seems that there was substantial resistance from the local Aboriginal tribe in the area they had selected and the party moved further west to Chetwynd. Thomas and Ann then settled at Nareen on what became known as the Bilston Springs property. By 1846 he held the publican's licence for the Bush Inn at Heywood (formerly Fitzroy Crossing) which he apparently acquired in exchange for Bilston Springs and in 1848 he was granted a Squatter's Licence over the Steep Bank Rivulet run (*Melbourne Argus*, 4 February). Two years later the *Argus* informed readers that he was offering both the Bush Inn and his pastoral run for sale. 'Applications as to terms must be made to Mr Bilston, on the premises, or to S G Henty, Esq, merchant, Portland'.

Perhaps due to the savage bushfire that ravaged the area in 1851 neither property was sold and he still held the licence in 1857 (*Portland Guardian*, 2 April). Steep Bank was abandoned and forfeited in 1874 and three years later Ann, who had been not quite 16 when she married Thomas in 1835, died at the age of 58. Thomas failed to make his fortune despite some brave attempts. He died in the Portland hospital in 1899, having spent 60 years of his long life as a well known and respected resident of the Portland and Heywood districts.

When George Stone Bilston was born on 7 October 1860 his father,

George Yarra, was described on his son's birth certificate as an Innkeeper. He had married Ellen McElligott in 1856 when he was 18 and she was 23. George Stone was the second of their 10 children. It was about this time that George Yarra became the licensee of the hotel at Mocambro, later renamed Henty. After his wife Ellen died in 1893 George moved to the Great Southern Region of Western Australia where a son, Henry Augustine, was farming and he lived there until his death in January 1916. The *Western Wimmera Mail* reported that he 'recently passed away at Katanning WA, of heart trouble, at the age of 78 years and six months' The article repeated the family story that he was 'the first white child born in Melbourne'. According to the *Casterton News* he was 'one of the very earliest settlers of the district and was well known to all the older residents among whom he was cordially welcomed on the occasion of a comparatively recent visit to this district'.

George Stone Bilston grew up in Western Victoria and married Ellen Bridget Margaret Ryan, an Irish Catholic, at Merino in 1891. They had nine children two of whom, Katherine and George, were born at Invercargill, New Zealand where the family lived between 1895 and 1899. George Stone was a carpenter by trade and after the family returned from New Zealand he worked mainly as a self employed carpenter and handyman in several townships in the Wimmera district of Victoria. Edna Margaret, my mother and George and Ellen's second youngest child, was born in the village of Gymbowen in 1907. After the First World War the family moved to the new irrigation settlement of Mildura where George purchased the Arcadia Cafe. In 1930 he retired to suburban Pascoe Vale in Melbourne and spent the last five years of his life in Bendigo where he died in 1940 aged 80.

My earliest memory of Grandfather Bilston, when I was four years old, was of him playing a bush ballad on his concertina and step dancing, his name for some sort of colonial jig. My only other memory is of viewing his body in an open coffin in the front room of their Bendigo home just a year later. Grandma Bilston, who was 11 years younger than her husband, died in 1951.

My father's grandfather, Wilson Cornwall, was an Ulsterman born in Armagh, Northern Ireland in 1811. He was sentenced to 15 years transportation at the Crown Court in Londonderry on Saturday, 23 March 1839. According to the *Londonderry Sentinel* of 30 March 1839, 'Cornwall and his accomplice, Moses Hutchinson, robbed Alexander Mitchell, a linen merchant, of four bank notes together with all his silver coins, his great coat and umbrella, after they all had shared a few beers and a half glass of whiskey at Mr. Mann's public house in Castledawson, County Londonderry.'

When he arrived in New South Wales on the *Middlesex* in 1840 with 200 other convicts the record shows that he could read and write. He was sent to Victoria (at that time still part of the colony of New South Wales) and granted a ticket of leave in 1846 but it was revoked the following year when he was convicted of stealing a horse. In 1850, at the age of 39, Wilson married Sarah Ann McIntyre in a ceremony at the Independent Congregational Church in Collins Street, Melbourne. My grandfather William Cornwall, born in Melbourne in 1861, was one of their eight children.

I am unable to provide a detailed account of Wilson's activities, occupation or business activities but he was clearly quite ambitious and entrepreneurial. In 1855 he applied unsuccessfully for a publican's licence for the Labor-in-Vain Hotel in Fitzroy but was refused, presumably because of his conviction for horse stealing. However, he appears to have become a man of some substance. An entry in the electoral roll of 1856 recorded his 'Place of Abode and Occupation' as 'Brighton, Farmer' and a second entry described him and his brothers, John and Edmund, as 'Yeomen'. This strongly suggests that they not only lived at that address but owned and farmed the land in an area in Melbourne that would later become valuable residential property.

On 17 November 1869 a Law Report in *The Melbourne Argus* described him as a cattle dealer living at Pakenham. He had launched a successful claim against the Colony of Victoria and a farmer, James Martini, for malicious prosecution and false imprisonment following another charge of horse stealing. He was awarded damages of £100. By the 1870s Wilson was probably quite a wealthy man but when he died in December 1900, aged 89, he was living frugally in the Melbourne suburb of Kew. His fortune had been wiped out in the property busts of the 1890s depression.

My Grandfather William Cornwall married Mary Grace Warren, whose family originally came from Cornwall, at the home of the bride's parents at South Gembrook on 21 July 1883. My father Joseph Wilson Cornwall was the second youngest of their 12 children. Grandfather Cornwall was already an old man when I was born. I was only 11 when he died in 1946 at the age of 85 but I remember his white beard which was always neatly trimmed and when he went out he dressed in a suit with butterfly collar, tie and hat. Despite his formal attire, however, he was an honest bush battler rather than a man of property. He made his way before the First World War, by working as a fencing contractor and on road construction while working his small farm in East Gippsland but he was badly affected by the 1914 drought.

We visited him at Gembrook, a village in Victoria's Dandenong Ranges, on several occasions and at least once he came to stay with us in Bendigo. As a small boy I remember him extolling the virtues of macadamised (high crown) roads in debate with the retired shire engineer. I also have a picture of him relaxing at home with his favourite pipe, a benign old grandfather who told some trite little jokes and posed simple riddles for the amusement of his grandchildren: 'What's the definition of nothing?' 'A legless stocking without a foot.'

I know little about Dad's mother, Mary. She died of cancer in 1923 when Dad was 19 and Grandfather remarried some years later in what seemed like a union based on practical considerations rather than any romantic notions. I remember Aunty May, as we called Dad's stepmother, as a blunt, practical woman and a sound housekeeper, but quite charmless.

Endnotes

1 The strike initially followed industrial unrest over pay and conditions but was ultimately a wildcat strike, precipitated by the Police Commissioner's use of 'spooks', four senior constables working in plain clothes throughout the city and suburbs to spy on constables on the beat. In an act of astonishing retribution following the strike, about a third of the force - 636 policemen - were discharged or dismissed, never to be re-employed as members of the Force.

2 *The Melbourne Argus*, 19 July 1930.

3 This was Melbourne's morning tabloid newspaper from 1922 to 1990 when it became the *Herald Sun*.

4 The last thing that Barbara Paynter's husband said to her as he boarded a train at Paddington Station, London, in August 1939 was 'Get a farm going darling'.

5 The fascinating story of ribonucleic acid (RNA) and deoxyribonucleic acid (DNA) was just emerging in scientific literature. In 1953 James Watson and Francis Crick discovered the molecular structure of DNA for which, with Maurice Wilkins, they were awarded the Nobel Prize in 1962.

6 In the context of the intensification of the Cold War in Europe, communist insurgency and success in South-East Asia, and the declaration of war in Korea, the Menzies Government introduced the *National Service Act 1951*. All Australian 18 year old males were required to do three months continuous military training followed by a series of short camps and training sessions, a further 90 days in total.

7 Frank Forde was the Deputy Prime Minister and Minister for the Army in John Curtin's wartime Government, positions he retained when Ben Chifley became Prime Minister following John Curtin's death in office. In 1946 he was appointed Australia's High Commissioner to Canada.

8 From 1 May 2014 the Australian Racing Board banned the use of anabolic steroids in any horse for any purpose (in or out of competition) other than as a therapeutic treatment for foals under six months of age.

9 The Bretton Woods agreement between the leaders of the allied nations acknowledged that international economic cooperation was the only way to achieve peace and prosperity. Between 1944 and 1947 it created the International Monetary Fund, the World Bank and the General Agreement on Tariffs and Trade.

10 Ian Verrender, 'Think Whitlam ruined our economy? Think again', The Drum, Australian Broadcasting Corporation, 27 October 2014, www.abc.net.au/news/2014-10-27/verrender-think-whitlam-ruined-our-economy-think-again/5842866, accessed 17 December 2016.

11 Graham Freudenberg, *A figure of speech: a political memoir*, John Wiley & Sons Australia Ltd, 2005, p173.

12 *ibid*, p175.

13 Paul Kelly, *November 1975: the inside story of Australia's greatest political crisis*, Allen & Unwin, 1995, p392.

14 Labor lost the 1968 election but Corcoran held the seat of Millicent by one vote over his LCL rival Martin Cameron. Cameron protested and a by-election was held, with Corcoran winning more comfortably, leaving the new Steele Hall LCL government to rely on the casting vote of Independent Speaker Tom Stott.

15 Sir Percy Spender had a long and distinguished career. He was the Minister for External Affairs in the first term of the Menzies Government (1949-1951) where he was credited with being the leading architect of the Colombo Plan and the ANZUS Pact. He was Australia's

Ambassador to the United States from 1951 to 1958, followed by his appointment to the International Court of Justice in 1958, serving as the Court's President from 1964 to 1967.

16 see Peter Grabosky, 'Political surveillance and the South Australian Police', in Peter Grabosky, *Wayward governance: illegality and its control in the public sector*, Australian Institute of Criminology, Canberra, 1989.

17 *ibid.*

18 Des Ryan and Mike McEwen, *It's grossly improper*, Wenan, South Australia, 1979.

19 In 1980 the Tonkin Liberal Government re-negotiated the detail of the land rights legislation and it received assent on 19 March 1981.

20 Through the 1980s Rod Cameron of Australian Nationwide Opinion Polls would be pivotal in propelling the ALP nationally and in the states to the greatest electoral success in its history.

21 Rod Panter, 'Chronology of ALP Uranium policy 1950-1994', Background Paper No 17, Parliamentary Research Service, Department of the Parliamentary Library, 1994.

22 Douglas Coster et al, *Report on the management of booking lists in Adelaide's public hospitals*, Flinders Medical Centre, August, 1988.

23 *An Enemy of the People* is the Henrik Ibsen play written in 1882 in which a doctor stands against an entire town when he discovers their medicinal spa, projected to be a major source of revenue for the town, is polluted and causing serious illness. Dr Phil Landrigan gave me a well-worn copy of the play soon after he arrived from the United States to review the work of the task force established to examine the environmental lead problem and make recommendations concerning its amelioration.

24 *South Australian Parliamentary Debates*, 14 October, 1987.

25 Stephen Leeder, Extract from the Foreword to Anne-Marie Boxall and James Gillespie, *Making Medicare: the politics of universal health care in Australia*, UNSW Press, 2013.

26 Anne-Marie Boxall and James Gillespie, *Making Medicare: the politics of universal health care in Australia*, UNSW Press, 2013, pp140-141.

27 *The News*, 29 February 1984.

28 *Sunday Mail*, 7 August 1988.

29 Hal Swerissen and Stephen Duckett, *Chronic failure in primary care*, Grattan Institute, 6 March 2016.

30 *ibid.*

31 Mike Rann first identified this as one of John Bannon's major strengths in his maiden speech after he was elected to the South Australian House of Assembly in 1985. He recalled and reinforced this sentiment in an address he gave at the launch of the Bannon Collection at Flinders University a generation later.

32 see Sharon Mosler, *Heritage Politics in Adelaide*, University of Adelaide Press, 2011.

33 Chris Kenny, *State of Denial*, Wakefield Press, 1993, p86.

34 *ibid*, p87.

35 Honourable Samuel Joshua Jacobs AO QC, interviewed by John Emerson, 23 May 2009, https://www.lawsocietysa.asn.au/LSSA/Lawyers/Publications/Articles/Jacobs.aspx, accessed 21 June 2016.

36 Michael Jacobs, *The New Daily*, 14 December 2015.

37 Chris Kenny, *op cit*, p103.

www.ingramcontent.com/pod-product-compliance
Lightning Source LLC
Chambersburg PA
CBHW071738150426
43191CB00010B/1626